FASHION MAKERS
FASHION SHAPERS

Thames & Hudson

THE ESSENTIAL GUIDE TO FASHION BY THOSE IN THE KNOW

with 265 illustrations in colour

FASHION MAKERS
FASHION SHAPERS

Anne-Celine Jaeger

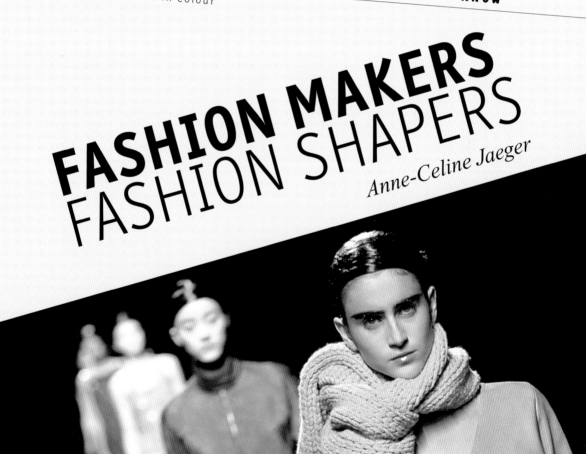

Autumn/Winter 2007–2008

First published in the United Kingdom in 2009 by
Thames & Hudson Ltd, 181A High Holborn, London WC1V 7QX

thamesandhudson.com

British Library Cataloguing-in-Publication Data
A catalogue record for this book is available
from the British Library

ISBN 978-0-500-28824-5

Printed and bound in China

CONTENTS

The Essential Guide to Fashion by Those in the Know

I'm no philosopher, but it seems to me that women – and men too – instinctively yearn to exhibit themselves, **Christian Dior, 1957**

Long before fashion magazines, runway shows and summer sales existed, the Roman philosopher Seneca announced, 'We live not according to reason, but according to fashion.' Though he may have been wearing only a toga when he said it, he had a point.

One of my earliest style memories is of heading to school in an alarmingly bright orange corduroy outfit on a fierce January morning. Despite the cascading snow, I left my jacket at home. It wasn't quite as extreme as the tale of the Emperor's new clothes – I wasn't naked to the bone – but given the arctic temperatures, it was foolishly close. Not unlike the Emperor, I wanted to be seen; I wanted people to notice the outfit and perhaps even admire me because of it. Although I was only 10 years old, I already had some notion that clothes make the man.

I came home that night with a furious fever. Reason, as Seneca had declared two thousand years ago, had not been part of the equation. Making a fashion statement, on the other hand, had.

Asserting individuality and status using garments dates back to a time long before the Romans. Even in prehistoric times, when making clothes meant skinning an animal, members of a tribe would accessorize their wears using bones and feathers to set themselves apart from the rest of the pack. These days, we don't have to pluck a wild bird to be in fashion, we can simply walk into a shop and buy ourselves some individuality. But how do we decide what to wear? How do trends come about? And, more importantly, how do the designers come up with new concepts and ideas to lure us into buying their collection, season after season?

above: Björk styled by Katy England and shot by David
Sims for *Dazed & Confused*, May 2000

Fashion Makers, Fashion Shapers is the first book to analyse the fashion industry as a whole. Not only does it delve into how the world's most celebrated designers approach their craft, but it also unravels who and what is behind the success of a label – whether it be a ready-to-wear, contemporary, sportswear or retail label.

Using a Q&A format and over 260 carefully selected images, the working practices of famous designers are explored, unveiling the processes involved in creating a successful concept, collection and brand. In these pages you will discover why handcraft is important to Dries Van Noten, what Paul Smith learnt about the fashion industry by setting up his own shop in Nottingham in 1970, and why the founder of A.P.C., Jean Touitou, 'doesn't make bags for bitches'.

In order to become successful, it appears, designers must master the fine balance between walking alone and having no followers. When Jean Touitou first launched A.P.C. the retailer Joseph said to him, 'Jean, I love you, but you won't get anywhere with these clothes. They are for firemen.' What's more, Italian buyers would look at his collection and exclaim, 'But this is not a jacket! Can't you include some more colours?' To which he would reply, 'Grey is a colour and so are white and navy blue.' Touitou's pioneering

below, from left to right: Missoni, Autumn/Winter 2008–2009; inspirational picture used by WGSN; Dries Van Noten menswear, Autumn/Winter 2008–2009; Stone Island, Autumn/Winter 2008–2009; detail from a Paul Smith shop; and Dries Van Noten womenswear, Autumn/Winter 2008–2009

aesthetic hadn't yet reached the masses. Today, his much-copied brand is a multi-million pound business, which retails all over the world.

Similarly, Luella Bartley is against playing it safe. She maintains, 'When you care too much what people think you don't push yourself to create something that's new or exciting.' Another firm believer in following your unique vision is Carlo Rivetti, the owner of Stone Island and C. P. Company. He says, 'Lots of designers say they take ideas from the street, but I think if you do that you're already too late.' Nevertheless, your creations can't exist in a fashion vacuum. According to Jane Rapley, head of Central Saint Martins College of Art and Design, it's important to be fresh. 'It's no good going out there and doing a pastiche

of what's out there already,' she says 'but it's not a revolution. It's difficult to be unique. If you're far out, no one else will buy into it or identify with it.'

And yet, no matter how inimitable your vision, it takes more than that to make or break a brand. In *Fashion Shapers* fashion editors, stylists, buyers, PRs and fashion icons are asked what they are looking for when choosing a garment to feature on the runway, in an editorial or on the shop floor. How does Alexandra Shulman, the editor of British *Vogue*, decide which designers to feature in the next editorial spread? What does the renowned PR agency, Purple, do to ensure their labels get the best possible press coverage? How does Catriona Macnab, head of trends at WGSN, decide what colour will be big next season?

According to the stylist Katy England it takes a lot more than thinking you know about clothes to become a successful designer. She says, 'It's easy for kids to say they want to go into fashion – they think they know all about it because it's all around us, to the point where it's practically rammed down our throats. But if you want to make a career out of it, it needs to go a lot deeper than that. There's a lot of hard work to do before things get remotely glamorous and you start making any money. It's about passion, obsession, hard work and dealing with lots of egos.'

Jane Rapley witnesses that google-eyed hunger for success time and again among college applicants. 'Many students who come here do have the ambition to become the next glam front-runner vanguard designer, so we have to spend time explaining that they're not going to be that, or that it's not that easy.'

According to Cathal McAteer of Folk the creative part of being a designer and owning a label is the easy part. The real challenge, he says, lies in controlling those innovations, managing your business, building a collection, being patient and not spending too much money. In his words, 'All the boring stuff that keeps you in business'.

Although often forgotten, a business is exactly what fashion is and many designers make a point of emphasizing the rather less romantic, but equally important aspect of the industry in the pages that follow. Christophe Lemaire of Lacoste maintains that you can be as creative as

you like, but if you don't figure out how to reach your public, you won't have much of a brand. According to Paul Smith it all boils down to having a point of view. 'Nobody needs another writer, architect, designer. The world is full of them.' However, 'if you've got a point of view, you've got a bit of a chance.'

And that's exactly where *Fashion Makers, Fashion Shapers* comes in. In-depth interviews guide you precisely to that all-important point of view. You'll read about the creative freedom that comes from being independently owned, how global trends come about, whether style is innate, how it is that an entire nation can suddenly be interested in wearing harem pants, what the rise of China might mean for the fashion world, how using a pencil can

enhance the way you see and therefore create, why accessories can be the turning point of a brand and much more. Whether it is design technique, garment production or the creation of a signature style, the makers and shapers of the fashion industry provide a unique and indispensable guide to their working methods and what it takes to create a successful label.

I, for one, now understand how American Apparel underpants, harem pants and Folk cardigans first came into existence and, more importantly, why it is that I am wearing them as I write this.

below, from left to right: Acne's original Mic Jeans; Folk cardigan, Autumn/Winter 2008–2009; a dress from Luella's Spring/Summer 2006 show; Gisele, an Alexandre de Betak light design; American Apparel classic briefs; a Paul Smith chair

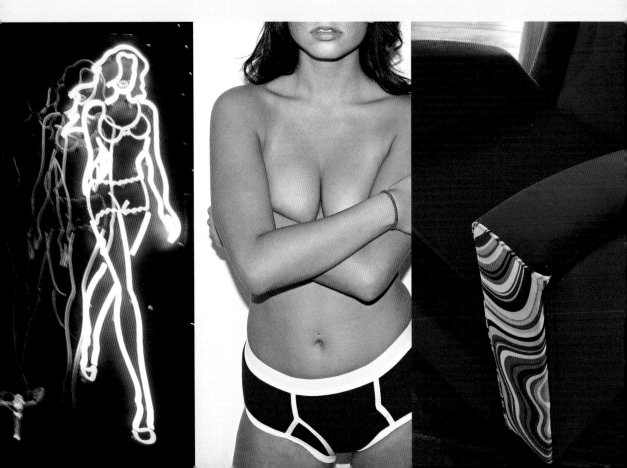

ION
ERS

PART I
READY-TO-WEAR
CONTEMPORARY LABELS
RETAIL
SPORTSWEAR AND
CASUALWEAR
NEXT GENERATION

Luella
Luella Bartley

Luella Bartley studied Fashion Communication with Promotion at Central Saint Martins College of Art and Design in London and left in her second year when she was offered a job as a fashion writer at the Evening Standard *in London. After working for several years as an editor for both the* Evening Standard *and British* Vogue, *she took on a dare to start her own label. Her first collection, which she 'cobbled together in a friend's flat', remained unseen. Her third collection, 'Daddy, I want a pony' got rave reviews. And 10 years down the line her quintessentially British label, which always embodies a twist of quirkiness, is sold in 50 different shops in 120 countries and is worn by the likes of Chloë Sevigny, Cameron Diaz and Agyness Deyn.*

opposite: From Luella's Spring/Summer 2009 collection, inspired by the notion of 'a proper English lady', but with an added 'wonkyness'

When did you first get interested in fashion?

It was quite late on. I remember my mother being quite an eccentric, 1970s hippy character, so that kind of style felt normal to me. She was a mature student so we always had arty, poetry types round the house. There was a creative feel to my childhood, but fashion was never really part of that. English was my thing, but I started hanging out with kids at the local college who were doing Art Foundation courses and it looked much more fun. My teachers at college noticed my interest and suggested I do a week at art college rather than a work placement. I never went back to finish my A-levels... The foundation course got me interested in fashion, but it was still very English-led for me: I was interested in the journalistic aspect of it.

What did you study at Central Saint Martins?

I did a Fashion Communication with Promotion BA. But in my first year we studied everything from design through to print.

Why did you leave before you'd finished the course?

I was very interested in the image-making process of fashion, but Saint Martins was also quite an intimidating place to be when I was still formulating my ideas. Lots of students ate, slept and breathed their vision of fashion, but I wasn't there yet. It was almost too early for me. I was 18. In my second year I got a work placement at the *Evening Standard* and I never went back. I was at the *Standard* for four years and then went on to British *Vogue*, working as a fashion editor. Katy Grand and I were commissioning shoots. It was very tongue-in-cheek and playful.

What made you decide to launch your own label?

It was quite a vague decision. Some have a very strong calling towards something and others just sort of fall into it. I don't feel like it was a lucky break, I was sort of coming at it from a different angle. I think that comes through in what I do now as well. I haven't taken the serious path of intellectual fashion. It's more of a wry take on culture and style in general.

I always had it in the back of my head that I wanted to do a collection and create something that wasn't about writing. I spoke to my peers and James, my boyfriend at the time. I'm a real commitment phobe, and James said, 'Why don't you just do it. Just draw some stuff and get it made. No harm in that.' That was about the level of commitment I could handle.

So I drew some stuff, found this pattern-cutter, Lesley Poole, who was larger than life. He had worked with Ossie Clark. It was all very amateur. I didn't do anything with that first collection, it was like being back at college and I had no idea what I was doing.

For the next collection I wanted to make shirts and shirt-dresses, but I had no idea where to get the fabric from and so on. I got a good response when I showed at London Fashion Week in 1999. So I just thought, let's have another go. I had grown tired of being in an office, and I was freelancing for *Dazed*

opposite, left: From Luella's Spring/Summer 2006 collection; opposite, right and below, left: Englishness and equestrianism with a twist from the Autumn/Winter 2007–2008 collection; below: Inspired by Luella Bartley's move to Cornwall, paganism and the local witchcraft museum, from the Autumn/Winter 2008–2009 collection

& *Confused* on the side. The next collection I did was the 'Daddy, I want a pony' collection. Katy Grand came on board and styled it. That show got a lot of attention and made me think, 'This could work.'

What was your vision for the label?

The first collection was about traditional English school sports and equestrianism, but it still had that edge to it. People referred to it as Pony-club Punk. I'm not too keen on that term, but it was that notion of tradition with a rock'n'roll edge. It was a bit naughty and subversive. It has sort of matured and evolved, but the key values are still the same.

Did you have a plan of action about how you were going to make it work?

I was quite lucky in that my boyfriend, who was a really philanthropic guy, was backing me at the time. I didn't have much of a business plan. It was a wonderful place to be, but it wasn't very realistic. I had no idea how I was going to make it work. But at the time there was a strong feeling between me and my peers that we could do anything. We had that youthful arrogance. Katy Grand started a magazine, lots was going on and we got swept up in that.

The 'Daddy, I want a pony' collection got lots of hype and attention. The spirit of it really resonated with people. With hindsight it was a very simple idea, not really a designed collection. After that collection we had to put a proper business plan together and we had to get a loan. I got Katie Hillier to come and work with me. We sort of fumbled through it together. We found a factory in England and got the collection made there. Production is so different now, it's such a huge, complex structure. It's hard to compete on any level with the labels that have a massive infrastructure behind them. But then we always had that youthful enthusiasm and we just got on with it. We never thought about the future, it just happened.

To what extent was the financial backing from your boyfriend crucial to getting the label off the ground?

You've got to have money behind you. It's impossible otherwise. I suppose the industry is slightly different now in that you can get support from Topshop and the British Fashion Council with setting up a business. You might even be able to get sponsorship, but I didn't know about it then.

How many of you were involved with Luella in the beginning?

It was me and Katie Hillier. Katy Grand was styling it and propping it up, and there was Lesley, the pattern-cutter, and one machinist. After the 'Daddy, I want a pony' season we also hired a production manager.

What did you your years as a journalist at the *Evening Standard* and British *Vogue* teach you about fashion and the way the industry works? Did it help you when it came to launching your own label?

below, left: Heart coin purse in lobster copper, Autumn/Winter 2007–2008; below centre: Elizabeth flats in grey and pink, Spring/Summer 2009; below, right: Hailed as one of the first ever It bags, the classic Gisele. Here in grey ostrich, Spring/Summer 2009; opposite, left: The multi-ribbon Bess clutch, Autumn/Winter 2008–2009; opposite, centre: Luella bows and hairbands, Autumn/Winter 2008–2009; opposite, right: Luella's Madge bag in black high shine, Autumn/Winter 2007–2008

I didn't have a grasp of how the industry worked from having written about it. Sure, I had contacts for designers and it was helpful in that I could ring people up who were showing in London and say, 'how do you do this?, where do you get fabric?' and so on, but that was about it. It put limitations on the collections we could produce. Having said that, if I had known how complicated the procedure was to create a proper collection I would never have done it. The licensing, the production abroad, buying fabric, distribution, it's mind-boggling and totally overwhelming. But like with all things, you start small and learn as you go along.

Were your years as a journalist useful in terms of contacts or detrimental in terms of not being taken seriously as a designer?
Probably a bit of both, it's hard to cross over. I wasn't that Central Saint Martins student with the vision. It wasn't so much what journalists were saying, but other people on the inside. But in a way, we were so arrogant, we didn't care.

In a *Guardian* interview you said that you were initially caught up in an ambition, hype and ego thing and then realized that that didn't work. What do you mean?
You just get caught up in that being cool thing. I remember going to London Fashion Week with Katy Grand and choosing ridiculous outfits and thinking we were being cynical and subversive, but people just thought, 'Who do they think they are?' It's funny to be here now and watch the younger generation do it. Agyness Deyn and Henry Holland, for instance. It's

that kind of 'we rule the world' mentality. And in a way, you can't do it without that arrogance because fashion can be a scary and intimidating environment. You need that to push yourself on; scenes come about. You couldn't feel like that on your own. It's that collective consciousness. We were the new generation. There was a lot of hype. The 'Daddy, who were The Clash' collection got rave reviews in 2000. Then we did the Fluro collection and Kate Moss modelled it and everyone was there. Katy Grand was standing backstage and spray-painting everything and the models were going out onto the catwalk in wet outfits. It was all very spontaneous. I think that was the collection when Sarah Mower brought us back down to earth. She said,

I loved the Gisele bag. It summed up everything about our aesthetic and the label. It was very classic, but had subversive elements, like the rings, which were S&M inspired. And good things happened because of that bag.

'Yes, it's very 80s referential. But it's also a lot of hype.' And she was right. It felt like, 'Hey, wait a minute, someone is almost catching us out here.'

Why did you move the shows to New York for several years between 2001 and 2007?

Katy Grand and Giles Deacon started working at Bottega Veneta and they invited us to do a show in Milan. It was very exciting. Here was a huge luxury goods house that was using young London designers. I did a skinhead collection. It was very edgy and young. Giles did a graffiti-esque collection inspired by Keith Haring. After that we didn't want to go back to London, it didn't seem like an exciting place. We were trying to build the business. I was living with Justine Frischmann of Elastica at the time and she was on tour and we thought, 'Hey, why don't we go to New York, get a tour bus. Just be on tour?' I called up the Council of Fashion Designers of America and they said, 'Great, we'll pay for you to come and show.' KCD, the biggest production company who do everyone from YSL to Marc Jacobs did our show for free. We got the cover of *WWD* (*Women's Wear Daily*) after our show, which is practically unheard of. We were riding on a high. And for a few seasons afterwards there was lots of home-grown new talent like Proenza Schouler coming out of the woodwork. I got used to choosing the girls I wanted for the shows in New York and those girls didn't come to London. I also loved Guido Palau doing the hair, and he didn't do shows in London. It just felt easier there. I ended up staying for six years.

What made you come back to London?

London was becoming more exciting, but it was also for personal reasons. I didn't feel like dragging my three kids across the Atlantic every six months. I also felt more confident as a person and about the collection that it didn't matter which models would be coming to London and so on. I felt like the collection stands for itself, without having all the other things that make a collection exciting. We were also opening a shop, so it was a good excuse.

Your collections often embody a twofold spirit of, say, punk-rock pony-club or ladylike-cum-psychedelic: what attracts you to those opposing characteristics?

I feel like those aspects are inherent in English style and culture. On the one hand, we're such a traditional society, but on the other there is always a sense of rebelliousness. I love all the symbols and traditions related to Englishness, equestrianism, etc. But it's also quite a personal thing for me. If you want to look at it from a psychological point of view...my mum and dad split up when I was two. He was very English and had a more posh, horsy, country side to him, whereas my mother was much more urban and cool and poverty stricken. I saw and wanted what my dad had but it was unattainable, so the rebellion was attached to it.

Where do you get inspiration for your collections such as most recently the asymmetrical orange frill dresses for Spring/Summer 2009?

That collection was very much based around the notion of a proper English – almost royal – lady, but I really wanted it to have a wonkyness. The detailing was bizarre, asymmetrical and ridiculous. That's what I love about Englishness. On the one hand, the collection was very proper, but it was also sick. The iridescent pink and orange and purple... I love that contrary aspect of fashion. There is so much psychology and inverted snobbery that goes on. Once you're in, you're out. And once you're out, you're in, etc. It's so ridiculous; I want to document that.

In terms of getting inspiration, it's more personal for me than going to an exhibition or flicking through an old *Vogue*. For example, the Autumn/Winter 2008 collection was inspired by my move to Cornwall and paganism and the witchcraft museum there. For the Spring/Summer 2009 collection, I wanted to change the silhouette of the collection and move away from the cutesy prom dresses. I wanted to take it to a more grown-up place, but wanted to have some wonky detailing in it.

opposite: From Luella's Spring/Summer 2009 collection; inspired by the look of a 'proper English lady', but with 'bizarre, asymmetrical and ridiculous' detailing

above: The Emily Dress from
the Autumn/Winter 2007–2008
collection; opposite: Kelly
Osbourne in Luella

How do you go about designing a collection? What is your starting point and how does it evolve into a collection?

It used to be just about the story for me: that comes from my journalistic background. It was about making an image as opposed to designing a skirt, but that's changed slightly now. I'm much more involved in the detailing. I think I've pushed the spirit of the label to where I want it to be and I can concentrate more on the details. Also, because we've now got proper backing and an infrastructure behind us, we're at the right place to be able to create a larger collection.

Do you have a muse or right-hand man/woman without whom your vision would not be complete?

I have my team. They are the most important thing to me. Because I lead a family existence in Cornwall I rely heavily on my team. At the moment, I come to London every week for two to three days and immerse myself in it. But Dave, my husband, is my other huge influence. We talk a lot and he has a big effect on what I do. He's the person I talk to most about fashion and creativity outside of my office. Although Cornwall is pure countryside and there are horses, you can be really creative out there.

You've been applauded for designing one of the original It bags – the Gisele – in 2002. Was it a surprise for you that the bag became such a success and what effect did it have on your career and label?

It was weird and it certainly had a positive effect financially in the short term. I was doing some work for Mulberry and rather than being paid I asked them to produce a bag for me. I wanted a bag on the catwalk to make the collection more polished. Then suddenly this bag made up 60 per cent of our sales that season. It was everywhere, but we didn't know how to control it. Bergdorf Goodman were ordering huge quantities. With hindsight, we should have done it slowly as it was everywhere for a while and then it was gone. But that's another learning curve. That kind of hype in fashion is quite dangerous. It can be over as quickly as it came...

I love that contrary aspect of fashion. There is so much psychology and inverted snobbery that goes on. Once you're in...you're out. It's so ridiculous; I want to document that.

I loved the Gisele bag. It summed up everything about our aesthetic and the label. It was very classic, but had subversive elements, like the rings, which were S&M inspired. And good things happened because of that bag. Club 21, who owned Mulberry, decided to back an accessory line for us, which was great.

How has having kids fuelled or altered your attitude to fashion and the industry?

My kids have given me perspective and confidence. I don't care about being cool or making mistakes. It's much more about having fun with the collection now.

Are you independently owned?

Yes, it's still owned by me. I've had a licensing agreement with Club 21 for the accessories and ready-to-wear side of the business for quite a few years. It's royalty based: I get a percentage of what we sell and they pay for the production, sampling, distribution and so on. I'm in charge of paying the team, though, and that currently consists of two designers on accessories, two on ready-to-wear and myself. We've also got a visual merchandising person. It's great to have a big infrastructure behind you, but no matter how big the structure, things can still go wrong...

What do you do to market your label?

We've got an in-house press office, but that's about it. We don't do any ad campaigns yet. We're lucky that people have liked the brand and continue to like it so we do OK on editorial.

How do you feel about celebrity endorsement?

It's a really important part of the fashion business today that cannot be ignored. You could feel resentful that people are only buying your clothes because they've seen a celebrity wearing them, but those celebrities wouldn't want to wear your clothes if they weren't great pieces of clothing... Most companies have a huge budget dedicated to dressing celebrities. We don't have the money to do that, but I'm happy for celebrities to wear my clothes as it converts into sales. We've made a few one-off dresses for people like Beth Ditto and Lily Allen. Then there are certain people we wouldn't

lend clothes to – not because they are not good enough – but in order to keep the aesthetic of the brand intact. It's very exciting for me when someone you really love wants to wear your clothes, it's like a mutual pat on the back. Someone like Beth Ditto, Meg White or Sofia Coppola. It's great too when the younger generation like Pixie Geldof and Kelly Osbourne want to wear Luella.

How do you feel you've improved as a designer?

I've just gotten a lot more serious about it. My first collection was like being at art college and now I feel I've grown in confidence and learnt so much I can play with the design element much more. I'm not paralysed and not so self-conscious about the process. When you care too much what people think you don't push yourself to create something that's new or exciting. What's the point in playing it safe?

What do you hate about the fashion industry?

The way it can make you feel about yourself can be hard. The whole model-size debate is out of control. It's very difficult if you want to do something for a normal-sized girl. They don't exist in the modelling industry. It's a catch 22. You want fashion to be making girls feel good about themselves, not bad.

It can also be quite hard to put yourself out there to be criticized. You can't help but take it to heart. It can feel like a personal attack if you've got your defences down. But in the end you're putting yourself out there for judgment, so you have to take it. And actually, there are a few writers and editors whose judgment I trust, and if I read a critical review, I take it on board. I tend to read the Style.com and *Evening Standard* reviews after my show in London.

What makes one label more successful than another?

I don't know. It's that elusive thing. What makes you buy one black jacket and not another black jacket?

What advice would you give a budding designer?

It's a hugely difficult industry to work in, but that shouldn't put you off. Go for it. It is possible.

opposite: Backstage at the Autumn/Winter 2008–2009 show, shot by James Cochrane

Paul Smith

above: Paul Smith with a mannequin in his first shop in Byard Lane, Nottingham, 1970s; opposite: Paul Smith's signature 'classic with a twist' detailing on a men's suit blazer, Spring/Summer 2008

When Paul Smith left school with no qualifications at the age of 15 he had dreams of becoming a professional racing cyclist. Following a serious accident, he fell into fashion almost by chance and opened his first shop in his hometown of Nottingham in 1970. Six years later he showed the first Paul Smith collection in Paris. Famous for his individual take on traditional British styling, where a distinct sense of Englishness merges with the unexpected and is often referred to as 'classic with a twist', Smith remains Britain's most financially successful designer. Today, his collections are wholesaled to 35 countries and sold in over 200 shops.

When did you first get into fashion?

I actually wanted to be a racing cyclist when I was young, but I had a terrible accident and ended up in hospital for months. It was when I came out of hospital that it all changed. I met up with some of the guys I'd met in hospital in the pub in Nottingham and by chance it was the pub where all the art students used to go. The conversation was about something called 'Pop Art' and something called 'Bauhaus'. At that time, London was just starting to do things in fashion, music, graphic design. It seemed like a fascinating world.

With hindsight, I realize now that I'd always been quite smartly dressed and interested in the way things looked, mostly in relation to cycling. Then one of the people I had met decided to set up her own business as a designer. She wanted to open a boutique where she could sell the clothes she made. She was excited about it but didn't know how to open a shop. I had absolutely no idea either, but I've always been an energetic and optimistic person so I said 'I'll help you.' I was convinced that it was an interesting way to make a living.

What did that first stint in the fashion trade teach you?

It was all new to me. I had to speak to people called estate agents, meet up with solicitors, look at buildings and shops. I'd never done anything like that, I was 18. It's all very much part of my story, though: learning something by doing it. Once it opened, I ran the shop, then started dressing the windows and decorating the shop. I really enjoyed it.

What made you decide to open your own shop – Paul Smith Vêtement Pour Homme – on Byard Lane in Nottingham in 1970, aged 24?

below, left and opposite, left: Paul Smith's Spring/Summer 2008 collection. A very British affair, with models wearing cricket-inspired cream flannels and David Hockney-esque spectacles; below, right: Men's shirt sleeve showing Paul Smith's signature 'classic with a twist' approach to design, Spring/Summer 2008; opposite, right: Lining and trim of a Paul Smith London Line suit

I had met my wife Pauline Denyer at an art college party. She had said, 'You have so much energy, wouldn't you be interested in running your own little shop?' At the time she was teaching two days a week. She had trained as a fashion designer at the Royal College of Art in London. Eventually I started working on my day off for people I got to know through running the boutique. I was styling photo shoots for magazines, fabric designing, colouring... I did really shitty jobs as well, like selling fabrics and suits. By this time I realized I had an eye for things. After earning that extra money for a few years I decided to open my own small shop. It was a tiny room, 12 feet square, not even a shop really, but it was all I could afford. I called it 'Paul Smith' because all the boutiques in the country at the time had really silly names like 'Birdcage' and 'Doll's House'. People knew me as Paul, and I added that silly title of 'Vêtement Pour Homme' because I was just striving to do something a bit different, to make people wonder why I'd done that. It

was just part of drawing attention to myself in a provincial town.

What did you learn from running your own business?

Pauline had been to see a lecture by an American man called Edward De Bono, a lateral thinker, who said, 'You can never change the job, but the job can change you'. In terms of my little shop, we interpreted that as meaning the job was going to change us if we didn't watch out. If we'd tried to keep the shop open every day of the week, we'd have had to start selling stuff we didn't want to sell in order to survive, so we'd have been compromising our concept for the shop. I think it's an amazingly good tip for any young designer starting out: try to realize your dream in a way that is subsidized by doing something else in those early days so you don't have to compromise. I basically worked doing anything I could to make money Monday through Thursday and on Friday and Saturday I'd open the shop. There was no

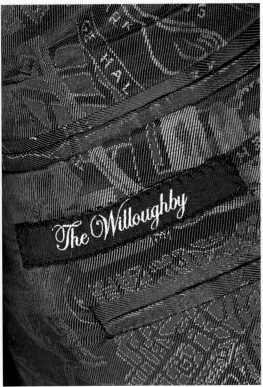

The Willoughby

compromise. It was very pure and unusual. That's probably exactly why I am where I am today. Slowly people started travelling from different towns and from London to see the shop because it had such unusual things. I got quite a reputation for being someone who not only had good ideas, but who also knew how to turn them into reality. In a provincial town you may get the same customer three times in one month, so you have to make sure the shop always looks different and that it's worth going to.

What made you decide to make and sell your own clothes in the shop?

Initially, Pauline was designing the Paul Smith clothes we sold in the shop. I would drive for miles to find a factory that could make me a few shirts, some trousers or some knitwear. At the time I was working for several London-based designers who didn't know how to get their garments made, so I'd say, 'I can make you some shirts'. Through Pauline teaching me about design and constructing clothes, I eventually started to be able to design myself.

Rather than going to fashion school you took the learning-by-doing approach and took evening classes in tailoring. To what degree did you learn the techniques needed to create your own collection?

I had no formal training, but Pauline had been to the Royal College of Art in London in the 1960s, just as the world of couture was starting to be a thing of the past and ready-to-wear was beginning to become popular. Her training had been about couture, that is, about the importance of pattern-cutting, the construction of clothes, proportion and balance in a garment, how to put sleeves in a jacket beautifully, how to put padding in a shoulder, etc. At night school my teacher was a tailor who specialized in ceremonial dress for the armed forces which is very much about making the wearer look regal and important. You try to make the wearer look tall and slim with good posture. It's all done through cutting and the way the clothes

are constructed. This along with Pauline's training and my learning by doing gave me a good basis.

Do you ever regret not going to fashion school?

No, I think what you get out of fashion school really depends on the individual. Some people need that academic approach to a career, but because I'm so lively and full of curiosity, the combination of learning from Pauline and the tailor and doing it myself and running the shop was the perfect balance. I don't think I would have been good at college, although I left school at 15 and sometimes I feel out of my depth when it comes to literature or maths.

What mistakes did you make along the way when you first started designing?

Luckily, I didn't make many. I think the big mistake people make is to leave college thinking they can immediately own a label without having experience of all the various aspects attached to it. If you design a collection, you have to make sure it's interesting enough to grab people's attention. But design is just one tiny element of the ingredients needed to create a successful brand. These days, fashion shows will be all over the internet within an hour of the runway show, so all the big brands who imitate and are influenced by smaller brands can see the clothes within the hour. Nearly all of them are far bigger than most designer brands, so it almost seems like you are copying them because they have such vast possibilities of distribution.

What challenges and triumphs were involved when you organized your first menswear collection to be shown in Paris in 1976?

Because I'd been working freelance for people such as Browns in South Molton Street in London, or doing colouring for Benetton and so on, I started to meet buyers from department stores and independent boutiques. So when I started my own tiny collection in 1976 I had a short list of people I could send invitations to. It was like, 'I'm Paul Smith. Do you remember me?' I showed the collection in a tiny hotel in Paris. Basically, nobody came [*laughs*].

From Monday to Thursday I just sat there on my own and then on the last day one boutique came in from Paris and another boutique came in so I had two small orders.

I was pleased that I got some orders. Luckily I was sensible enough to have a tiny collection and I'd established a relationship with a couple of factories. I'd been honest with them from the beginning, saying, 'I might only give you an order for 20 shirts, or it might be 200. I just don't know.' I asked them whether they might be able to put the order through the sample room rather than the mass production side of the factory. Many designers starting out think they'll take hundreds of orders and it can go hopelessly wrong. There is a real naivety about the industry. I'm not sure whether it's the fault of the colleges or because the designers are blinkered. I've had designers round my desk saying, 'I really need my own label' and I say, 'What do you think the first thing you should do is?' and their reply is 'Get a PR.' They have no money, no product, no relationship with factories, no

right: Sketch of a Paul Smith suit designed for actor Daniel Day-Lewis for the Oscars in 2008

My teacher was a tailor who specialized in ceremonial dress for the armed forces which is very much about making the wearer look regal and important. You try to make the wearer look tall and slim with good posture.

I am interested in all forms of creativity. There must be 500 books and objects in front of me now, ranging from paintings to architecture and old fabric books. If you are curious you can easily find inspiration.

understanding of costing. Take photography, for example. These days it's so easy to take a picture, but taking one that means something and that has relevance is probably harder than ever. It's the same with clothes really.

What was your vision for Paul Smith when you started the label?

When we first started out it was just a way of earning a living and having an enjoyable life together. There was no vision at all. That hasn't really changed, we've certainly progressed, but not because we had a five-year plan or a big mission to take over the world, just because we've been honest. It's weird, we've been really laid back about things. You'd think that would have a negative impact, but so many people in the world are so used to falseness and hype that when they come across something that doesn't have any of that it's almost more appealing.

What is your philosophy now?

It's still the same. We could easily be three or four times bigger than we are. We refuse offers such as designing phones, hotels, cars, ad campaigns, or being asked to open shops here, there and everywhere... It's what we say no to that has been our strength.

How would you describe your signature style?

Although we've never had a business vision as such we've always had a design vision. About 15 years ago we got approached by every big group out there, including Louis Vuitton and Prada, when they were trying to buy people. We were polite enough to meet them all and they'd say things like, 'We're going to open 20 shops for you next year and so on', but we've never been like that. We'll open a shop because we've found an interesting building somewhere. It's far more to do with letting things happen gently and naturally. Paul Smith clothes have always had this element of 'classic with a twist', although the phrase is really over-used now. We're not making groundbreaking, avant-garde designs, it's all very relevant to the season and we always move the collections forward, but they're incredibly

opposite: A Paul Smith Melrose chair; above: Paul Smith in his office engulfed by books and other objects he peruses for inspiration

wearable. They're unique, they'll either have a lovely lining or be a hundred per cent cashmere, or there will be a hidden print under the cuff...

We design clothes for people who are happy with their lot and not looking for an identity mark which says, 'I am fashionable' or 'I am wealthy'. People who are insecure often look for status, which puts them in a club, whether it's the car they drive, the clothes they wear or the restaurants they go to. It's all part of being a certain way. I hope that with Paul Smith clothes the wearer wears the clothes rather than the clothes wearing them.

What thought processes are needed to develop a signature style?

It's a hard question to answer because it should come from the heart and from your lifestyle and interests. If you love tailoring then that might be your specialist subject. You'd work out ways of developing a tailoring collection by relying on old-fashioned methods. Then there are people like McQueen or Galliano, who create attention-seeking pieces, it's about your own personal character.

My advice would be to try to dig into your inner self for what it is you love. If you're a humorous, jolly person, you might do things in bright colours with vivid embroidery. If you have a more serious nature, you might do things in a more monochrome

way. It doesn't mean that it'll work, it's not a guarantee for success, but an ingredient.

You wrote a book called *You Can Find Inspiration in Everything*: (*and if you can't, look again). You now have 12 different collections including Paul Smith Women, Paul Smith Jeans, Paul Smith Accessories and Paul Smith Shoes. How do you come up with concepts and themes for your 12 different collections each season such as, say, the David Hockney spectacles or the Cricket-inspired menswear collection in 2008?

It's something I've been fortunate enough never to struggle with. I am interested in all forms of creativity. There must be 500 books and objects in front of me now, ranging from paintings to architecture and old fabric books. If you are curious you can easily find inspiration. If you aren't then it can be very troublesome. What happens in many cases is that many designers and brands take their ideas from old magazines such as *Grazia* or *Nova* or shopping at Portobello market in London. It's one way of doing it and I suppose there's no harm in that, but it's slightly disappointing as humans were made with brains. There is so much of interest out there, whether it's going to a Louise Bourgeois exhibition (her family were seamstresses), or going to a Russian expressionist exhibition. You can find inspiration in art, books, someone's lifestyle, you've got to have a busy mind. Forcing a theme can be extremely dangerous and rarely works. It has to come naturally.

How much does the inspiration for the 12 collections have to merge into one coherent vision?

I think it normally does because the starting point is always 'classic with a twist' which is boring to hear time and time again. If you ask 'what is Paul Smith about?' I can certainly define what I do.

left and opposite: Paul Smith's unmistakable, quirky British sensibility is apparent in his Spring/Summer 2008 collection

I have a love of tradition, craftsmanship, producing nicely made clothes, attention to detail, but always with a sense of surprise. If I create 12 collections and one is about, say, Matisse and one is about cycling and one is about Louise Bourgeois and so on, they'll all still be built up of the same ingredients. They'll all be nicely made, no garment would have 18 zips or three arms, I don't do high fashion. You'd never find twisted seams or ruching because it's not what I do. Eventually you discover your own way of doing things. It's like making a soufflé, you have a recipe and then work out your own way to make it stay up.

How does designing for women differ from designing for men?

It was a lot more difficult. I had a reputation for being a men's designer, I am a man and started designing men's clothes based on what I liked. It was quite easy and continues to be easy. I know my stuff. With women's…a lot of women's designers are gay and have a strong feminine side to them. I have a feminine side like all human beings, but I wouldn't say it's a strong one. I don't live that life. I'm not turned on by hair, make-up, shoes, old movies. My approach to womenswear was always more male. It was about tailoring and simplicity. That's how I started, but then I had to get an assistant designer, who had a strong feminine side. Well, she's a woman. She now does the dresses and skirts and the more feminine pieces and I do the knitwear, the shirts and the tailoring. It was a tough call, but I had to do it to make it work.

Were accessories a natural design progression for Paul Smith? How important are they for the label both financially and as a marketing platform?

Many of the big brands out there are not actually clothing companies. They are accessories companies. A while ago I read that only 12 per cent of Gucci sales are in clothes; 22 per cent is watches. Prada is also an accessories company, as is Louis Vuitton. The amazing thing about Paul Smith is that

we are a clothing company. We sell clothes and we only recently started doing good business in accessories. We've always designed accessories, but we came from clothes first. Accessories are so important from a business and a human point of view. We all need cheering up from time to time. If it's rainy and dull and you've got a bit of money to spend on yourself, you might go out and buy a book, or a nice scarf, or a pair of socks, or a tie. They are low-cost items that can make you feel great. And from a shopkeeping point of view, going back to my early days as a shopkeeper in a provincial town, accessories are a great way of keeping a shop looking interesting.

You started selling products such as quirky penknives, Filofaxes and interesting pens you found on your travels in your first Covent Garden shop. What inspired you to sell clothes mixed with other artefacts in the same shop as early as 1970?

Right from my first 12-ft square shop I've always sold objects as well as clothes. I'd sell clocks, things I found on holiday, pen knives... I'd go to, say, Paris and buy some art posters at the Centre Pompidou, or I'd get pens from antique shops, or notebooks from stationers on a Greek island. The things always sold out in days. I don't know where it came from apart from my head. I never did it for commercial reasons, just to make the shop more interesting. I wanted to entice the customer to come back.

A few years ago, Carla Sozzani from 10 Corso Como in Milan and Sarah Lerfel from Colette in Paris said to me that the main influence on their stores was the Paul Smith shop on Floral Street in Covent Garden because it sold other things besides clothes. In the very first shop I opened in Covent Garden in 1979 I had a tiny cabinet with a small display, but the money that generated always surprised me.

You have over 200 Paul Smith shops in Japan and outsell every other European designer there. Why do you think you are so successful there?

Hard work. In the 1980s loads of designers and companies were invited to go over there. Lots of people just saw it as a way of making money. They went over once or twice and sent a few faxes, but never really embraced the market or put their heart and soul into it. I felt so privileged to be out there, I went two to four times a year and really tried to understand the culture. I did lots of interviews, I worked closely with the company that I made a licence agreement with. So closely in fact that if I wanted a bunch of flowers, they'd ask me what kind I wanted in the shop. I really embraced the job. So many designers were disrespectful and didn't do that. I've got an office of 25 people out there, run by me. I've approached it in a really honest, hands-on way. It's like a marriage, if you're always away, never wash up, not interested in what your partner has to say, then you'll fall by the wayside. Of course the clothes are important too, but it's not just about the clothes. It's about the aura that surrounds the name, the interesting shops, the interviews you give and so on.

Why do you think you are a global success?

Never over distributing, never being too greedy, always keeping people hungry for our clothes. Also, I've always worked hard at never being number one. You can only go one way if you're number one and that's down. If you analyse what was hot and popular 10 years ago, chances are they're not hot anymore. They might be doing well financially because of the fickleness of the press, especially in womenswear, but 10 years down the line someone else is the new darling. Fashion designers need to know that at the end of the day it's about somebody somewhere buying your clothes today, in five years and in 10 years' time and realizing that it's not just about today but tomorrow as well. If you want to believe your own publicity and think you're great you'll go bankrupt. It's about keeping up, inventing and continuity.

Other designers have long since started producing their clothes in China. How important is keeping the production of your collections in England and Italy and sourcing your fabrics in France, Italy and England?

It's not as important as it used to be because people are more familiar with clothes being made outside Europe. Morally we would love to keep our business in England, but it's not possible because nearly all the manufacturers have closed down. We do work in Italy, France and other parts of Europe and a little bit in the Far East.

Is your company still independently owned?

Yes. It's so important to me because as soon as you get shareholders on board they're only interested in their own personal greed and creativity is stopped, which is why we've got huge economic problems in the world today. I don't know why people don't just say it, 'It's because of greed.' It's because people are living beyond their means, over borrowing and so on.

Is there anything you dislike about the fashion world?

Just the fact that so many designers have egos that are far too big. It's an

important and enjoyable industry, but it is only clothes. We're not sewing arms back on or working in a cyclone disaster area. We're not saving lives. It's clothes and we're very privileged but, please, just keep your feet on the ground.

What makes one designer/brand more successful than another one?

On the one hand it's to do with practicality and clothes that are beautifully made on time, and it's about a company being organized enough to get paid and to have enough money to finance the next collection. On the other hand, it's also about image, re-inventing yourself and continuity. But in a way it's about neither and about both.

What advice would you give a budding designer?

I'd say try to keep your ideas pure when you start out. They won't necessarily earn you money to start with. You'll have to subsidize yourself by doing other things that don't only provide an income; if you choose a job carefully it will have a learning-by-doing aspect as well. And you have to have a point of view. Nobody needs another writer, architect, designer. The world is full of them. If you've got a point of view, you've got a bit of a chance.

left: Brown punched leather brogues, from the Paul Smith Shoe collection, Spring/Summer 2008; below: Postage stamp Union Jack holdall, Spring/Summer 2008

Accessories are so important from a business and a human point of view. We all need cheering up from time to time. If it's rainy and dull and you've got a bit of money to spend on yourself, you might go out and buy a book, or a nice scarf, or a pair of socks, or a tie.

Missoni

Angela Missoni

above: Siblings Angela, Vittorio and Luca Missoni are all part of the Missoni brand; opposite: From the Missoni Autumn/Winter 2008–2009 campaign

Founded in 1953 as a knitwear producer by Angela Missoni's parents, Ottavio and Rosita, Missoni is one of the most celebrated and long-standing ready-to-wear brands to come out of Italy in the 20th century. Angela worked in the company for over 20 years learning about every aspect of the business and brand, from designing through to production, before becoming creative director in 1997. Since her appointment, she has focused on updating the brand's signature knits and instantly recognizable stripes and zigzag patterns, thereby introducing a new and younger fan base to the label.

Your parents launched Missoni in 1953 and you were born five years later. You've been around fashion all your life. When did you first get interested in it?

I started assisting my mother here and there when I was 19, but my priority has always been to have children. I was 15 the first time I told my mother I wanted to have a baby. She freaked out. I ended up waiting until I was 23 to have kids and then had three in quick succession. After the birth of my children everything I wanted to do related to the

wellbeing of children, for instance, I opened a playground for children in Varese. When I was pregnant with Theresa I said to my dad, 'I really think I'm never going to work in this company, it's not my thing.' He asked me what I wanted to do and I said I liked designing jewelry and he said, 'You know you can always do a project independently, you don't need to work with your mom every day.' Until that point I hadn't realized that I wanted to do it alone.

I started looking after special projects such as leathers and lingerie and realized that I knew the process from beginning to end. After two or three years, when I was 29, I decided I wanted to work at Missoni and generate my own line, experimenting with texture, shapes, patterns and prints. Missoni was sponsoring me and after several seasons my mom

below, left: Ottavio Missoni was an athlete and created tracksuits in knitwear in 1948; below, right: A Missoni dress from the 1958 collection; opposite, left: Missoni's instantly recognizable zigzag patterns form part of its DNA: here on a creation from 1973; opposite, right: Famous for knitwear and stripes, this outfit was presented on the catwalk in 1981

said, 'What you are doing is what I'd like Missoni to be today. Why don't you do the same for the main line?' My mother was ready to hand over. She was tired and stressed about fighting with the commercial side of the industry. You have to have the strength, in fashion, to fight for your point of view.

What did being around your parents' company from such a young age teach you about the industry?
Everything. I realize now that I learned a lot just watching my mother go out to flea markets to buy 1920s and 1930s pieces. She was into Elsa Schiaparelli and similar designers. Missoni has never been an industry as such, though: that wasn't my parents' intention, they always thought of themselves as artisans.

You have had the best on-the-job training. Do you think it's important to go to fashion school?
Yes. One of the most important things that it can teach you is that there are so many other jobs out there besides 'designing', fabric research, the knitwear field, the arts... We are lucky in that we own our factory and the product is made here from beginning to end. So anyone working for us can witness how the garment is made from initial sketches through to production. It's not just about being in the studio and drawing, but also finding solutions to designs you've created that are impossible to implement.

What attributes do you need to become a successful designer?
You have to have a good eye and with that comes a certain sensibility. I don't know if everybody can

I realize now that I learned a lot just watching my mother go out to flea markets to buy 1920s and 1930s pieces. She was into Elsa Schiaparelli and similar designers. Missoni has never been an industry as such, though: that wasn't my parents' intention, they always thought of themselves as artisans.

do this. You need to have an eye for detail and for the big picture at the same time. The big picture is the label, which consists of both the image and the product. You have to learn not only how to create a garment, but also how to handle a party, how to put on a show, why one girl should go on the catwalk before another. You have to have a good psychological attitude in order to understand people and get the best out of them. You can't do it all on your own, you need to let others help you.

How would you describe Missoni's vision?
It's hard for me to describe it because there was never a plan. We're currently making big changes in the company and one of these is going to be communication. I feel that sometimes people don't realize how our product is made and that it is still very artisanal. I want Missoni to create a product that is fashionable but will also last. After all, we need to think how fashion will evolve after this frantic period of buying, always buying more shoes, more bags, more shoes. How many shoes do we need? Where are we going to put them? I'm looking at the next generation. Sooner or later we're all going to get tired of consumerism to such an extent. What will the next generation appreciate? I would like my product to become a cherished item in your wardrobe.

In a way it's a miracle that Missoni is still here. So much has happened in the last 50 years. There was no Gucci, no Tom Ford, no Zara, no H&M and no big accessories business. So many huge labels, in terms of money and accessories, have been created. We managed to stay afloat with our little budget and our primary product, which is clothes.

Where do you get your inspiration for new patterns or prints?
It could be anything: a postcard where you can see 13 colours together, or a coat that has a strong orange-red on which the entire colour code might be based. Sometimes it's more about shapes: I might build half a collection around the shape of a buckle on a bag.

above: Rosita and Ottavio Missoni; opposite: From the Missoni Home collection

But then again, it could be an exhibition, a time period, a movie, a woman passing on the street.

How do these prints then get created?

We design all our prints. I have an artist who has been working with me for eight years and he has designed all the prints we've done. We discuss inspiration, he draws and once he's finished we might pull four prints from that one drawing. It starts to grow and you start seeing other things...

How do you go about designing a collection?

We always start out with the colour card, and then we choose a yarn because we do our knitted fabrics before we choose our fabrics. Then we think about where we want to go in terms of shape and then we choose the fabrics and create designs specific to each fabric. Fashion moves so quickly these days, people have so many images on their mind, so the narrower the message, the more likely it is to stick.

How important are accessories to the label?

They are not very important yet. We started creating shoes a couple of years ago and we've added bags to the collection too. Accessories in general sell well because it's much easier to buy a bag than an item of clothing. You don't have to try it on, there are no sizes, one size fits all. It's the same with shoes: it doesn't matter whether you're skinny or fat, your shoe size will always be the same. Whether you are buying shoes or a bag, you can just nip into a shop and out again and you've got that same happy feeling as when you've bought a dress.

What is your best-selling garment?

Knitwear of course. I'm forever changing the knitwear and trying to do something new with it. For example, four or five years ago I started using some light knits and doubling them up, so they could be used as fabric. I used them to make trench coats, light jackets and blazers. These are now part of the collection every season. It's a new way of wearing Missoni.

Since becoming creative director in 1997 you have managed to attract a younger generation of consumers who didn't necessarily remember the brand from the 1970s. How did you achieve this?

I did it instinctively. I realized that Missoni had lost my generation and I started making things that I wanted to wear and that my girlfriends wanted to wear, but I wasn't just focusing on a younger generation. What makes me very happy is that there is something recognizable about Missoni. It's not about age, it's more about style. I think that Missoni is trans-generational. If, for instance, a mother, daughter and grandmother walked into one of our shops, they might not buy the same outfit but they could all find something they liked.

Do you think it's important to be innovative?
Of course. Fashion *is* innovation. Fashion looks forward.

Do you think you need a philosophy to create a beautiful collection?
I can only talk about myself here. I know that I like to work in harmony, in a harmonious place. I'm lucky in that when my parents built the company in 1968, they built it in the woods, in a place they would have loved to live. I think you can sense that in the label somehow. We take pleasure in creating the product. We smile and laugh a lot. My family has a big sense of humour. Of course we also disagree on things sometimes. Being able to go home to have lunch with my kids because I lived close to the factory also made a huge difference, and also living close to my parents. I felt like I had a normal life.

How important has financial independence been to Missoni as a business and as a brand?
I like being independent. There are always offers from people who want to buy us, but the Missoni factory is like my home and we don't want to sell it. Being financially independent is a privilege. It is a great responsibility, but on the other hand it keeps the brand free and creatively autonomous. Maybe with a financial partnership change can happen faster, production can get bigger, but the risk is missing out on integrity, quality and the total involvement and control of what you are doing. Nevertheless...we're

opposite and right: Missoni Autumn/Winter 2008–2009 collection

currently trying to re-organize the company so it can be self-sufficient in case none of the kids wants to take over. You need a lot of passion to be in this business because it can get very stressful and it can drain you a lot. You have to wake up every morning and be excited about every little detail.

To what degree has your strong family unit been part of the family's success?

Being a family unit has been absolutely part of our brand's success. It is something very Italian so there are many other families behind the 'made in Italy' success and the family business has identified our culture, our unique way of living and working, around the world. And because people always liked the idea of a family unit, it was always very much part of Missoni's image – to the point where Missoni quickly evolved into a lifestyle brand rather than just being a fashion brand. The unity and complicity of our family inspired a wider range of products and collections, including home, sport, baby and kids, perfumes, etc. They are products and collections inspired by our family's trans-generational way of life.

And we are all still involved. My eldest brother Vittorio looked after the commercial side for many years and now he is like the ambassador for the brand and is in charge of the openings. Luca used to design the menswear label but now he looks after the Missoni Museum. We're probably also going to start a foundation. Before we re-organized the company, we were actually slow in making decisions because we didn't have anybody to help us. We've had the same general manager since 1964, who literally unlocked the doors every morning. Now we've hired a financial director, a commercial director and managers for all the stores. Although my mother no longer designs the main line collections she still looks after the Missoni Home collection and my dad is still involved with some aspects of the fabric side. Aside from the strong family tie, I think another reason for the company's success was that my parents always had interests outside of the company. My mom used to go mushroom hunting and they both love sports.

How has the fashion industry changed since your parents created the brand in 1953? What aspects do you love/despise?

Missoni was born at the very beginning of Italian prêt-à-porter and I think they are the only brand left from that era. What I love about this work is that you need to have a good eye. Also, every day you are dealing with all the different aspects of production. You have to recognize problems quickly, make decisions and find solutions. Also, I love that it keeps me constantly in touch with matters of design, aesthetic improvement, beauty and femininity. Perhaps what I despise about it is its frantic rhythm, the constant short-term deadlines. I also hate the globalization of fashion. I hate that all shops look the same no matter what town you are in. I think it's boring and people will get bored with it. I have a new concept for our stores. I'd like each shop to embody a sense of the city it's in and I'd like people to be able to buy certain products that they can only find in that specific shop. For example, it might be nice to sell special Missoni plates in Capri and Positano that are made in Amalfi.

What makes one designer or brand stand out more than the next? Why do you think Missoni survived?

I think my parents invented something truly genuine. They were experimental. They did something in knitwear that hadn't been there before, so when I took over I wasn't afraid to experiment. My father started doing knits because he was an athlete and he did tracksuits in knitwear because he wanted to be comfortable, so comfort will always be part of the Missoni DNA.

What advice would you give a budding designer?

Listen, listen, listen. Designers always want to talk too soon. You can learn so much from listening and watching. But on the other hand, when you really feel like you've got something to express, don't be worried about expressing it.

opposite: A Missoni weaving machine

I think my parents invented something truly genuine. They were experimental. They did something in knitwear that hadn't been there before, so when I took over I wasn't afraid to experiment.

Dries Van Noten

above: Dries Van Noten, portrait by David Turner; opposite: Dries Van Noten womenswear Autumn/Winter 2007–2008 collection

Born in Belgium in 1958 and often referred to as a member of the 'Antwerp Six', Dries Van Noten was introduced to fashion at a very early age. His grandfather, a tailor, opened the first ready-to-wear store for men in Antwerp and in the 1970s his father opened a large up-market fashion store. In 1976, aged 18, Van Noten enrolled at the Antwerp Royal Academy of Fine Arts to study fashion design. When he launched his debut collection of shirts, blazers and trousers 10 years later, it was an immediate success and was bought by prestigious retailers such as Barneys in New York and Whistles in London. His work is characterized by a creative use of prints and colours and is inspired by tailoring, printing and handcraft practices from around the world. Besides selling in the company's own stores in Antwerp and Hong Kong, his collections retail in approximately 400 shops worldwide. Van Noten has never advertised and his label has been financially independent since its inception.

When and why did you first get interested in fashion?

For three generations my family had worked in gentlemen's 'outfitting' so it was natural that I gradually moved towards this passion.

Your grandfather opened the first ready-to-wear shop for men in Antwerp and your father opened a large up-market fashion store some years later. How much time did you spend in your family's business as a kid?

As a young boy my mother used to take me with her to attend fashion shows in Milan and Paris. I remember feeling a sense of wonderment through my participation in this exciting world. My grandfather and father instilled a sense of respect for the rites and traditions of dressing. It was this foundation that nurtured the eye and hand with which I still look at and feel fabrics and textiles today.

To what degree did it influence your decision to become a designer?

Evidently and absolutely.

Describe your time at the Antwerp Royal Academy of Fine Arts.

We shared the idea of breaking, challenging, thwarting and embracing tradition in an attempt to create a new and personal expression through clothing – all this in our own and financially independent way. This experience of nurture and challenge at the Academy was shared by six of us, who would later be referred to as the 'Antwerp Six'.

What did you learn there?

While there I captured the idea of a garment as an attitude or stance and not just clothing.

How important is going to a fashion school if you want to become a designer?

For some vital, and for others entirely superficial.

When I create a collection what concerns me most is that my designs transcend trend.

How did working as a buyer for your father's boutique help you when you came to designing your own collections? What did it teach you about the industry?

With hindsight it probably instilled a practicality in the way I design: the fact that designing isn't just necessarily about creating beautiful items that I like, but also about creating items that women and men will enjoy wearing. Garments that will, hopefully and ultimately, become key pieces within their wardrobe.

How does one develop a signature style?

I don't think that a signature style is the ultimate goal one hopes to achieve or develop throughout one's career. I think it's probably something people attribute to designers when they have stronger elements within their collections. Certainly I hope that people can see beyond what is ascribed to me and not focus simply on any one element or style.

How would you describe the Dries Van Noten signature style?

I always aim for the idea of elegance without ostentation.

Do you think you need a philosophy to create a beautiful and coherent collection?

I don't think that it is necessary for everyone. But I know that when I create a collection what concerns me most is that my designs transcend trend. What might be considered beautiful today should also be beautiful in five or even 10 years' time.

You've been described as designing collections item by item to offer individuality – why then is it necessary to create an entire collection?

Since I began designing I've always wanted to offer the idea of creating an entire wardrobe for men and women. The 'all encompassing' wardrobe has been the philosophy behind our work.

Your designs are often described as 'art- and ethnic-inspired'. Where do you pick up the ethnic references that end up in your collections?

opposite: Detail shot from the Autumn/Winter 2007–2008 collection; overleaf: Sketches from the Spring/Summer 2008 collection with the creation that followed

THE HENLEY COLLEGE LIBRARY

I have always used elements from all over the world within my designs. I'm fascinated by the idea of 'another place' and yes, I suppose it can be said that there have been collections that have been strongly inspired by ethnicity. Given, however, that I don't have that much time to travel anymore, I try to create my own stories.

How important is handcraft in your work – the beautiful scarves you create, the embroidered elements, etc?

The foundation of everything I do is on the basis of being inspired by ideas and practices of tailoring, printing and artisanal know-how from around the world. Many of the key pieces I present within my collections come not only from Belgium, where I choose to produce, but also from around the world where the masters, tailors or craftspeople we have discovered while doing our research come from.

When is a design finished?

How long is a piece of string? When conception fuses with utility and realization.

To what degree does one need to be innovative and bold in fashion?

To a heightened degree.

How does designing for men differ from designing for women? Do you enjoy one more than the other?

The techniques and approaches are very different. For women, designs tend to challenge 'the daily' and men's tends to be more founded in the reality of our surroundings rather than the dreams and aspirations of a designer. Neither eclipses the other for me. I am simply lucky to have both complementary challenges in my life.

Describe your ideal customer or Dries Van Noten wearer?

Someone who is comfortable with their own style and not afraid to be themselves.

Why have you never advertised?

At the beginning simply because we did not have the money and, later and now, the idea that someone would buy clothes simply because they are attracted to the tag concerns me somewhat.

Why is being financially independent important to the brand and to you personally?

This question comes up constantly. The only answer I can give is that having financial independence lets me move at my own pace, grow as I want to grow. In other words, it permits me to feel comfortable about the development of my company as it expands. Financial independence ensures creative independence.

Why did you decide to stay in Antwerp despite your worldwide success? What does the city give you?

Antwerp is and always has been my home. It's not too far from London, or from Paris, which means that should I wish to visit the big metropolises I can do so easily. The discretion of Antwerp is a big plus for me and it is here that I am most at ease. Home is where the heart is!

What do you love most about your job? What element of your job drives you up the wall?

I love the variety of work that comes my way each day. No day is the same and that's exactly what keeps it so exciting. Intransigence and dulled vision can cause frustration.

What advice would you give to a budding designer?

Consider clothing not as an element of social status but more as an expression of one's personality.

What makes one designer more successful than another?

Individuality, idiosyncrasy, intrepidness, inspiration, introspection and...a sense of humour!

Consider clothing not as an element of social status but more as an expression of one's personality.

opposite: Dries Van Noten is inspired by ideas and practices of tailoring, printing and artisanal know-how from around the world, Autumn/Winter 2008–2009

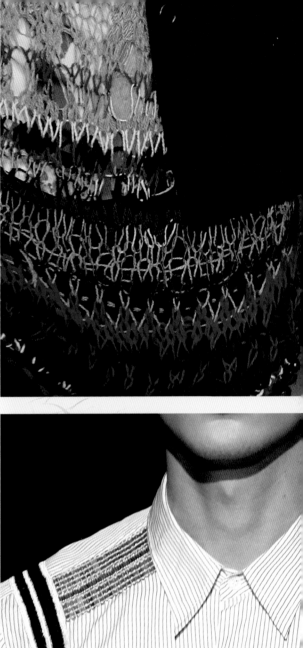

Acne

Jonny Johansson

Founder and creative director, Acne

In 1997 Jonny Johansson, the founder of the Swedish creative collective Acne, decided to distribute 100 pairs of jeans to his friends, family and clients. Soon afterwards orders came in from several boutiques who wanted to stock the raw denim jeans with bright red stitching. And so what began as a marketing idea for his creative collective ended up being the inspiration for an entire fashion label. Ten years on, Acne has developed into one of the world's most renowned contemporary labels and is sold in 485 shops in 40 different countries.

When did you first get interested in fashion?

Self-expression has always been really important to me. I never studied fashion as such, I'm actually from a music background. My sister is a music teacher, my brother is a guitarist and my father played in different bands, so I always thought that I would be a musician or an artist. However, along the way I got more and more into the idea of self-expression and fashion and the way I dressed was a big part of the way I expressed myself.

What made you come up with the idea of distributing 100 pairs of raw denim jeans with bright red stitching to family and friends?

First of all we had the idea of creating a 'creative collective'. That was in 1994 to 1995. Our aim was to design everything in the creative collective ourselves: from the office to the conference table and so on. We wanted to explore all these different fields, including photography and consultancy. The first major breakthrough was when somebody from *Wallpaper** magazine happened to pass by our offices and loved them so much they did a feature on us. All of a sudden our work became very public. And given that fashion is one of the biggest media, we then went on to discuss how we could make something within the fashion genre that was about fabric and was more closely linked to what true fashion actually was. We discussed which product would have the most energy. I felt that jeans were the perfect canvas. For me, they are the starting point of fashion as we know it today. The movement that occurred in the 1950s, which separated youth culture from how people dressed traditionally, is still relevant today. We wanted to choose something from that period and make it work for the present day.

Did you come up with the design for that initial pair of jeans?

Yes. And that was kind of hard because I had never designed a single item of clothing. As you move on

you sort of learn... I had some friends who were pattern-cutters. It was a creative collective idea and we thrived on the whole social thing. For us it was all about 'the group'.

Once the jeans were successful did you think, 'let's continue with this?'

It wasn't that straightforward. Initially we had to do a lot of other things such as directing commercials and doing brand consultancy to survive. We worked with all the Swedish brands, from H&M to J. Lindeberg. I can't say we had planned to start a big business because it was sucking a lot of money away from what we were doing. We just felt that we wanted to do our own products and we didn't take any salaries at the beginning. The timing of our starting up was very fortunate because it was the period of deconstruction and the period of the 'do it yourself' mentality – which was good for me because I never trained to be a fashion designer. But fashion and music are a similar kind of thing. You sell an illusion, or a feeling, or an idea.

Are there advantages to being a 'non-trained' fashion designer?

Ten years ago I would have said, 'yes'. But today I would say that it's not advantageous. Obviously, I have a different perspective on fashion from someone who has been 'taught' a perspective, but I would say I have more disadvantages.

I felt that jeans were the perfect canvas. For me, they are the starting point of fashion as we know it today. The movement that occurred in the 1950s, which separated youth culture from how people dressed traditionally, is still relevant today.

opposite: The original Acne raw denim jeans, with red stitching, first created in 1997; overleaf: From the Acne Spring/Summer 2008 lookbook

What are the disadvantages?

Learning pattern-making takes a long time. Today the competition is so hard that you need all the tools you can get. Fashion today looks totally different from how it did even 10 years ago. The construction of garments is more worked through, the fabrics are very well chosen. I wouldn't recommend launching into the fashion world today without any training, especially if you are not an artist.

Where do you get inspiration for new collections?

For me inspiration is a way of giving energy to your creative mind. It's all about finding a new method. For me the research process is very important. I like brands where the research process and ideas actually flavour the collections. I don't like seeing the same idea every season.

Can you name a brand where that has been the case recently?

Prada is doing very well right now. It's very conceptual. They work on ideas and take them to the next level. In the fashion industry that would be considered a sacrifice because essentially what people want is the same thing over and over again.

So where exactly does the inspiration come from?

It's all about the method. For example for one season we all rented an apartment in Paris, in St Germain, for one month and lived there together. It was like a social experiment. We just stayed there until the collection came together. But it could also just be a regular book that you find: anything that makes you find a new method to give you energy.

Do you need a philosophy to create a beautiful collection?

I think you discover what it is while you work. It's easier now for me to say that we have some kind of philosophy, but I couldn't have said that 10 years ago. The only thing we had at that moment was that we wanted to attract creative and strong people. Now I can see it in retrospect. For example, part of our philosophy stems from the fact that we are not from Paris and that we are not an American brand. Whilst still being global, I feel it's important to be local because everything is so known today. As a designer you work more and more with your history

Learning pattern-making takes a long time. Today the competition is so hard that you need all the tools you can get... I wouldn't recommend launching into the fashion world today without any training, especially if you are not an artist.

and your background. You might get inspiration from your mother's or father's clothing, or from your roots. I think what people like about us is that we are a bit more local and that our clothing has this personality linked to the creative collective. Philosophy for me is always about giving energy rather than taking energy. Some clothes are designed to be beautiful for a very short moment and those clothes can be very hard to wear because you have to be in a certain mood to wear them. I don't really like that. Creating a classic garment is more interesting to me than creating a party piece.

Can you talk me through your design process?
It's quite basic. We do patterns for everything, we have a pattern-making room, we have computer patterns, we do research, we go to all the fabric fairs... It's very boring. It's the same structure that everybody follows. The difference, perhaps, is that we pride ourselves on always keeping one foot on 'the street', unlike some of the high-end prêt-à-porter brands that are leaning towards couture. Those brands are very extreme now – not only in the way they design, but also in the way that it's all about luxury. It's far removed from what's happening on 'the street'.

Acne expanded its jeans collection way before jeans became a multi-million pound business. What made you think this was where fashion was heading?
We took the jeans in 1996 and said, 'This is the most important garment there is'. We were the first brand to come out of the 'streetwear' genre and say, 'Hey, it doesn't matter if you're streetwear or whatever you are, it's about the experience'. That's why I knew we should bring in the jeans. There are a lot of prêt-à-porter brands now, who see jeans as a cash cow and are turning them into sub-labels. After we made the move all these brands suddenly wanted to sell to prêt-à-porter stores, but I think we were the first to make that move.

Did you just have a hunch that it would be successful?
It's related to how we bought and consumed fashion ourselves. For me it has always been about the whole mentality. It wasn't about luxury or glamour. For me, the people behind the scenes are usually more interesting than what's happening in the foreground. A lot of brands have gone down the Hollywood route in the last decade and are trying to dress stars and portray a glamour that is long gone. We never went down that route. We obviously have many stars who wear our clothes, but they don't wear our label because we pay them to.

How often do you need to change styles in your denim collection?
We do four collections a year.

opposite and left: Design sketches created for the Autumn/Winter 2008–2009 collection

Do you have key items that remain the same from season to season?

Not really. The jeans generally have a longer lifecycle, they blend in more easily. In fact, the first pair of jeans we ever did – the Mic pair – which are the ones we sent out to friends and family, are still one of the best-selling styles.

How do you decide how to price a garment?

Again, it's linked to our heritage. We are a Swedish brand. The Social Democrats have ruled this country for many years… It's a lot about group work here. Our basic idea was that we wanted to have the same margin on everything, so that if you were attracted to a garment that was cheaper to make, the price would be cheaper and if you were attracted to a more expensive fabric, for instance, the garment would also be more expensive. I would never price a T-shirt at 200 euros just because it's made by Acne.

Acne created items such as the mismatched David Hockney-inspired socks or the 'flattering' lattice dress. How important is it to maintain a sense of humour and adventure in the fashion industry?

That's what it's about. I like to take the whole industry seriously but, at the same time, I think that it's quite intense. It's also about having fun and living in the 'right here, right now' frame of mind and just seeing what happens, which includes taking risks every now and then.

How important are accessories for the brand?

We never sold that many accessories. It's always been just one piece here and there that changes the look of the collection or gives it a contradictory twist because I think that's really important. At the moment we're pushing shoes. I think it's the most important accessory to change a look totally. We also included really wide 1970s ties in our collection although the collection itself had nothing to do with the 1970s. To me it's about trying to create a clash of

left: Acne's 'flattering' lattice dress, Spring/Summer 2008 collection; opposite: The plimsolls produced in collaboration with Tretorn, Spring/Summer 2007

sorts, because opposites attract. For us proportion is always more interesting than decoration.

Why are collaborations, such as the one you did with Tretorn, important to you?

We're not interested in collaboration per se, but we were interested in Tretorn's product. It was something we couldn't make ourselves. We actually tried to make sneakers ourselves in the Far East, where every brand these days is manufacturing their sneakers although it might say something else on the label. But we couldn't get it right with the factories. It was a lot of work. Then we were approached by Adidas and Puma and others, but in the end we decided on Tretorn. They are Swedish and they have a casual approach to sneakers, which is what we were after. We grew up with the brand: it's in our history. We felt there was a reason to create something with them. It goes back to the method I was talking about. Why does one do something? For me there has to be a reason. If somebody just told me I had to design sunglasses I'd find it really hard. There are so many sunglasses out there. Why should we do it too? If you have an idea or a dream then it's a totally different story.

How would you describe Acne's brand identity and vision?

I have no idea. I think it's very important for us to be able to explore. We have a saying that's quite ridiculous, but we always say it, 'Discover how far you can go.' It's a tagline we use internally to get people to go further. I think often it's much more about the experience than the result. I love the idea of the creative collective. I want people to utilize their creative potential. I work with people who are better than me. It excites me to experience the ideas that other people put out. I want to be constantly amazed. We launched Acne Paper because we wanted to capture the ambiance of what we talked about while we were doing a collection. We wanted to show people what's not shown in the collection. We're open about where our inspiration comes from. We know we only have

Why does one do something? For me there has to be a reason. If somebody just told me I had to design sunglasses I'd find it really hard... If you have an idea or a dream then it's a totally different story.

10 years of history. We know we are not Vuitton, we don't have that power or muscle.

Acne creates simple and functional clothes, which are effortlessly stylish. It sounds so easy and yet most fashion companies fail to hit the spot – what is it about Acne that catches people's imagination?

You can participate more in what we do than with the regular fashion labels. There's also a lot of input that comes into this house, which we try to give out. I think there will be more and more of that in the future. I want people to feel and see that we are more honest in our approach.

How important do you think it is to be innovative in fashion?

You have two ways of doing things: one is going for handcrafted garments; the other is to pour ideas on people and give them inspiration.

Unlike most other fashion brands, you refrain from running ad campaigns. Why?

On the one hand, it would be really nice to do a picture of what you've created that season, but at the same time it's an industry. And it's ridiculously expensive. When we did Acne Paper people said, 'Well that's not a free magazine'. No it's not, but instead of having lots of ads, we have our name on the magazine. And we try to attract people that we like and want to work with. A regular fashion magazine would have advertisers and the stylists would have to use the clothes that are advertised. And if they don't like the stuff for an editorial, they have to use it in a still life because they have to make sure the brand is in there.

Acne tried to expand quite quickly in its early stages. How did this affect the company?

I've learnt that you have to expand organically. We wanted to become an international brand really quickly and we sold to lots of international shops. These in turn weren't paying us and so on and

below: Acne studio, the brand's retail outlet in Paris

because we were a small brand nobody really cared about us. In fashion it takes a lot of working through your ideas to get somewhere. And it's not just about design. It's about the factories, finding the right people to stitch the garment together. For example, the first couple of years we went to fabric fairs nobody wanted to work with us. Now we work only with the best.

Why have you decided to base Acne in Sweden, away from the main fashion capitals?

The best thing about working here in Stockholm is that you don't have to participate in what's happening in the fashion industry – in London, Milan, or Paris. It's quite nice to sit on the sidelines and just get on with work without being distracted. The problem is getting people here because nobody wants to work in Sweden. I more or less only recruit people who have been working abroad. I think it's important that you have an international perspective.

It appears that your employees are very loyal. What do they like about working for Acne?

I feel that's the best criticism I can get. That's my goal. I like working with people over a long period of time. Why do they like staying with us? Probably because we're quite open-minded, we're quite human.

Why do you think Acne does so well in the German market?

Germany is not our biggest market. Norway, Sweden and Denmark are our biggest markets, followed by France. We dreamt about selling in France from the moment we started: that's where haute couture has its history. We really tried to make it work there early on. We went there all the time and we put in the hours. You have to put in the hours. In Germany we work with Andreas Murkudis, who is a close friend of ours, that's why it's working there I think. It's all about the people you work with and the relationships you have with those people. It can't only be about business.

What makes one designer/brand more successful than another?

There is so much focus on fashion these days that people get attracted to the business. But there are very few slots available. The only advice I'd have, if you want to create your own brand, is to work for different companies first. Because it's not just about design. That's only 10 per cent of the process. Unfortunately, there is a whole cycle involved, which includes production, logistics, finance, PR, marketing. In the 360 degrees of the cycle of creation, design is only a very small part.

What's the biggest lesson you've learned in your first decade as a designer?

I personally had to learn to focus on fashion rather than thinking about being a musician. I've learnt that you really have to focus. As for the company, I'd say it's all about the people you work with, it's about having good relationships.

What advice would you give a budding fashion designer?

First of all, you need to find out what fashion is all about in general: in other words, that it's not just about designing. But the other thing is learning to present and finish a concept. I see so many ideas that are only half worked through, when people come here with their books. Usually they come with their schoolwork, which they've worked on for three years. But in fashion things move quickly. Working on something for three years is easy, but when I throw a job idea on some of these people and say come back in two weeks and show me what you've come up with, usually it's nowhere near as worked through. To survive in this business you have to have the tempo. And you have to surround yourself with other things too intellectually. You have to be interested in more fields than just fashion to be a good fashion designer. There is so much fashion out there that looks exactly the same as everything else. I believe fashion schools are for finding your inner creativity, not for adapting to the business: that comes later. But what usually ends up happening is that students adapt to the business first, but end up not finding their inner creativity.

A.P.C.

Jean Touitou

Founder of A.P.C. (Atelier de Production et de Création)

above: Image, created by Bruce Weber and M/M Paris in 2008, used as a poster and in a limited edition A.P.C. book; opposite: The shoot inspired by the book *Christiane F.*, shot by Horst Diekgerdes in 2003

Formerly a member of a communist group, Jean Touitou founded A.P.C. in 1986 as an antithesis to the ostentatious luxury of the 1980s. Synonymous with minimalist chic at its inception, the label maintains an entirely individual approach to fashion, not only through its design, but also through its refusal to run ad campaigns or engage with the marketing ploys of mega brands. There are currently 30 A.P.C. shops worldwide, including 14 in Japan.

You stumbled into fashion almost by accident. Can you explain the evolution from being a history student at the Sorbonne in Paris to launching a fashion label?

That's easy, I didn't want to do anything that was related to money because I was quite idealistic. I decided to be a teacher and after I finished my studies I went travelling to South America and California for a year and when I got back I realized that I couldn't be a teacher because even if it would involve wearing grey suits, which I loved, it would also mean taking the 7am train to the suburbs, where people wouldn't care so much about history. I thought about doing something else. My sister was working at Kenzo at the time and I could see that

the people there were lively and funny. There must have been of 15 different nationalities, all of them with real personalities and real style, nothing like fashion today. I was attracted to that: if they had been manufacturing screwdrivers or tyres I would have gone there too. It was the group I was attracted to.

At what point did you create your own brand?

It took me many years, it was about 10 years later. First I became a partner at agnès b. in New York. I knew her husband from school and he gave me a lot of freedom to launch in America. It was fun. Later on I became a partner for the Japanese designer, Irie, who had been Kenzo's assistant. After a while, however, I got sick of all the coloured prints, so in 1986 I started A.P.C. (Atelier de Production et de Création). It was so minimalist, dark and beautiful. It was very strong, but it was too radical. But

below and opposite: From the A.P.C. Spring/Summer 2008 lookbook

because I needed to feed my people and pay their salaries I made a lot of money designing for other people at the time. I didn't want to ask friends to work for free because it's better to keep your friends as friends and employ employees.

A.P.C. was created as a backlash to the excess of the late 1980s. Do you think a brand such as A.P.C. is as valid today as it was then?
These days there is no more fashion, there is just finance. There are It bags and perfume and shows where people don't care about the proportion of clothes and the fabric. There is no more art either. There is only the history of the market of art. The world is driven by finance people, who sit down for a meeting and put their Blackberrys on the table. That's when you know you're in trouble. They are cowboys and I'm against that. But I must say, following 10 years of grey and heavy fabrics,

I couldn't sustain my own philosophy. After a while there was so much fake minimalism around, which was used as a pose rather than a philosophy that I had to shift my vision. That change happened five years ago and I hired an extremely gifted, sweet and beautiful designer from Germany called Gabrielle Greiss to help me. She's now the head designer at Sonia Rykiel's studio.

How has being 'untrained' been beneficial to you?
At Kenzo I could tell that pattern-cutting was important, even if I didn't have my hands on it. But in our trade only Azzedine Alaia, Jessica Ogden and Alexander McQueen know about cutting. Everybody else knows jack. I think most designers don't even know what a pattern is. I may not have been prepared for cutting patterns when I started A.P.C., but I knew about fabrics and prints and exactly what kind of styles I wanted. Even if I'm technically

not the best designer, I know how to give proportion to clothing on a piece of paper.

Did you ever experience any difficulties setting up the brand?

I remember the retailer Joseph said to me in 1987 when he came to see my first collection, 'Jean, I love you, but you won't get anywhere with these clothes. They are for firemen.' At the time I was designing the cheesiest leopard print leggings for him – exactly the opposite of what I was trying to do for A.P.C. – it was like Mr Minimal by day, and leopard print by night. Jekyll and Hyde. But two years later Joseph opened an A.P.C. shop in London. Similarly, Italian buyers would say, 'But this is not a *jacket!*' Or people would say, 'Can't you include some more colours?' and I would say, 'Grey is a colour and so are white and navy blue.' But they didn't get it in the beginning. But other than that, starting out was easier than it is now. In those days you just had to be brave and hit the road at 3am and go to the factories. These days, you have to go to incredible lengths to manufacture a garment, especially if you want to keep your visual integrity and have your own fabric woven for you. You have your fabric woven in one place, finished in another, then sent somewhere else to make up the garment, then sent to another country for the washing…it's a huge production. It has changed dramatically since I started. I'm glad we have the power to do those things, but it must be tough to start out now if you don't have tons of money.

How difficult were those first years?

I was designing for other people to earn the necessary cash: I can't stand being in debt. We had the means to be patient and wait until success came.

below: Jean Touitou and Jessica Ogden discussing designs at the A.P.C. studio

How long did it take for the brand to become a success?

When you sell 20 items of something it's concrete, but when you sell 20,000 it becomes abstract and doesn't talk to you as much. I could tell things were going well when I started seeing people on the street in my clothes. That took about seven years, you need patience.

How many collections do you design each year?

We design four collections for the four seasons plus two Madras collections with Jessica Ogden. It's much better for a retailer to have something new every three months rather than a new installation every six months.

Where do you get inspiration for a collection?

Nowhere. It's what you've been living until you get there.

To what degree are you still involved in the design process?

Frankly, if you saw the studio where we work you wouldn't call it minimalist. There are so many fabrics, styles and prints. To be minimalist implies that a monk cut it. Maybe what people mean by minimalist is when you don't go out on a catwalk and show your torso at the end of a show.

I mostly oversee the creation of fabrics because I'm good at that. People who weave fabric now are very gifted at making them look sexy so you're tempted to buy it, but then the garment might fall apart after one wash. I'm also a partner at the weaving plant we use, south of Lyon. It's a small company. We create 60–70 per cent of the fabrics for our clothes. You won't find them anywhere else on the market. Of course I have no guarantee that people won't copy them but I don't want to spend time on the legal thing. There is so much copying that goes on in this trade. Sometimes when I get really mad at a brand that's been copying I just call the general manager and say to the guy, 'Do you really want to get into trouble or can we just talk?' It usually works.

A.P.C. is often described as minimalist. Do you agree?

Frankly, if you saw the studio where we work you wouldn't call it minimalist. There are so many fabrics, styles and prints. To be minimalist implies that a monk cut it. Maybe what people mean by minimalist is when you don't go out on a catwalk and show your torso at the end of a show, or you don't go to every art opening and buy everything on the market.

What do you think when people say your clothes are 'French'?

I don't feel very French. 'French' to me is dog shit on the sidewalk and rude people with no manners when they eat and so on. Yes, A.P.C. may be designed in France, but I would do exactly the same thing if I were living in Oslo or Rome.

How would you describe A.P.C.'s aesthetic?

It's tricky because from an image point of view we're trying to be as advanced as possible in our choice of art direction, photographers, how we print things. I'd say we're a very creative brand in that respect. Regarding the clothes themselves, I'd say we're a creative brand that wants to be affordable while being visually challenging and wearable. You can't be an avant-garde artist and then say I'm going to sell clothes. It has to fit into people's day-to-day life.

Are there any things you wouldn't do design wise?
I wouldn't shout out against fur, except that it's too expensive so we don't do much. I wouldn't shout out against doing underwear either, except that it's too complicated. Bras are very challenging technically, but I definitely would shout out against the It bag.

But you also make bags. What's the difference?
What's the difference? My bags are not for bitches. There are a lot of clothes out there that are made for bitches, literally bitches. I don't mean the image of a bitch. I mean a bitch, a prostitute, a call girl. I don't mind call girls, but I'm not a call girl designer.

Are there any living designers who inspire you?
Eley Kishimoto and Jessica Ogden are doing good things. But when it comes to the big luxury brands sometimes they create excellent things, and other times the nutcase finance people decide to fire the designer and the brand becomes garbage. It's impossible to judge.

You've been quoted as saying, 'You can't imagine the work involved in

> My bags are not for bitches. There are a lot of clothes out there that are made for bitches, literally bitches. I don't mean the image of a bitch. I mean a bitch, a prostitute, a call girl. I don't mind call girls, but I'm not a call girl designer.

creating a normal, unexceptional garment'. Can you explain what exactly is so difficult?
Let's take T-shirts as an example. Have you noticed how T-shirts twist? How the side seams go in front of you sometimes? Well to make a T-shirt that doesn't twist takes a lot of time, but the effort is invisible. Nobody would say 'Great brand, their Tees don't twist'. It has to do with the very nature of the yarn you're using and the twist of yarn and the way it's knitted. The reference to architecture is accurate. In general, a good architect is known for his beautiful building, but not for his engineering. But believe me, good architects are good engineers. Otherwise their buildings would just fall apart.

How do you go about pricing your collections?
Oh! That's such an issue right now. It's not poetic to talk about it, but the decrease of the Japanese yen and the dollar is creating a huge problem because margins have to be lowered when exporting. So right now, in order to stay in business, people have to give up their own price policy. I try to be affordable to people with a little bit of money and it's very frustrating for me if a piece costs too much.

Are you referring back to your communist ideologies?
It's not nice if you're only selling things to jerks, dealers' wives, or real estate people. It is not funny to sell to people with no culture. There is so much big money now with no culture. If, for example, I see a journalist on TV, who is clever and speaks well, I just want him to have a proper jacket. So sometimes I just call people like that and say, 'I really like what you're saying, but I think your jacket sucks.' I then say, 'I'll help you buy a good jacket'. We never give any clothes away for free. I don't have this Hollywood policy of catching a starlet, sending them a bag and then saying, 'If you go to that café at that time of day, we'll snap you.' We don't do that.

Is clothing merely a pragmatic tool or does it have another function?
For me paradise is when you have a clever person who is also sexy. Fashion is not just a pragmatic

opposite: Leopard pouch from the Spring/Summer 2008 collection; above: An A.P.C. shop in Tokyo, Japan; overleaf: Mood board used as inspiration for an A.P.C. collection

thing, but it does have to be pragmatic. In other words, if you're going to make a pair of jeans they should be both beautiful and last 10 years. People are either considered geniuses with no style, or style icons with no brains. That's not the definition of a human being to me.

What is the worst part of your job?

I try to avoid talking to finance people as much as I can, they are the worst. In my own company my financial director and general manager are cool people, but, in the outside world, I try to keep away from those guys. They don't get anything.

Who according to you has a good dress sense?

You can't beat Samuel Beckett. I defy you to criticize the proportion of his V-neck and lambskin jacket. I've also never seen Wes Anderson dress badly. The amazing thing is that he looks different all the time although he only owns two suits. He's always got the right sweater and tie to go with it. He is the definition of what masculine chic could be. Slight nuances, not going for big trends. A guy who tries too hard is never sexy – gay or straight. For some reason, though, women can pull it off. Maybe it's because woman is the most beautiful creation of creations to me. However, if a girl has no style and only follows the magazines then you're in trouble too.

How innovative do you think one needs to be in fashion to succeed?

You need to be very innovative. You have to surprise yourself with beautiful things all the time, but you can't radically change proportions every season.

How important are collaborations with people such as Jessica Ogden to you? What do they add to A.P.C.?

They ensure that my life is not boring. The aim of life is to find a way not to be depressed. Depression is bad. I like opening the window and having fresh people around me. When you work on a movie your team changes with each new project. In fashion you're supposed to have the same company and work with the same people. When I called my company Atelier de Production et de Création I wanted to have people around me. I saw myself as someone who has ideas, but I'm also very happy to push other people's ideas. Right now my recording studio here is my biggest satisfaction. At the

moment we're doing the soundtrack for Wes Anderson's next movie – an animated feature film called *Fantastic Mr Fox*. Once a week Wes, my sound engineer, Jarvis Cocker and myself get together and make music for the film.

You have also produced CDs, DVDs and published books on such diverse topics as your mother's cooking and Japanese pornography – in what way do these creative outlets help your creative process in the fashion realm?

It's like opening windows and letting in some fresh air. We've also done a karaoke DVD. I don't create other products to make the press talk about them, sometimes they sell and sometimes they don't. You know you have to do them so you do. I'm lucky enough to have the means to do it.

How important is your independence, i.e., not belonging to a fashion group?

It's huge, if I belonged to a fashion group I'd be totally muted.

Can you see yourself ever being bought out by a group?

I have no idea what will happen in the future. All I know is that the day A.P.C. is not mine I won't be there either. I think the most beautiful way to stop is to just stop. That's what Balenciaga tried to do. He said, 'I'm finished.' But then 30 years later it started again. His decision was not respected.

You have criticized luxury brands for endlessly creating the next It bag and yet you sell accessories such as handbags, belts and shoes yourself. Why are accessories important to you?

The word accessory is a bad word. We don't focus on accessories like every other brand just because they sell. I love making bags, shoes and scarves. Our trade is to sell clothes, so we make clothes. Right now I'm working on a perfume with a small company based in Los Angeles, who work only with natural oils. The brief was 'the inside of a guitar case' because sometimes it's made from very precious

The aim of life is to find a way not to be depressed. Depression is bad. I like opening the window and having fresh people around me.

left: From a 1994 collection

wood and that mixed with the velvet of the case creates something special. It's a unisex scent because I don't get the male/female divide. To answer your previous question, if I belonged to a group, they would have a marketing plan and launch date set in place. I can just play it by ear. The first thought I had was to call the scent 'Old Playboy'. No finance/fashion group would allow that.

Why do you think your brand is so successful in Japan, where you currently have 14 stand-alone stores?

It's easy to explain, but we have to go back to the bubble economy of 15 years ago. Everybody was milking the Japan cow and putting logos everywhere. I guess they liked me because I wasn't playing that game. When nutcases talk to nutcases they understand each other. Japanese people are not intellectual, they are into perception. Maybe they could feel that I was pure and just trying to be myself, that I wasn't doing the marketing thing and trying to invade Japan. I've learnt that you need to build a lot of cultural bridges to get through to the Japanese. They take things quite literally. Five years ago when we decided to change our image I was really inspired by Christiane F. We created images inspired by the character and the Japanese would say, 'Mr Touitou wants us to become junkies and prostitutes.' It took me 15 years of fighting to have my concepts understood and then this year I gave up and thought, 'Yes, in Japan I do have to hire the best PR people.' We hate hiring external PRs because I think they are the worst, they don't know anything. They are like mercenaries with no cause. But in Japan we gave up because we found good ones. The only comparison I can think of is one in 1920s politics: in the 1920s Lenin described a socialist leader as being, 'made of rotten wood but we need this guy to get through to the masses.' In Japan sometimes you need to use things that seem a bit rotten to you, to make your point.

above: I love NY T-Shirt, Spring 2008, photograph by Olivier Placet

Have you noticed how T-shirts twist? How the side seams go in front of you sometimes? Well to make a T-shirt that doesn't twist takes a lot of time, but the effort is invisible. Nobody would say 'Great brand, their Tees don't twist'. It has to do with the very nature of the yarn and the way it's knitted.

What percentage of sales come from the internet and mail order?

I'd say approximately 20 per cent of our sales are by mail order and the internet. There are way too many shops in this world right now. Unless I work with a really good architect and do something really different, I won't be tempted to open another shop.

How do you reconcile your former Trotskyite beliefs with the capitalist fashion world?

I gave up the revolution when I was 30 years old. The conditions for the revolution were ready but they're

above: Created by Bruce Weber and M/M Paris in 2008, this image was used both as a poster and in a limited edition A.P.C. book

totally rotten now. The revolution should never have started in a country like Russia. We didn't plan it that way.

And you found there was no point in holding onto that ideal?

You can be good around your own people and projects. I believe I'm behaving in a dignified way, being honest with my employees, but I can do no more than that. Capitalism is here. I just opened a pre-school in Paris: in a way it's contradictory, as it's expensive to send your kids there, but I'm not making money from it. I just wanted to open the perfect pre-school, where the furniture is beautiful, the teachers are excellent, there are nice cotton cashmere blankets, the kids get taught

I have so much freedom, it's pretty amazing. It has its price too, because there's always the risk of the company collapsing one day.

theatre, English, etc. The only reason why I could do that was because I'm rich and totally independent.

Why don't you take part in Paris fashion week?
Like everybody I try to break the rules, but the rules are unbreakable there. There is so much advertising out there now that editors will only go to the shows of brands that advertise in their magazine because the ads pay their salaries. It's frustrating for me not to do a show because I do like the energy around them, but it's a waste of money. Because I don't advertise, since I would rather invest in the quality of fabric or the interior of a shop, it would mean some people wouldn't come. And I don't really play that game of who sits in the front row. The celebrity thing has taken on ridiculous proportions. People in Milan will now pay so-called 'underground' actors around $1 million a year to sit in the front row. It's so cheesy. They'll fly some dummy rapper first class, make him stay at the Ritz...just to have him in the front row. I try to focus more now on the quality of images we shoot.

How do you ensure you don't get caught up in the fashion circus such as using celebrities to endorse your product, etc?
Even if I wanted to, I don't think I could do it. There are some people that I just can't talk to. I don't know what a celebrity is. Everybody is a celebrity, it's a nightmare right now. On other hand, if someone famous wants to buy my clothes I'm not going to say no, but I wouldn't start throwing names around. That's a very miserable thing to do.

You created a limited edition book with Bruce Weber this season. What was the thinking behind that?
I was on a really tight budget and I asked Bruce whether he'd be able to create four images for us. He delivered 89. They were all so beautiful, so I would have found it frustrating not to use them, so we published 500 hundred copies of the book and sent them mostly to people I love and respect.

What excites you most about being a creative director?

> People in Milan will now pay so-called 'underground' actors around $1 million a year to sit in the front row. It's so cheesy... I try to focus more now on the quality of images we shoot.

I have so much freedom, it's pretty amazing. It has its price too, because there's always the risk of the company collapsing one day. But for the last 22 years I have had total freedom. One day, 10 years ago, when I was sad and depressed, I just decided to record an album called 'Abstract Depressionism' with various musicians. I asked them all to write the saddest music they could. That's the kind of freedom I have.

What makes one designer more successful than another?
There are a lot of bad designers who are successful. Sometimes I jog early in the morning; it's like a Stalinist nightmare. The high school girls all have the same way of wearing their little red bags and jackets with four huge buttons... What amazes me with fashion is that there are so many designers out there, but the looks on the street aren't getting any better. Fashion groups rule the show and people buy clothes around the It bag.

What advice would you give a budding designer?
You'd better have loads of money or a job working for a big brand. It's pathetic if you have to feel the pressure of meeting the payment terms of production and research. If you're a young designer and you have loads of money, you can afford to launch and not be successful for two or three years. If you don't, it's impossible to start a new brand now.

American Apparel

Tory J. Lowitz Director of product development

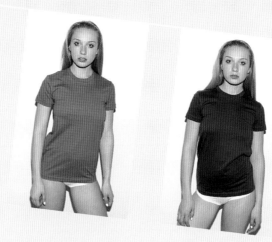

above: The women's T-shirt comes in a range of bright colours, like all American Apparel basics; opposite: American Apparel's campaign images are often, but not always, shot by the company's founder Dov Charney

Tory J. Lowitz began working for American Apparel in 2004 after Dov Charney, the founder of the company, took a liking to the jacket he was wearing at a trade fair. Fast forward four years and Lowitz is now overseeing American Apparel's entire design department, which consists of 22 people. Famous for its colourful cotton and jersey basics, American Apparel is sold in 189 shops around the world.

When and how did you first get interested in fashion?

At college, painting was my first love and that's what I studied. I soon realized I could apply the thought processes I'd learnt in the art world to different industries, and fashion was something I fell into. I started designing for California T-Shirts right after college. It was a $40 million T-shirt company in the early 1990s. After that I worked in TV animation designing characters for nine years. Then I worked for Universal Studios as a signwriter for a few years. At some point I realized that the simple grey jacket I'd been obsessively wearing for 10 years was falling apart. I wanted to make a replica of that jacket and a friend and I decided to start our own jacket collection. We called it VIKK.

How did you start working for American Apparel?

In the same year that we launched VIKK I went to a trade show wearing a jacket I liked and I ran into Dov Charney, the founder of American Apparel. He asked me where I got my jacket. After I told him I'd designed it, he photographed me and said, 'Come work for me on a jacket or two.' We designed the windbreaker together in 2004, and I never left.

What does your job involve?

Initially Dov and I worked closely together, along with another product developer. Then I developed a team of people and now I'm running a department of 22 people, including pattern-makers, technical package writers, etc. My job is to develop and source fabrics, design products, develop and engineer them, design trims, direct traffic with other developers, oversee the pattern room, the sample-sewing area and the sample-cutting people. I am also putting together a sample library to support production on the factory floor.

> Designing by season inhibits the creativity of a collection. Dov would consider that to be an institutional faux pas. Why would you falsely create something new?

American Apparel is a 'vertically integrated' company. What exactly does that mean?

In short it just means that we do everything under one roof – everything from knitting, cutting and sewing, to shipping garments to our locations.

To what extent is the set up of the company the reason for its success?

There are various aspects that contribute to the success of the company. In China, for example, factories do something called 'line production' where you might have 45 sewers in a row, with a medley of five or six garments back to back. What we do is very different, we do something called 'modular team manufacturing', a system that was devised by Marty Bailey, who used to work at Fruit of the Loom and now works for us. We can produce over 210,000 garments a day, with 60 teams or so comprised of people working within our modular teams dedicated solely to T-shirts. We are the largest manufacturing company in North America. About 5,000 people come through our doors every day, working on three different sewing shifts 24 hours a day. This gives us the ability to calibrate our selling costs because a person on the manufacturing team gets paid for each piece they've worked on. It's an incentive to work hard and both parties win. Also, we're the only company that I've heard of that has such a prolific design base. We can put together 30–40 new designs each month. We'll create the fabric, make the silhouette, fit the silhouette, create five sizes and put it to bed.

You claim to be sweatshop free. How important are your factory workers to the success of the label, and what benefits do you provide?

Very. Our workers really care about what they do. And we try to establish a real sense of community by having a large cafeteria, for instance, where workers can socialize. Many people have moved here to work for us because they have the opportunity to send money home to their families. It's a big deal,

opposite and right: Although famous for its basics, American Apparel now also creates other essentials including dresses, jeans and hoodies

employees earn a minimum of $12 an hour, which is well over twice the federal minimum. We also offer parking, subsidized public transport, subsidized lunches, free onsite massages, a bike-lending program... We also guarantee job security and full-time employment, which is an anomaly in the garment industry. What's more we provide all of our employees and their families with company-subsidized, affordable health insurance and we just opened an onsite medical clinic, which offers primary care services along with paediatric, urgent and preventative health care. It's the first of its kind.

When and how do you introduce new garments to your collections?

Sometimes we introduce new products because we feel that a silhouette is missing, or the weather might be changing: it might be getting warmer, so we'll gear up to pump out some summer styles. We might switch the fabric of an existing style, or build a new pair of shorts, which might trigger a whole idea for a dress, or it might give us spin-off ideas for different colour stories. We're not really into superfluous details, for us it's about the bare minimum. The less time a garment spends in the machines, the less it costs to make, which means there is a bigger profit margin, but also that it's more affordable for us to stay in the US. We couldn't support this kind of prolific production if we had to sew on details such as 10,000 buttons because we felt that it would look cute.

How many collections do you design each year?

We don't design by season like other brands. We're only just getting into the rhythm of building cold and warm weather items. In the past we just designed what we felt like designing, designing by season inhibits the creativity of a collection. Dov would consider that to be an institutional faux pas. Why would you falsely create something new rather than wait for the ideas to come naturally? One of the hardest things for us to do is to send the products to the right location, depending on the weather in that location. We're opening shops in Australia, China and Berlin, but we're stuck in Los Angeles. So it's a question of finding people to work out the allocation of stores. A simple concept but one that needs some work; it continues to get better daily.

Where do you get inspiration for new garments?

Often a fabric can be an inspiration, for example, when we made the digital hologram leggings. I mentioned to Dov that we should do something metallic and he agreed. He was at a trade fair and saw a metallic fabric he liked and bought a few thousand yards of it. It could have been a total nightmare because we don't have the manufacturing capacity to work with slippery fabrics at our company, we do mainly jersey and cotton, but it worked. For the most part we don't look at other companies or designs for inspiration. Some companies who are inspired by us will directly

Accessories are huge sellers for us. They are impulse buys when you are in the store. You're not sure what you need or if you need anything at all when you walk in there, but you walk out with a headband. You need to keep the customers' interest alive, it's like having Tom without Jerry.

follow products we've developed and it makes me feel bad for them because they are reactionary rather than genuine in their approach to design; it should come from within. The A-way jacket, for example, was something I was interested in developing because I love jackets. Dov has fond memories of young men wearing an old brand called K-WAY; this sounds ridiculous because I said we aren't reactionary, but this is more of a 'homage to'.

How many different types of fabric do you use?
We work with everything from denim and nylon to jersey and cotton, as well as combinations of all of the above. Ultimately it seems that colour is our strong point.

Talk me through American Apparel's use of colour?
We have the ability to be agile and choose different colours based on the demand of the market. We have people I think of as colour psychics. There are a few of us at American Apparel who have an intense vision of the future when it comes to colour. Mostly, however, we tend to go for bright colours because it's part of who we are and Dov has taken many losses on muted browns and dirty colours. The organic cotton line is a little less bright simply because of the saturation of the dye. In some cases you need chemicals to get brighter colours, but we work across the palette, while trying to avoid

earthy tones. I'm not a big fan of burnt orange or brown either or maybe I don't want us to take a sales hit gambling on a dirty orange, for instance. Bright colours are part of the brand, muted colours may seem dedicated to slightly older customers or seem less exciting. At the moment we're getting back into fluorescent colours again.

How important are accessories to the label?
Accessories are huge sellers for us. They are impulse buys when you are in the store. You're not sure what you need or if you need anything at all when you walk in there, but you walk out with a headband. You need to keep the customers' interest alive, it's like having Tom without Jerry. We have a hosiery department; we make socks, underpants, wristbands, and headbands. We also make backpacks, wallets, duffel bags, tote bags, etc. Recently we bought lots of 1980s style sunglasses from an overstock house and are now reselling them. My personal biggest contribution to American Apparel in terms of accessories is the men's brief and perhaps assisting in the technical designs of our bag collection.

What is your best-selling garment?
The 2001 fine jersey T-shirt and the 4415 men's baby rib brief.

How much research goes into the production of a new garment?
It really depends on how complex the product is, but for the men's brief, for example, we went through 150 different tries before

below: American Apparel design sketches by Tory J. Lowitz

finalizing the product. Thanks to Marty Bailey we were able to hammer out certain aspects of the economies and the design. It's a complicated production process because you have to get the elastic around the waist and leg just right so that it's not too tight, but also so that it doesn't lose elasticity.

How would you describe American Apparel's brand identity and vision?

We're a T-shirt company disguised as a 21-year-old girl. At the end of the day it doesn't matter what you buy, we're still a T-shirt company.

What is American Apparel's philosophy?

We pride ourselves in providing social responsibility combined with honest design. And we aim to be affordable. It's hard to nail it down to one thing. We're not just sweatshop free, but we champion the opportunity to make garments in America and support its economy by creating safe jobs and fair wages.

What are the delights and difficulties of your job?

I get a great sense of satisfaction when I see my friends in clothes that I've worked on. Another delight is the fact that because American Apparel is virtually integrated we get to see the garments being manufactured right in front of us, in the very same building. We can make adjustments in the machining rather than waiting for the garments to come back from, say, China. It gives us lots of control. The hardest thing in fashion is to galvanize the garment in production exactly the same way you delicately designed it. Anyone can make one gorgeous item of clothing, but to see an item mass produced to a high standard is the most difficult thing, especially when production happens abroad. There are so many variables that are hard to control. As for the hard part of my job...it's devastating when you see something failing that's taken you ages to develop. For example,

opposite: Models from American Apparel shoots are often chosen from within the company. Tory J. Lowitz says, 'They're usually friends, or friends of friends, or store employees.'

right now we're developing, among about 39 other styles, a men's button-up. It's no way near ready to be sent to the store, but I've been working on it for three months. I'm extremely happy with the design, but the manufacturing element is extremely difficult. I may have to simplify the garment, but I certainly won't give up.

How important do you think it is to be innovative in fashion?

That's the definition of fashion, if you don't come up with new things you're dead.

Who is your ideal customer?

Nineteen to 23-year-old women, or someone who is very educated in fashion and music: trendsetters and tastemakers.

Does American Apparel do advertising?

We advertise in magazines and on billboards. If you see our garments in a film it's because the stylist bought them. We spend most of our advertising budget on print ads.

How do you go about marketing the label?

We use print ads, our sales staff wear American Apparel in the store, a lot of it is word of mouth...

Talk me through an American Apparel photo shoot? How do models get chosen? How does Dov decide to shoot? How did he come up with the idea of the look and feel?

Dov only photographs the lifestyle shoots. We have many lifestyle photographers, but he's the best and has the most experience of working with models. His basic inspiration is his obsession with classic men's magazines. Dov chooses models from all over the place; there's no real theory besides their natural style: hair, lack of make-up, sex appeal, and so on.

The hardest thing in fashion is to galvanize the garment in production exactly the same way you delicately designed it.

Many people at American Apparel bring in models, who are usually friends, or friends of friends, or store employees. We also shoot photographs of the garments we've got coming onto the store floor in-house on a daily basis. The models are almost like still-life images that we use for, say, the website or for PR purposes. Our website is comprised of models featured in basic frontals, some close-ups, and three-quarter views.

Do you do fashion shows?
No, it's something we've never done. It would be fantastic to have a show, but it's never happened so far, it's not part of what we're about.

Dov has said in past that the company is quite disorganized but that it allows things to happen. Can you explain what he means?
We don't design by season, our designing is more off-the-cuff, i.e., it's linked to what's inspiring us at that moment in time. I guess that aspect could appear disorganized but I would actually call it a way of being creative. We are able to make quick moves within the market place and most companies can't do that. Often a company's design space is completely stifled because it is too organized.

right: American Apparel's campaign images have caused controversy in the past due to their at times suggestive nature

What makes one designer or brand more successful than another?
For me it's linked to a collection singing in unison. It's very easy to go outside of the boundaries you are trying to create for a label. It's much harder to keep one unified vision and have every style fall under that voice you've created. If you look at some of the nicer collections out there, say, Balenciaga or Mandarina Duck, everything they create is inspired by the exact same vision and they don't stray from it. Part of my job as the final editor of a collection is

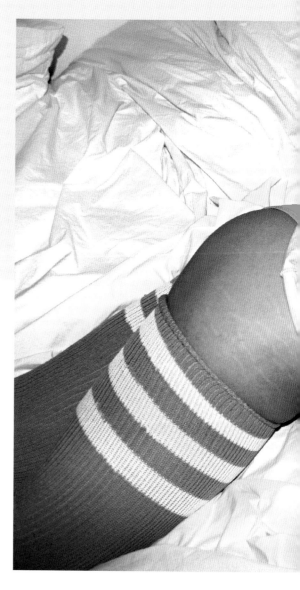

It's very easy to go outside of the boundaries you are trying to create for a label. It's much harder to keep one unified vision and have every style fall under that voice you've created... one voice...is what makes us successful.

to pull people back if they stray from the one voice. This is what makes us successful. We run by the seat of our pants and we've failed many times. Sometimes we'll spend a long time developing a garment and we may have to drop it because, beautiful though it may be, it's not in line with our vision.

What advice would you give a budding designer?
Stay in tune with your unique vision and don't be reactionary. Challenge the timeline of fashion history. Understand its history before you approach it, at the end of the day, a garment is just a silhouette. You can do many things with it: just because a garment is a T-shirt it doesn't mean you can't break the silhouette in a way that could be extremely avant-garde. If you challenge history you might find yourself making things you never thought you could. And be sure to seek influences and inspiration outside of fashion, for example, I listen to a lot of Metal and I also like hardedge painting.

H&M

Margareta Van Den Bosch

Head of design for 21 years and now creative advisor

above: H&M dress from the Summer 2008 collection; opposite: Red coat from the Spring/Summer 2008 collection, photograph by Peter Gehrke

After graduating from Beckmans School of Design in Stockholm, Margareta Van Den Bosch worked as a designer and design consultant in Italy for companies such as Ticosa, Centro Design, Gruppo Finanziario Tessile, Hettemarks and Rosier for many years before moving back to Sweden. She was appointed head of design for H&M in 1987 and held that position until 2008. Today, she is the brand's creative advisor. Famous for offering both affordable basics as well as garments inspired by high fashion, H&M currently has 1,500 shops in 28 countries, and will shortly be opening shops in Egypt, Japan, Oman, Bahrain and Saudi Arabia.

When did you first get interested in fashion?

I've always loved drawing ever since I was a child. My father was a political cartoonist, so I'd watch him at work and draw myself. Before I went to primary school, I started drawing clothes for paper dolls. When I finished school, I went to the Beckmans School of Design in Stockholm. After graduation, I moved to Italy where I lived for many years and started working as a designer and consultant. In 1987 I became a designer for H&M in Stockholm.

Do you think it's important to go to fashion school?

I think you can definitely learn how to be a designer by working rather than studying, but it might take you longer. Years ago nobody went to fashion school because it didn't exist, you were taught by someone who was better than you. I think it's important to learn about pattern-cutting, sewing and fabrics.

I would really recommend going to fashion school because it allows you to work more freely than if you are working for someone. You have the opportunity to be entirely creative, artistic and experimental. Of course there have been many great designers with no formal education, such as Christian Dior...

Although formal education is great, it does not mean you are ready when you come out of school. You still need to learn about actually making the product. You need to learn about fabrics, treatments, compositions. If you start working by yourself straight out of school, it's not as easy as if you start in a company – even if you start in a little company. It allows you to learn about the customer and how to be commercial: without that knowledge you won't go anywhere. You really have to have an idea of what it is you want to sell.

How has the H&M brand developed during your 21 years there?

When I started there were very few designers. We had buyers and were working more with agents in the Far East. Designers at the time were more responsible for creating colour cards and coming up with new ideas. Now we have a team of over 100 designers and we also have about 20 print designers and about 60 pattern-makers. We design entire collections in teams. We have also set up production offices in, for instance, Italy, Turkey, Romania and China, who follow the production cycle and control the quality. This means we can create a drawing in Stockholm, cut the pattern here, send it over to a production office by computer and it then goes to the supplier, who make the garment and send it back. We'll then make changes on the computer and send the new garment back.

If, however, we have something that's very difficult to make then we make it in-house. We also work according to a different planning schedule now. We do long-term planning, but are also able to react quickly to what's selling in the shops. Right now we are working on the trends and colours for summer 2009, so we're a year ahead. But at the same time we might still be working on winter 2008 and even on garments that are in season now. If, for example, a look is big on the catwalk, we can make it big in the shops – whether that be a colour such as pink or a cut such as a pair of Bermuda shorts. Our strength is that if something is selling well, we can buy more immediately and restock the shops. We can react to sales figures. New stock goes into our shops every day.

opposite: Opening of a Hennes shop in 1952 on Kungsgatan, Stockholm; below, left: H&M shop, Harajuku, Tokyo; below, right: H&M shop, Ginza, Tokyo

What makes H&M different from other affordable high street brands?

I think we have a broader customer base because we design collections for men, women, including maternity wear, children and babies. We also try to offer value for money and we are very customer-oriented. We can really see what the customer needs and wants by what's selling in our stores. Right now, high-waisted jeans are back in style, but many customers are not quite ready for them yet, so we can provide what they need, even if that means selling more skinny jeans until they feel they want high-waisted jeans. Once high-waisted jeans pick up momentum, we can buy more. When you're dealing with big volumes, it's important to know what the customer wants, otherwise you're set to lose lots of money. We operate a sort of triangle system where we buy lots of the garments we are sure will sell and fewer of the garments we are not so sure of.

Do you think you need a philosophy to create an interesting collection?

You certainly have to work in a creative way at all times to stimulate ideas. We often look at what the company sold well in previous seasons and we think about how we can make that garment again in a new way because we're sure to make money on it. We tend to create ideas or themes around collections. Recently we've been working around sport, art and romantic 1970s influences. We decide as a team what these themes should be and then everybody works out how they want to use the theme in their own department, whether that be men's, women's, children's, babies'. We also have a colour card theme where about 15 designers decide which colours we should be using that season, and that will filter

below: From the H&M menswear Spring 2008 collection, photograph by Enrique Badulescu (left) and Peter Gehrke (right)

through to all the garments from pants to knitwear, etc. We don't have trend scouts as such. We are our own trend scouts. I don't think you can get inspiration from anyone other than yourself.

Where do you look for inspiration?
Magazines, books, exhibitions, the street, boutiques, interior design, vintage markets, travel, contemporary culture, fabric fairs. It's always great to look at new fabrics at the beginning of the season and see which direction the season is heading in. Celebrity culture, TV and the music world are also hugely important. If you're not really a fashion person, you may not know who is designing what, but you'll know who is who. It's a new phenomenon. I also try to ascertain what people will want and need. I look at what's selling and create new things from old bestsellers. I think that's how everybody's working.

You've worked at H&M since 1987 – what were some of the best projects you worked on?
The design collaborations with designers such as Karl Lagerfeld and Rei Kawakubo who set up Comme des Garçons have been really exciting to work on. I've also loved launching H&M in countries such as France, America and Japan. We tend to present ourselves as we are in new countries to show what our identity is. However, in countries such as Japan we will include smaller sizes and we may focus on the younger and trendier parts of our collections. I've also really enjoyed working on the big fashion shows we did. We did one in New York in Central Park in 2005 and another one in 2001 in Dalhalla, Sweden, which was a limestone quarry. I also truly love the atmosphere in the offices here and working with my colleagues: the print-makers, pattern-cutters and so on.

What have been the biggest challenges?
When I first started working for H&M it was more difficult to get your designs through because we had fewer designers and many buyers. It's always challenging to figure out what is going to be the next bestseller, because you never know. You can react to what people want, but you can also make a mistake when you're buying. Sometimes I'll come up with an idea and if nobody believes in it then I'll sit on it for a while. I may be too early with it. I figure, if I can't convince my collaborators, I won't be able to convince the customer either. We're not that avant-garde.

A lot of high street brands get accused of copying the catwalk. To what degree do you alter the catwalk trends to suit the mass market?
We are such a big company, we really can't copy things. We'd lose a lot of money if we did because we'd have to pay the person whose work we'd copied and take all the relevant clothes off the shelves and so on. This season, for example, there were a lot of flower prints on the catwalk. Copying is when you create exactly the same flower dress as, say, Prada, with exactly the same prints. If something becomes fashionable we have to make sure we make it different: we have to pick our own flower print. As most shapes have been done before, you can't own a silhouette. For such

Celebrity culture, TV and the music world are … hugely important. If you're not really a fashion person, you may not know who is designing what, but you'll know who is who. It's a new phenomenon. I also try to ascertain what people will want and need. I look at what's selling and create new things from old bestsellers. I think that's how everybody's working.

I think when you're looking at vintage clothes for inspiration, it's really important not to copy something straight off. You can get inspired by it, but then you have to make your own print.

Is H&M more visionary or reactionary?
We are both. I don't think we'd have been able to make all the changes we have if we'd only ever looked at the customer. We had to have a vision too. We are always ready to do something new.

To what extent is your design process computerized and digitized?
We use computers to send our design sketches and scans of original prints to the production countries. Some of our designers draw by hand and then scan the drawing, others use the computer.

How did the collaborations with designers such as Karl Lagerfeld, Stella McCartney and Viktor & Rolf come about?
Our marketing department wanted a change. We used to have an underwear campaign in November and they wanted to try something

general things there is no copyright. We've been accused of copying before, but it was when we bought sunglasses from suppliers and unbeknown to us, they had copied someone else's design. I think when you're looking at vintage clothes for inspiration, it's really important not to copy something straight off. You can get inspired by it, but then you have to make your own print.

new, so they came up with the idea of designer collaborations. We thought it would be great to start with a design icon like Karl. Someone on the design team knew him and asked him and he was interested immediately. We discussed how big the collection should be and that we wanted typical Karl Lagerfeld designs. Stella started off by designing dresses and we asked her to add some tailoring since she's also famous for that. We always have to have some accessories too. There's lots of dialogue between us and the designers. The collections sell really well. We always buy a limited quantity. The most recent collaboration we did with Roberto Cavalli sold out in two hours in Stockholm. Right now we're working with Rei Kawakubo of Comme des Garçons for the launch of the Japan store. Collaborations are great for the brand because it helps our image,

increases traffic to the stores and creates a lot of press coverage. And the designers are happy to work with us because it's nice for them to have a bigger audience. They can reach customers they wouldn't have otherwise and it's great publicity for them.

How do you decide which designer to work with?

We try to choose designers who are different from the ones we've worked with before. So it was great to start with a fashion icon like Karl Lagerfeld. Then, with Stella, we went for a younger designer. After that we went for more of a couture/Paris influence with Viktor & Rolf. Cavalli was nice because it had a feeling of glamour and now with Rei Kawakubo it's more avant-garde.

According to the trade press, you focused too much on design in 2000 and not enough on basics

and the company made a loss. What have you learned from that experience?

It was when bohemia was coming into fashion, but we were too early with our colours and detailing. We forgot to buy more wearable basics. Since then, we always make sure we follow the triangle set up, so we buy big quantities of the garments we are sure will sell and we buy less of the garments that are more expensive or very high fashion. If the new, high-fashion items end up selling well, we can always increase the quantity we buy. We did make a mistake, but we really learnt from it.

How do you go about marketing new collections?

The store is our primary information channel where we communicate the latest fashion and our offering to the customer. Other channels include the internet, PR activities, the *H&M Magazine* and advertising. The main medium for our advertising is the store, followed by TV and cinema commercials, billboards, newspapers, catalogues and the internet. We launch a number of major campaigns every year plus a number of smaller campaigns in-between. Our total market communication budget is around 3 per cent of group sales excluding VAT which amounts to £6.7 billion.

How do you manage to keep prices so low?

We have a lot of experience: we buy big volumes, we work with very few middlemen, we buy the right products from the right market, we have efficient distribution and we own all our stores.

Where do you think the fashion industry is heading?

I think fashion is quite an individual thing nowadays. Whereas people used to be happy to buy, say, an entire Chanel look, today it's much more about mixing and matching and putting an individual look together. You can see that happening in the design world too. People are mixing old furniture with modern pieces. Most people don't want a complete change from one season to the next. They might want to change an aspect of their look, but they don't want to change their entire style. It's important to think about this modern way of dressing. People aren't spending so much on constantly following the latest trends, they're thinking about fashion as a long-term thing.

What makes one brand or designer better than another?

To be a good designer you have to be a good self-critic. You have to analyse why something isn't working. And if something is a success, you always have to renew yourself and not rest on your laurels so you can keep that success going.

What advice would you give a budding designer?

Work for a while when you leave fashion school because you need the practice. You also need to learn about the practical aspects of doing a collection and really thinking something through. You need to think about your customer and to have a complete idea about what you want to do: who is my customer? What should the collection look like? What are the ingredients? How do I want it to look on the shop floor? What kind of person do I want to reach? I'd also say, even if you have a good idea, don't work on your own. Work with someone else who has a set of skills that you don't have, so if you are artistic, find someone practical and vice versa. Find someone to share your vision with.

opposite: H&M swimwear, Spring/Summer 2008, photograph by Alexi Lubomirski

I think fashion is quite an individual thing nowadays. Whereas people used to be happy to buy, say, an entire Chanel look, today it's much more about mixing and matching and putting an individual look together.

Uniqlo Yukihiro Katsuta

Head of the international design team

below: UNIQLO jeans, Spring/Summer 2008;
opposite: UNIQLO flagship store, Ginza, Tokyo

Yukihiro Katsuta was vice president of men's merchandising at Bergdorf Goodman before joining UNIQLO as senior vice president of global research and design in 2005. Following Katsuta's appointment as the head of the international design team, UNIQLO underwent a drastic image change and is now considered one of the world's leading must-have basics brand. UNIQLO is sold in 810 shops worldwide and has a turnover of £2.6 billion each year.

When and how did you first get interested in fashion?

When I was about 12, I started buying a fashion magazine called *Popeye*. It was my introduction to US fashion. They featured deck shoes, heavy-duty outdoor clothes, mountain gear, L.L.Bean... Everything looked so fresh to me, I'd never seen anything like it. I started to buy some of the items by mail order. And when stores like Beams, which started out as a very small shop on Harajuku and is now a big chain, started to import American casualwear, I used to head there straight after school. Ironically, that kind of fashion has made a comeback now.

What is your design experience to date?

I don't actually have any design experience as such. I never went to fashion school, for example. My background is in merchandising. My first job in fashion was as a sales associate in the shoe department of Japan's most fashionable department store, Isetan. From there I went to Barneys in New York and Japan. Then I worked in the Polo Ralph Lauren HQ as a merchandiser and then became vice president of men's merchandising at Bergdorf Goodman, before joining UNIQLO. When I was working at Bergdorf Goodman I was not only buying designers, but also developing a private label. I started learning about the process of product development. I feel like I understand both sides of the business now: the creative side and the merchandising point of view. The challenge for any brand is to create the perfect balance between the two.

Were you a good salesman?

I was. I always say to people, 'To be a great salesman, you need to have some humanity. Anyone can learn to sell a product, but you can't learn to have a personality.' These days, when you can buy everything, anywhere, it's even more important to have a good attitude as a salesperson because people are paying more attention to whom they are buying from.

opposite: Merchandise in UNIQLO's UK flagship store, Oxford Street, London

Do you think it's important for a designer to go to fashion school?

It's a very interesting question for me because I never went. I don't think there's anything wrong with going to fashion school to learn how to be a good designer, but if you look at the successful designers out there, people like Tom Ford, I don't think they went to fashion school. Everyone is now talking about Thom Browne, saying he's the next Tom Ford, but he didn't go to fashion school either. He was a merchandiser and sales rep for Giorgio Armani. It's important to know how to create great designs, but it is even more important to be able to create a great concept for your brand, in other words, creating a better image for the brand, and deciding how to send the right message out to the customer... Tom Ford is a genius for being able to create a great package. To me he's not a great designer, he's a great concept-maker.

You moved from being vice president of a luxury department store to a high street brand. Why?

Five or six years ago I felt that consumers were developing new attitudes. People were starting to think about what actually made them happy. Was it really that Rolex watch or the jacket that cost a couple of thousand dollars? They started moving in a different direction, spending more on education, home improvements, organic food and travelling. According to the *New York Times*, that was what 'happiness' was for the new generation and not going to a five-star French restaurant in Manhattan. I tend to agree with that philosophy. When I used to work for Bergdorf Goodman, I used to buy and sell those luxury clothes, but I started feeling, 'Do I really need a new suit every year?'

But even if people's motivation in life changes, they still want to look nice. So I started thinking, if somebody were to make a garment that looks great, made from great quality material at a cheaper price, I'd buy it. That's where UNIQLO came in. They contacted me. They had a background of making great quality clothes at great prices; somebody just needed to insert creativity and great taste into that equation. I felt the brand had the potential to change a lot in the years to come. That's why I joined.

How would you describe UNIQLO's style and philosophy?

UNIQLO's philosophy is about creating great basics made from great quality at great prices. Even when you're creating basics, you can create fashion. You need to make changes every season. Let's say we're talking about a simple white T-shirt: you can change the fabric, the shape of the neck, the silhouette. You have to find the perfect length, fabric and so on for *this year*'s T-shirt. You can improve that white T-shirt season upon season.

How does it differ from say Gap and Marks & Spencer?

Formerly, Gap used to adhere to a similar concept as ours, but then they started carrying more 'fashionable' things. If you add the wrong concepts to those basics, those basics can end up not looking so good. I think occasionally our competitors get it wrong in that way.

Tadashi Yanai has said he wants UNIQLO to become bigger than, say, Gap. How do you intend to do this?

Nobody is trying to create and present great collections of 'New Basics' today. If we can spread our concept globally, as we are doing now, slowly but surely, I think we can turn it into a big success and potentially be bigger than Gap. From my 20 years experience in the industry, I'd say it's a huge challenge. At the same time nobody has completed this concept in the past, creating clothes of great taste and quality at a good price and updating and improving upon those basics every year. That's why there is a big chance for us.

How did you go about changing the perception of UNIQLO in the last couple of years? It went from a little-known label to one worn by trendsetters...

> Even when you're creating basics, you can create fashion... Let's say we're talking about a simple white T-shirt: you can change the fabric, the shape of the neck, the silhouette. You have to find the perfect length, fabric and so on for *this year's* T-shirt.

I always say product comes first. Sometimes people forget about the product because they're thinking more about the business. I hired a talented team of designers in New York, Paris and Tokyo because I knew it wouldn't be possible using just the original team in Japan. I shared the philosophy and vision I had for the brand and provided them with a clear direction. We just did what we're supposed to do. We are focused on upgrading the taste level whilst maintaining good price and quality. Of course marketing was also involved. But if you don't have a great product to start with marketing is not going to help you.

Were there any key pieces that helped turn the company around in the last few years?

I think our first huge success was what we called our 'skinny' jeans. We designed an up-to-date basic pair of jeans made from great quality materials and sold them at a great price. In Japan alone we sold about 4 million units. We also promoted our cashmere collection last year which sold about 700,000 units in Japan alone. I'd say that's our business trick: providing great basics at great prices that are constantly updated. Everybody needs that. If we were to chase purely fashion,

few people would follow us. We're constantly thinking: how can we create new and updated basics so lots of people can wear our clothes easily? Not just regular people, but fashion people too. We want them thinking, 'I must have that'.

How do you manage to sell your garments, such as the Pantone Cashmere collection, at such great prices but made from good quality materials?

We tend to buy cashmere a year in advance to get the best price. We also have an advantage because we produce such vast numbers. It helps keep production costs down.

What do you think Western consumers like about the UNIQLO brand?

I think people understand our style and philosophy and buy into that. They see that we make simple clothes at affordable prices, but that there is a great level of taste and quality. Our name is becoming popular so now customers are coming because they know us, thinking, 'Wow this is much better quality than H&M'.

How did the UT T-shirt project come about?

I think that a printed T-shirt is a vehicle through which one can express creativity, character, passion and emotion. It's like a blank canvas. We work with

above: UNIQLO's logo

about 40 creatives each season and they come up with over 700 exclusive designs for UNIQLO. Most recently we used designs by Keith Haring and Jean-Michel Basquiat and we also introduced some Japanese manga characters this year. They're all selling very well: the reactions have been great.

How do you choose the designers for your limited edition T-shirt range? Who would you like to work with in the future?

We keep a look out for people who have an interesting way of life. That's how we tend to choose. I'd love to work with a very influential politician for some of our designs in the future. We could print a message to the world on a T-shirt and hopefully people would get it.

What is the idea behind using people such as Chloë Sevigny and Samantha Morton in your advertising campaigns?

Our global advertising campaigns are concepted and produced by MP Creative in New York City. The idea behind associating ourselves with credible actors, designers and artists, renowned for their own personal style, is to reinforce the idea that UNIQLO

above and opposite: UNIQLO's Pantone Cashmere collection offers cashmere garments at high street prices

We also promoted our cashmere collection last year which sold about 700,000 units in Japan alone. I'd say that's our business trick: providing great basics at great prices that are constantly updated. Everybody needs that. If we were to chase purely fashion, few people would follow us.

is a brand for everyone. We have also worked with talent such as fashion photographer Terry Richardson, *W* magazine creative director Dennis Freedman, writer Neville Wakefield and fashion stylist Melanie Ward to ensure we are aligning the brand with the art and design industry, again reaching a wider audience and appealing to niche sectors.

Can you talk me through your design process?

We design four collections each year: spring, summer, fall, winter. But summer and fall tend to be the biggest collections for us. The spring season is getting shorter and shorter. We still have snow in Tokyo, London and New York in March, but according to the fashion calendar, spring is from January to March. People these days have a hard time selling spring items because consumers aren't ready for them in those months. Then in April things suddenly change.

In terms of design, we might change small details, the stitching, the proportion or shape of a garment. Even just three or four millimetres of stitching can completely change the look of a garment. We're always checking trends too. For example right now we're noticing that after years of jeans, the skirt is making a comeback. We might observe it in magazines, on the street, at the fashion shows and so on. Fashion seems to go in cycles of five to seven years. So if women are starting to wear more skirts, we need to think: how can we update our jacket for next year? What is the perfect shape and length to wear with a skirt? That's how we go about updating the collection: we call it 'styling'.

Is UNIQLO more of a visionary or a reactionary company?

The ideal thing for us is to create a trend, but the reality is that we try to provide clothes 'on time'.

If the luxury brands are doing a garment on trend, we want to be able to provide that same trend but sell it at our prices and with our quality.

Your brand is famous for creating basics – how do you choose what cut/style to go for each season to ensure new interest from the customer?

Styling is getting more important for us. Of course if you take each individual item, you might just think, 'It's a navy jacket. This is white T-shirt…,' but it's the way we put the items together that shows you a new look.

From where do you get inspiration when you are designing?

I always send my key designers everywhere: to Europe, New York, Tokyo. We also get a lot of answers by seeing what people are buying in our stores. Sometimes people will also come in and ask for items we don't stock yet. We watch what goes on in the important fashion capitals: New York, London, Tokyo, Milan, both on the catwalk and on the street and we observe how people are dressing.

Who is your ideal customer?

People who know how to 'wear' clothes. A lot of people just buy labels because it's made by a famous designer, but they may have no style. For them it's a lifestyle choice. They don't necessarily know how to 'wear' clothes. We never put emphasis on our label.

Is your customer different in Japan, New York, London?

Our customers in New York and London buy our clothes not because of the label, but because they recognize that they are great. In Japan some people are still not proud of buying UNIQLO because in Japan the brand still suffers slightly from its previous image of being a cheap brand. But even in Japan customers are starting to recognize that the label has changed.

Where do you think fashion is heading?

I think there will only be two ways to go. You'll have the luxury brands and the mass-market brands such as UNIQLO and H&M, but I don't think the people in-between will have a future. They tend not to have a strong point of view and also they can't provide

a better price. They might provide a better price than luxury labels but the quality is only ever OK. I see a lot of middle-market companies struggling.

How important is the exact location when you are choosing a new site for a store?

We look for the best retail locations to communicate the right brand message. We opened the UK flagship store in Oxford Street, Europe's premium shopping street, and in New York we made the decision to open the global flagship store in SoHo, rather than on Fifth Avenue, to introduce the brand to a 'cooler' audience.

What advice would you give a budding designer?

A designer needs to have a clear vision and philosophy. It doesn't even matter if it's good or bad because nobody can evaluate that. There is no standard in the fashion industry, it's all completely subjective. Taste is a personal thing, so you need to be able to send out a clear message with confidence to your customers, otherwise people will get confused.

What makes one designer better than another?

Good question. To be successful you have not to care. You just have to believe in yourself. You have to put your entire passion, emotion and soul into what you believe in. Take Polo Ralph Lauren, for example. They are the sixth biggest volume fashion company in the world. It has a true, clear vision that never wavers. And UNIQLO is right behind them; they are seventh in the world.

Vans Steve Van Doren

Vice president of events and promotions and son of founder, Paul Van Doren

In 1966, Steve Van Doren stood by his father Paul's side as he launched the Van Doren Rubber Company in Anaheim, California. The company made shoes in its own factory and retailed them in their own stores to maximize profit. The basic canvas, vulcanized shoes called Vans quickly became a success. Van Doren learned all about the business by working in the factory and on the shop floor after school. By the time Van Doren was 19 he was in charge of half of Vans' 50 stores. When Vans was sold to VF Corporation in 2004 for $396 million, Van Doren became vice president of events and promotions. Today, Vans is sold in over 175 Vans retail outlets and has 10,000 wholesale accounts in 60 countries worldwide. The label turns over $700 million a year.

above: Steve Van Doren in his office; opposite: Skateboarding legend Steve Caballero competing in 1980 wearing Vans, photograph by J. Grant Brittain

When did you first get interested in your father's business?

I was 10 years old in 1966 when my father opened his first factory. I started helping out from a really early age. My four siblings and I would go there after school and we'd help my grandad paint the walls. At 14, I started working in the warehouse in the holidays. I'd do the inventory of the entire warehouse once a week and I'd also work on the production schedule with my dad. By the time I was 19, I was married and in charge of 25 of our 50 stores. I tried to go to college a couple of times,

but I remember a professor talking about business in a way that was so different from how we were doing things that I just wasn't into it. I knew I wanted to work with Vans. It was my passion.

Vans had its own factory and retail outlets. Lore has it that your father opened 10 shops in the first 10 weeks of opening the factory in 1966 – what was the thinking behind that?

The bottom line was my dad had to produce shoes to make the factory work. With one store, we might have sold 100 pairs a week. With 10 stores, we had the potential to sell 1,000 pairs a week. It all moved

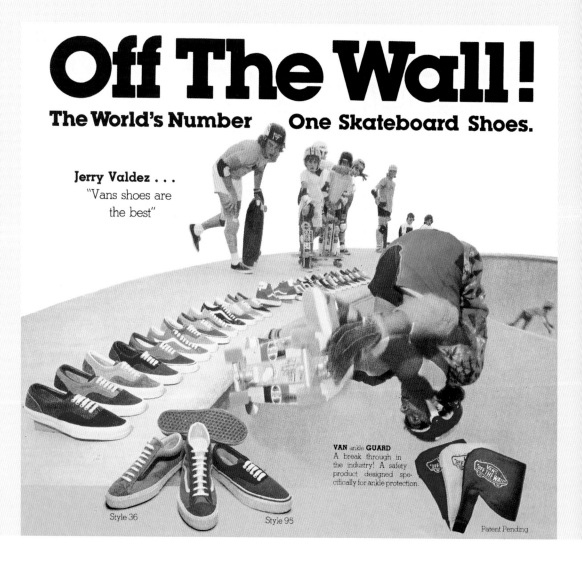

Off The Wall!

The World's Number One Skateboard Shoes.

Jerry Valdez . . .
"Vans shoes are the best"

Style 36

Style 95

VAN ankle GUARD
A break through in the industry! A safety product designed specifically for ankle protection.

Patent Pending

very quickly. My dad would find the new location on Monday, sign the lease on Tuesday, start painting and putting up shelves on Wednesday and open shortly after that. And that was happening every week. His accountant was telling him, 'Hey, Paul, six of those 10 stores are losers.' And my dad replied, 'Well then I need 10 more losers.' His whole idea was that if he was only making one pair of shoes, the manufacturing was costing him $10,000 for that pair, but if he made 10,000 pairs of shoes, it was costing him $1 a pair. He needed to get capacity up for cost efficiency.

Why do you think Vans was so successful straightaway?

My dad worked for a shoe manufacturer called Randy's – the third largest in the US – for 20 years before he opened his own factory. He knew how to make a shoe. He decided to make the soles twice as thick as the average shoe and use pure crepe rubber and a number 10 duck canvas thread, which was a far better material. He wanted his shoes to last longer. He couldn't afford to do advertising so he had to win his customers over through quality and fit.

Our Vans stores were very simple in the way they were fitted, but my dad realized early on that going the extra mile was worth it. On one of the first days after he opened the shop, a woman came in and saw our colour range. Among others we had a pink, a loden green, a navy blue and a white shoe. And she said, 'That pink is not the right pink for me.' My dad was thinking, 'Lady, I can't make 20 different pinks…', so he told the lady to buy a piece of material she liked and come back and he'd custom make her a pair. He charged her a dollar extra for the custom-made shoe, and so began our customizing efforts. It was unique. You could come in with a Hawaiian shirt print and we'd make you the shoes to match.

opposite: A Vans ad from the mid-1970s, showing their range of styles and colours; right: The black-and-white checkerboard Vans Slip-On first came out in 1981, but has since become a design classic

We made shoes in school colours, we made shoes for cheerleaders before everyone went athletic. Skateboarders adopted us and so did the surfers. We welcomed all the sports that other people left alone.

Since you started customizing shoes from the very beginning, including one woman who wanted her mink coat turned into a shoe after divorcing her husband, to what extent did this aspect of individuality help the company's image?

You could come in with a Hawaiian shirt print and we'd make you the shoes to match. We made shoes in school colours, we made shoes for chearleaders before everyone went athletic. Skateboarders adopted us and so did the surfers. We welcomed all the sports that other people left alone.

It helped tremendously. People don't like wearing the same things as everyone else. It was a way for people to express an attitude. I've just finished making my niece a pair of shoes for her wedding. It's got her and her fiance's name and the print of the wedding rings on the white rubber sidewall of the shoe.

In 1975 the skate legends Tony Alva and Stacy Peralta from Santa Monica wanted custom-made Vans. What did they come up with?

For them it was mostly about colours. They wanted the left shoe to be red and the right to be blue. Then they got into two-tone shoes: beige and brown, royal blue with white. They'd wear out their right shoe three times as fast as the left because of the ollies and tricks they were doing and we'd just give them another right.

Vans are to this day associated with Skatewear and that free lifestyle – what made you think at the time that it was a good route to follow and not too left field?

The skaters came to us and were loyal to us and we were loyal to them. And also, we didn't know any better at the time. We just did things that people liked. Stacy was the first skater we paid to wear our shoes. We put him in *Skateboard* magazine ads in the late 1970s. In 1988 we did our first signed model skate shoe. We consciously asked Steve Caballero to design a shoe for us and it's still a great shoe. At 42 years of age, all these years later, Steve still skates on our team. The strategy works like a pyramid, where you have five top pros at the top – currently that's Geoff Rowley, Anthony Van Engelen, Tony Trujillo, Dustin Dollin and Johnny Layton – underneath them you have a bigger group of established skaters who are exceptionally good but not as famous yet. And below that you have the amateurs and kids who aspire to be as good as their heroes. They want to look and be like those guys they respect. In the same way, we keep our classics and special edition shoes in our top stores to keep our core customers happy. Last year we probably could have sold three times as many shoes as we did but we made a conscious decision not to farm them out to any old shop in order to keep the image intact. That means that today you'll get a kid aged 12 who is just as likely to wear them as a skateboarder or a 52-year-old guy like me.

Your dad's philosophy was to make shoes to last by making the waffle soles twice as thick as normal... Is this still how you make the shoes today?

Yes, we still use the same technique. If you have a good recipe, why change it? It's like Entenmann's Cookies. When production was moved overseas to China and Indonesia in 1995 they wanted to change the last, that's the mould the shoe is created on. I had to fight hard to make them go back and re-create the original last. We make vulcanized shoes rather than cold cure shoes. It's the technique my dad learned at Randy's. During the '68 Olympics in Mexico, the first non-vulcanized shoes started coming out by people like Adidas.

When Vans were still manufactured in California what were the advantages of having your own factory close by?

Of course it's always nice to be able to say 'Made in America', and to keep US citizens employed, but it was also great to have such a quick turnaround. It took us 19 days from when we came up with a new style to having it on the shop floor. We were the quickest by far. We could react to the market place really quickly both for our own stores and also for our wholesale customers. If I walked out of the factory and realized that a gold and brown checkerboard style was doing well, I could make sure it was available as a stock shoe. We could also crank production in the factory up or down, depending on demand.

Why did your father Paul Van Doren not want to sell Vans outside of California before the shoe appeared in the film *Fast Times at Ridgemont High*?

My father knew from the outset that he never wanted to be at the mercy of the big retailers. When he worked at Randy's all those years, they were at

Jim dreamed of being a brand like Nike or Adidas. He went nuts trying to make shoes that we were not good at. He was trying to make break-dance shoes, sky-diving shoes and so on, but they weren't selling because nobody knew we were making them. We weren't advertising.

the mercy of JC Penney's and so on. He needed those orders to come through from New York and other places. Given that he had his own factory and his own retail stores he was at the mercy of himself.

Before *Fast Times* came out we were selling Vans in Arizona and the Sun Belt, but once the movie came out *everybody* wanted those shoes! Our former PR lady, Betty Mitchell, who is now 92 and retired, but was with the company for many years, walked up to Universal and handed over some boxes of Vans while they were making the movie. That was in 1982 before we spent money on major advertising. But, in fact, Sean Penn had had the same idea before she even dropped them off. He'd walked into a store and told Universal, 'This is what I want to wear in the movie'. This was when kids were doing their own checkerboard designs on the rubber of their Vans shoes.

below, left: A Vans BMX print ad used in 1980; below, right: Vans has been offering a successful customizing service since its inception and continues to do so today via its website

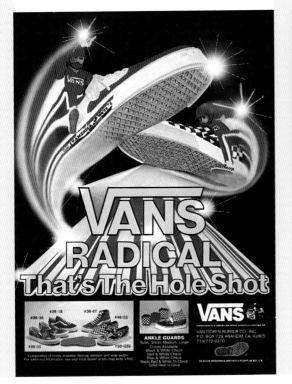

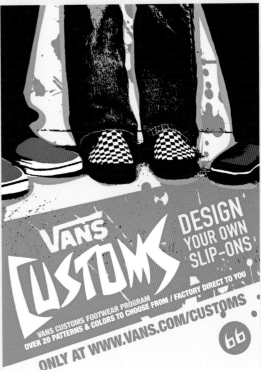

At what point do you think Vans became a fashion item?

I think from the moment *Fast Times* came out. Sean Penn played this Spicoli character. He was a surfer dude, who plays in a band and dances on stage with those checkerboard slip-ons on. At one point in the movie he takes a pair of checkerboard Vans out of their box and his friend says, 'What's that?' and Spicoli hits himself over the head with the Vans saying, 'That's my skull. I'm so wasted.' In the list of top 50 shoes of all time published by numerous magazines, that shoe comes in at 6th place.

How do you turn something into a lifestyle brand?

The one thing you need to make a brand succeed is passion and patience. If you don't have those elements you're quickly going to think, 'I'm working too hard for nothing.' If you love something passionately enough and believe in it, you'll get others to believe in it. Between 1966 and 1994 it was very profitable for us to manufacture Vans in the US. In 1994 we decided to shift all production overseas and in 1996 we became a marketing-focused company. We started getting involved in the Vans Warped Tour, a concert/amateur competition tour that goes across the US and kids can see up to 40 bands in one day. We also started the Vans Triple Crown of Surfing competition plus skateboarding and snowboarding events. At the end of the day, Vans is a canvas shoe, but people associate it with quality and style. They know that we support skaters, surfers, the music industry and that we are trying to make those industries better.

In the early 1980s Vans diversified and made everything from baseball shoes to skydiving shoes to try to keep up with the Nikes and Pumas of the world. To what degree do you think that was a mistake?

My father's business partner at the time was his younger brother Jim. He was an incredibly talented engineer, who designed the waffle soles. He took over a bit as my dad was easing off. It was about 1982 when the checkerboard was doing really well and Jim dreamed of being a brand like Nike or Adidas. He went nuts trying to makes shoes that we were not good at. He was trying to make break-dance shoes, sky-diving shoes and so on, but they weren't selling because nobody knew we were making them. We weren't advertising. We went off track. In 1984 we were suddenly spending more than we were bringing in. The banks didn't like what they saw. My dad and uncle had to go to court and my uncle was told to leave the business. The company filed for Chapter 11 (bankruptcy) and my dad owed $15 million dollars. In the space of three years he paid back all his debts to both the bank and the suppliers at 100 cents to the dollar. The few companies that get out Chapter 11 usually do so by paying 10 cents to the dollar, but my dad didn't want to do that. For him it was about integrity. Six months after we were out of the red, the company sold for $75 million dollars.

You attempted to battle against the Nikes and Pumas of the world and failed, and yet the company is due to turn over $700 million by the end of 2008. What is the secret of diversifying a classic shoe and keeping it fresh?

Our mission statement is youth culture. We focus on action sports. We have a core group of women and men who want to be our regular Vans customer. It's about 65 per cent male and 35 per cent female in the 11–18-year-old sector. And we stick to what we know. We collaborate with incredible designers such as Marc Jacobs to create unique lines, which then retail in high-end stores such as Colette in Paris. The Vans Vault series will be made from special leathers and materials and be sold specifically in those boutique stores. Other Classic shoes will go to the mall and our stores. We try to keep the shoe desirable. I try my best to build the brand and keep my face at the forefront of all the events we do.

Has the manufacturing of the shoe changed since its inception besides going overseas?

above: The famous Vans waffle sole, which is twice as thick as the average sole and made from pure crepe rubber; below: Three classic Vans styles: Sk8-Hi, Old Skool Skate Shoes and Authentic

The 'vulcanized' process has been around for over 100 years. It's how tyres are made. It's pretty much still done the same way as when we started.

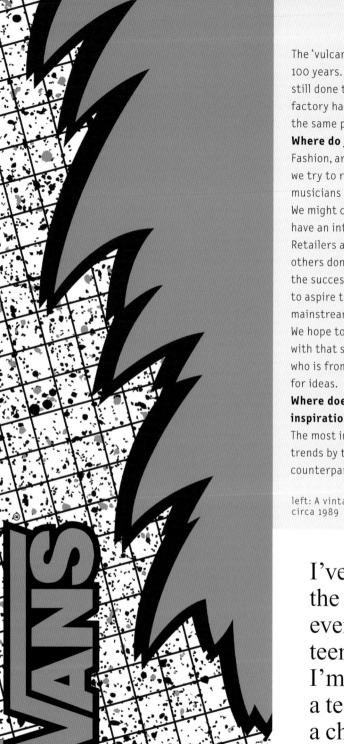

The 'vulcanized' process has been around for over 100 years. It's how tyres are made. It's pretty much still done the same way as when we started. Each factory has their own little way, but essentially it's the same process.

Where do you research fabrics for your shoes?

Fashion, art, sport and music are the four corners we try to reach. We do lots of collaborations with musicians such as Iron Maiden, Bad Brains and KISS. We might collaborate with a shop like Colette if they have an interesting designer they are working with. Retailers always like to have something special that others don't have. It's a really important factor in the success of the company. We want the top stores to aspire to selling our shoe and also the more mainstream shops, who will sell the classic pairs. We hope to still be selling Vans in 50 years' time with that strategy. Steve Murray, our president who is from the UK, also travels the world looking for ideas.

Where does your design team look for inspiration?

The most important thing is watching up-coming trends by travelling and talking to our Vans counterparts around the world. Our designers

left: A vintage Vans shoebox; the design first came out circa 1989

I've got the best job in the world. I get to go to events and hang out with teenagers. Although I'm an old guy, I feel like a teenager. It gives me a chance to talk to interesting people and do unique things.

also shop the world over looking for new style ideas. They might speak to the buyers of certain stores to gauge what is coming next. We work with trend forecasters such as WGSN in terms of what colours are going to come out, but then we also try and gauge whether it's more of a year for solid colours or prints. Also at certain times it's the slip-on that's more popular, other times it's our lace-ups. We work about 18 months in advance.

Who heads up the design team and what is the design process?

Bill Bettencourt is currently in charge of all production. We have different departments who work on different aspects of the process. We have a sourcing department, who finds fabrics, a design department, etc. They all work according to briefs. They then create prototypes from drawings. From there they bring in stores and salespeople from the different divisions and they show them the collection. Then it gets tweaked and production starts on the popular styles. The design process has gotten a lot more complicated than when we produced the shoes in the factory in the US.

How did Vans develop after it was bought by VF Corporation in 2004?

VF Corporation own Lee, Wrangler, The North Face, Nautica, Reef, etc. They are all apparel brands. We never had much apparel but since we were purchased we've started developing apparel lines. Our goal is to make 20 per cent of our business apparel, i.e., sweaters, pants, shorts, tees, fleeces, etc. It's something we never dreamed would happen, but VF Corporation has spent their whole existence in apparel so they have helped us take the brand beyond the shoes.

Samuel L. Jackson was on the cover of *USA Today* wearing a custom-made pair of Vans. How did that come about?

I had this idea of getting him a pair of custom-made Vans made for when his film *Snakes on a Plane* came out in 2006. They were a pair of classic slip-ons with snakes hand painted on them. The next thing I know, he's on Jay Leno with his legs crossed talking about the movie and his shoes are in full view. And then he was pictured on *USA Today* in the same pair. I remember also being in the same hotel as Julia Roberts when she was filming *My Best Friend's Wedding* in Chicago in 1997. Her birthday was the same day as mine. I organized a long stem rose box and put a couple of pairs of Vans girls' shoes in there in size 9. After she finished filming for the night, we were still in the bar and she came over and said, 'Where is Steve Van Doren?' And I was like, 'That's me!' and she was all happy about the shoes and wondered whether she could have a few more pairs for her friends. Next thing I know she's wearing the high-top Vans in *Notting Hill* in the scene where she walks up the stairs in Hugh Grant's flat.

What makes one brand more successful than another?

We try hard to make sure we have the right combination of coolness. The right writers commenting on the brand, to have a great visual merchandising department... We've now got a team of people who drive around in a van to the different shops that stock our shoes and they are in charge of setting up displays in shop windows to try to make the brand look its absolute best, so people can see what Vans is about as soon as they walk in. If you're stocked in some dark, back corner nobody is going to see you or notice you. We're now competing with the biggest shoe companies in the world for shelf space. You've got to keep up with the Joneses.

What advice would you give to a budding designer?

Find something that makes you happy and that you have a passion for. You have to have fun. I've got the best job in the world. I get to go to events and hang out with teenagers. Although I'm an old guy, I feel like a teenager. It gives me a chance to talk to interesting people and do unique things. You've also got to enjoy who you work with.

Lacoste

Christophe Lemaire

above: Christophe Lemaire making final adjustments to a collection before the show; opposite: Lacoste catwalk show, Spring/Summer 2009

Christophe Lemaire worked for Thierry Mugler and Christian Lacroix before launching his own label, 'Christophe Lemaire', aged 25. He became the creative director of Lacoste in 2000. Since his appointment, he has been lauded for giving the brand with the famous croc logo a new look, while managing to maintain its traditional values.

When did you first get interested in fashion?
My mother and grandmother were always very elegant and dressed in Yves Saint Laurent. Plus my uncle was the director of *Vogue Paris*, so during the summer holidays I was always surrounded by chic people and I became interested in 'the look'.
I was more interested, however, in design in general: furniture design, industrial design and so on and I wanted to prepare to go to art school. However, my father wasn't willing to support my studies so I had to find a job. I started working for Thierry Mugler when I was 19. I was the assistant of the head of accessories and I suddenly realized that it was fun. It took a bit of time, though, because I was also working as a DJ organizing club nights once a week.

I was always good at sketching so I didn't feel the need to go to school. The only thing I've always regretted was not learning the technical skills needed, such as pattern-making. Of course you learn through experience but I think it's always great when you can achieve something completely on your own, so that you can say to a pattern-maker, 'No, you can't do it that way' or 'Why don't we do it this way?' That way you can really push your ideas to the limit. I'm very interested in simplicity and I think the more you want things to be simple, the more you have to master the technical side of things.

Do you think it's important to go to fashion school?
I think for certain elements of design – such as knitwear design – where you have to learn technical things, it's beneficial. But when it comes down to pure style, I don't think you can learn that. At end of the day, it's just a matter of taste, of point of view, of culture, of keeping an eye open, of being observant.

Can you think of anyone in the fashion industry who is working but doesn't have style?
There are too many people to mention. I'm against this whole podium craze, where fashion is designed to become a spectacle on the runway but has no connection with reality. I love one specific period of fashion that dates back to the late 1970s. It's

below and opposite: Lacoste catwalk show, Spring/ Summer 2009

not because I'm nostalgic, but it's because I feel that the designers created an interesting balance between practicality, functionality, aesthetic values and sophistication. Women tended to be more emancipated, and the clothes were made so they could move freely in them. Of course I loved Yves Saint Laurent and French designers such as Marie Beretta, Guy Paulin, Christiane Bailly, Sonia Rykiel and non-French brands such as Missoni. I also love that

> I like things to be real. The same goes for culture, it needs to be real. I hate it when it's in a museum or art gallery. I hate fashion made for the runway.

American style book called *Cheap and Chic* (1976) which is a style bible for me! Armani, Halston... I always like to look back at these references. I like things to be real. The same goes for culture, it needs to be real. I hate it when it's in a museum or art gallery. I hate fashion made for the runway.

What did you learn when you were working for Christian Lacroix and Thierry Mugler?
At Christian Lacroix I learned about pleasure. My previous experience had been a bit frustrating. Because I wasn't gay or hysterical about fashion, I felt like a bit of an outsider. I didn't really fit in to the milieu, but with Christian Lacroix I met some very open-minded and intelligent people who were full of culture. He recognized something in my book and he asked me to become his assistant. I felt very lucky. I travelled to America and, of course, I learned all about colours working alongside such a great colourist. He also had a certain approach to fashion, which might be considered French, a 'désinvolture', a 'légerté'. The feeling that a sort of lightness and sense of humour has to remain,

despite fashion being a business with commercial issues. It's so important to keep a bit of poetry and playful fun. I've always tried to maintain that spirit.

What did launching your own label 'Christophe Lemaire' teach you?

After working with Christian Lacroix for a while I realized that I was interested in much more real fashion. Haute couture was great when you had a great creation and great clientele. The clientele used to have taste and they were mostly aristocratic and rich, but by the end of the 1980s people with money didn't necessarily have taste. I became more interested in working to create a more daily, affordable style. In 1990 I won a prize from the Ministry of Culture called ANDAM. The purpose of the prize was to give support to young designers. I was 25 and decided to make my own collection. I presented the collection at the Salon du prêt à porter in Paris and immediately had orders from Japan. It was like jumping in water and learning to swim straightaway. I had good distribution in Japan, but I think perhaps I wasn't considered to be 'designer' enough in France: in 1991 everything was super-experimental. The business grew and after seven years I found myself working with 15 people. I started integrating more sportswear and military details into my collection, playing with the colours and focusing more on the functionality. That's probably why Lacoste picked me up.

What was your vision for the brand when you were hired to become creative director of Lacoste in 2000?

My vision hasn't wavered since the very beginning, but it wasn't that easy to implement straightaway. I grew up as a French bourgeois boy on my father's side. I was very into golf and tennis, so very much in a Lacoste environment. I knew what the brand was about and immediately had a clear vision. For me it was about the unique balance of easy wear and style, sportive elegance, simple but fresh with colours, affordable yet good quality. For me it was a very French vision of sportswear. It had to become the ultimate sportswear chic brand.

What changes did you make to the brand to attract a younger audience, as well as keep the old customers?

Having a vision is one thing but then having that vision accepted by the company is a whole different thing. The managers at Lacoste took a big step by recruiting an artistic director. They understood that it was necessary in order to create a more coherent image and to improve the style. The problem was that sales were good; the money was there, so commercially there hadn't been a decline. However, the image of the brand was rather old fashioned and dusty. I had to be extremely patient and stubborn when it came to cutting the old business and creating a new one. It took me four years before I could really share the confidence I had in the new vision. When I started, the existing team wasn't very modern or open-minded. They were very proud of working for Lacoste and not so young.

I'm proud of the fact that I could change the perception of the brand without changing what it is. I was always very keen to remain faithful to what Lacoste is about. I didn't want to do anything too fashionable, extreme or hyped. The brand is unique in that people of so many different ages, social groups and backgrounds are attracted to it. People recognize its simplicity and quality. It's democratic, despite having a preppy heritage. The people at Lacoste didn't believe it was possible to make Lacoste modern again without betraying the philosophy of the brand. But we did it.

In France the image is still rather BCBG (bon chic, bon genre) isn't it? Are you trying to shake that as well?

It's definitely more difficult to change the image in the country where Lacoste started. In France, it was considered a provincial, safe, bourgeois, catholic and traditionalist brand. But then again, you'd also have the North African kids from the suburbs wearing it, and they were from a different social background. At one point it became an issue, as you'd see kids on the news who'd just done a robbery or some such, and they'd be wearing the croc. The company was embarrassed by this, but I didn't really think it was a problem provided we made the effort to communicate again what Lacoste was about: its history, René Lacoste and showing the new style, etc.

How do you go about designing a collection?
We have to start incredibly early, the system is very rigid. The company doesn't like risks so only those items that the forecasters and people in the sales team believe in go into production. It's a big problem. Right now we're in September 2008 and we're already starting designs for Spring/Summer 2010, so we work almost two years in advance. The samples get approved by the sales team in March and shown to distribution people in June. We usually start by deciding on the colours. We work with a design team using inspiration boards and so on. We do sometimes work with a trend forecaster because it's interesting to have an outside point of view. But essentially we all work in fashion and deal with style so we don't desperately need to look at trends. For colour trends, we use our intuition. In a lot of companies there is a constant battle between the product managers and the sales people and the design team. I'm quite proud that we've managed to find the right balance at Lacoste, where there is respect and dialogue between each of the teams.

right: Formerly seen as a traditional French brand, Lacoste has had an overhaul since Christophe Lemaire became creative director in 2000

The people at Lacoste didn't believe it was possible to make Lacoste modern again without betraying the philosophy of the brand. But we did it.

Can you talk me through the importance of colour at Lacoste?

Lacoste is a colour brand. We have between 30 and 40 colours for the polo shirts every season and we change at least half of those.

Do you design with your audience in mind?

I think the best way to design is *not* to have your audience spectrum in mind. It's sort of there unconsciously but if you try to please everybody, you end up pleasing nobody. Too many brands today are driven by merchandising. At the end of the day all the brands end up looking like each other. And that doesn't just go for clothes, it goes for cars and so on too. I'm convinced that if one car company had the courage to go out on a limb and create a more original design, it would work. Marketing departments are obsessed with the mass market. They want to please everybody. Fortunately, at Lacoste we still possess a sense of naivety, which is perhaps what makes us attractive. We are able to design each collection without thinking too much about what people expect and think we should do. As designers we have to be down to earth and understand what's real in everyday life and what's not.

Where do you get your inspiration?

From archives of course, from movies, pictures and books. I'm inspired by musicians and their style. I was very into the book *Back in the Days*, which documents the emerging hip-hop scene between 1980 and 1989. I'm also into electronic music. We have this very new label called Red, which is dedicated to the younger, trendier, urban clients. It comes out in Summer 2009.

How did Lacoste transform from a sportswear to a fashion label?

I think it was an iconic label in the 1980s. The polo was part of the upper-class wardrobe. I think that it's only really in the last 10 years that Lacoste became a fashion label. It's partly because we've developed the ladies' collection and we've started doing fashion

opposite: Lacoste became famous for its polo shirt made from cotton pique

shows, which has really helped a lot to share the vision of the brand. Our advertising is now sending a strong message about Lacoste being a sportswear brand and also playing in the field of fashion.

Now that Lacoste is a fashion label, as well as a sportswear label, how important is technical innovation and performance wear to the brand?

It's extremely important. We have a team dedicated to technical and fabric research for the sports line and we are planning to develop that part further. And with the main line, functionality and comfort is always at the forefront. There is no way that we'd ever design a trench coat that isn't waterproof, for example. It doesn't make sense.

You use players such as Andy Roddick and Richard Gasquet to endorse your product? Do you still focus on sportspeople more than on celebrities?

It's a matter of reminding people that we were originally a tennis and golf brand, but I'm not personally involved in the sponsorship side of things.

What made you decide to present Lacoste on the runway and what was the response?

We did our first show in Paris in 2002 and the next one in New York in 2003. Paris was great, but I think we did it too soon because I felt that the product wasn't really there yet. I wasn't super enthusiastic but the managers wanted to send a strong signal that something was happening at Lacoste after they'd employed me. For the Paris show I wanted to demonstrate the huge variety of individuals who wear Lacoste, from the hip-hop kid to the little bourgeois, from the young kid to the old grandad golfer. We created a huge tennis court, had a huge band playing live. Unfortunately, the French press

> The polo was part of the upper-class wardrobe. I think that it's only really in the last 10 years that Lacoste became a fashion label.

was saying that the reality of Lacoste was still pretty old and fusty. In Paris they expect the avant-garde, we weren't understood.

We then decided to make the move to New York in 2003. It was a big risk because it was at the start of the Iraq war and the French were not very popular. But we had a huge welcome and the show was a great success. It was very poppy and colourful. The brand had disappeared from the market for 10 years because of distribution issues, etc., and it was our chance to come in and say, 'We're back.' The men's press and women's press are together there, which works for us. Also, New York is a great commercial playground for a sportswear brand like Lacoste to show its line. We gave it a playful, sexy twist.

Who is your target audience?
It's difficult to say who our target audience is. I think we're more of a concept. I'm very sceptical about the marketing way of thinking that puts people into categories. Reality is not like that. Categories exist but it's more important to understand people's social habits and movements. I try to work with an idealistic silhouette and then turn that into reality. I'd like to develop a Club Line, which would be more refined, sophisticated and expensive. It would be timeless, easy chic, such as comfortable cashmere tracksuits for, say, people travelling around the world.

You have over 1,000 boutiques in 112 countries – what is the global appeal of Lacoste? What does it stand for?
Distribution is one of our biggest strengths but also our weak point. Lacoste is distributed worldwide and renowned all over the world. Although, or because, the logo is rather strange everybody knows it. The biggest challenge now is to make sure the new designs we are coming up with actually hit the shop and don't die before going into production and that depends on the sales and distribution teams.

Does each country have the same bestselling items?
The polo shirt is still our bestselling item worldwide. It's the key piece of each collection, but people now understand that we're not just a brand that sells tops. Our knitwear and shirts are also a big success.

What effect has your campaign 'Un peu d'air sur terre' where people are jumping through the air in Lacoste had on sales?
David Sims, Tom Munro and Phil Poynter have all worked on that campaign. More recently we

> There are many good designers out there, but most of them don't have the philosophy or backbone needed to create a great brand. René, who created Lacoste, was the incarnation of his own style...a very elegant, chic, creative, healthy, modern sportsman, who enjoyed life.

left: The famous croc logo; opposite: René Lacoste placed a crocodile emblem on his left breast as people had begun to refer to him as 'the alligator'. According to Lacoste, it was the first time a brand name ever appeared on the outside of an item of clothing

employed Terry Richardson for our new campaign. The 'air sur terre' campaign was about lightness on earth, about people being dynamic. I feel that the message is much clearer this season after Terry's photo shoot. The effect on sales has been great.

How important are accessories to the brand?

Extremely important as Lacoste is a lifestyle brand. Shoes, bags, belts, eyewear, watches...they're all part of the equation. You can apply that Lacoste aesthetic and quality to other products.

What is the advantage of licensing some elements of the brand such as fragrance and sunglasses out to other companies such as Procter & Gamble? To what degree do you still have creative control?

With Procter & Gamble creative control doesn't exist. It's a huge machine. I think that deal was made without thinking about the global message. Procter & Gamble have huge financial power and huge media planning departments, but I think the brand image and the advertising side of things on the fragrance side is a disaster. It would have made sense if it were coherent with where we wanted to situate the brand, but at the moment it's sending contradictory signals. It's not good. I can't really do anything about it as I'm just a humble soldier, but everybody in the system understands the problem now and we're working on it.

What makes one designer/brand stand out more than the next?

Success depends on how a style and concept are accepted by the public. You can have great designers but if they don't have the means to reach their public through the right distribution channels it won't work. If the concept is flawed and you have strong distribution it won't work either. You need

below and opposite: The Spring/Summer 2009 collection

the right balance between what you have to say and what the people want to hear. For Lacoste, I would say what makes it such a great brand is its uniqueness.

Great designers such as Coco Chanel, Yves Saint Laurent, Martin Margiela, Armani...have a unique point of view about life and about style. They are original in their way of thinking. There are many good designers out there, but most of them don't have the philosophy or backbone needed to create a great brand. René, who created Lacoste, was the incarnation of his own style. He was a very elegant, chic, creative, healthy, modern sportsman, who enjoyed life.

What advice would you give a budding designer?
I would say you need to be stubborn and determined because it's a very tricky business and it's not an easy job anymore. It was never easy as such but even back in the 1980s it was more light and playful and there wasn't so much pressure. It's a very stressful job now because the economic issues are more cruel than ever. The problem with fashion is that at the end of the day it's still a business. You have to be creative and have fun but it's super competitive. It's not just about being talented and having a vision, you also have to reach your public. You have to be passionate, smart and determined. I don't want to sound pretentious, but I think you need to be intelligent to understand all the issues involved. All the great designers were always very smart and had a point of view about society and how it worked. Or you have to have a partner who does the financial and planning side of things for you. But that's a luxury. A lot of journalists writing about fashion never mention the economic side, but it's such a huge part of the business. These days magazines are so difficult to digest because it's just a media circus. It's not inspiring, nothing stands out anymore. It's all just a spectacle.

C.P. Company and Stone Island

Carlo Rivetti _Owner_

left: Carlo Rivetti, owner of C.P. Company and Stone Island; opposite: Stone Island, Autumn/ Winter 2008–2009

A descendant of the founders of Italy's second ever wool mill, Lanifici Rivetti, Carlo Rivetti has been immersed in the manufacturing of clothes from the day he was born. Not only did he watch his father open the first Italian factory that produced garments on a production line, but he was also involved in distributing Giorgio Armani from the late 1970s until the early 1990s with GFT, the largest manufacturer and distributor of formal clothes in Italy at the time. In 1993 he bought Sportswear Company, the sportswear division of GFT and with it C.P. Company and Stone Island. Ever since, he has made it his quest to ensure that the two brands are on the cutting edge of technical innovation and functionality by dedicating 70 per cent of his staff to researching new textiles, fabrics, cuts, dyes and designs. Rivetti's approach to design is completely different from the rest of the fashion world. For him, design is more about research than fashion. Today, Stone Island and C.P. Company are sold in 1,300 shops worldwide, including 12 flagship stores in countries such as China, the UK, Italy and South Korea.

When did you first get interested in fashion?

It's a long story, but my family have been in the textile business for generations. It goes as far back as the end of the 17th century, at the start of industrialization in Italy. Quinto Rivetti, my forefather – I come eight generations later – founded the second ever wool mill in Italy and called it Lanifici Rivetti, which means Woolmakers Rivetti. Between the two World Wars, Lanifici Rivetti was the largest company in Italy; it was even bigger than Fiat. After the Second World War my father went to America and learned all about the production of men's suits in theoretical sizes. When he came back to Italy he convinced the family to sell their shares of Lanifici Rivetti in order to buy GFT, which was the commercial part of Lanifici Rivetti. In 1950 we opened a shop in Turin to teach potential customers about the new size system. Until then people had only ever bought suits from a tailor, but between 1950 and 1965 we sold 4,000 blue suits every single Saturday. We only had one style and one colour, but it was the perfect starting block from which to start an industry because it was very simple. So my father started the first Italian factory, which produced garments on a production line: he just copied the way cars were being produced. In other words, the garments or suit jackets and so on were assembled. In the 1950s and 1960s GFT became the largest Italian factory making formal clothes. Then suddenly, in 1975, came the oil crisis. It was then we knew we had to do something to revamp the market, we had to inject the suits with a new element and that was FASHION.

My cousin, just by chance and it was lucky timing, got a call from Milan and a journalist told him about a young talented guy who was about to go bankrupt because he was growing so fast he couldn't finance his own business. He met the guy and they decided to do something together. That guy was Giorgio Armani. And together they created the 'Made in Italy' concept. The very idea of having a 'designer' and the concept of royalties and licence agreements first came about because

of the set up between GFT and Giorgio Armani. GFT became the producer and distributor of the biggest designers in Italy: after Armani, there was Ungaro, Valentino.

At the beginning of the 1980s GFT was the most powerful formal dress company in Italy, but I thought the future was in non-formal wear. We looked into who and what was the best Italian company doing non-formal wear and that was C.P. Company. We bought 50 per cent of the company in 1983 and managed C.P. Company and Stone Island until 1993, when GFT ran into financial difficulties. The company decided they wanted to concentrate on their core business, which was formal wear, but my belief was in non-formal. I was kicked out in 1992 because I wanted to go non-formal, so I bought Sportswear Company – the Stone Island and C.P. Company sector of the GFT business – and it became a medium-sized Italian company, which I was very happy with.

Do you think it's important to go to fashion school if you want to work in the industry?

I think if you know marketing, it won't kill you. In my opinion, there are some problems here in Italy. Generally speaking, schools are not involved in the real side of the industry. Students are strong when it comes to theory, but they don't have the opportunity to get their hands dirty working in the business. And that means that they don't know fabrics, they don't know how to stitch and sew, they just don't have the experience. The way it runs in Italy is that most factories are small independently family-owned businesses and because they are family-owned, they are too small to be managerial companies. It's like the old Italy. They are usually based in small towns and each factory's company has its own language in a way. You really have to work for a company and learn from them.

We have lots of schools that teach you how to be a designer, but to be a designer you must first be kissed by God. At the end of the day, how many Giorgio Armanis can we have in this country? We have the technical schools here, but they are all

above: Bordeaux hooded Stone Island jacket in Raso Gommato, structured with pleats and seams to make it virtually flat, Autumn/Winter 2002–2003

empty. And they are empty because the only aspect of fashion that reaches young people's minds is the sparkling, shining world of fashion. The catwalks, the glitz, the bling. Nobody is communicating the vital fact that the biggest advantage and selling point of the 'Made in Italy' label is that besides being extremely creative, Italy is able to cover the entire textile supply chain involved in producing a garment. Of course the catwalk and the designers are important, but the real business is the people working to produce the garments. It's the largest part of the industry and it's simply not communicated to the younger generation.

I always say to my students when I'm teaching the industrial fashion design course at Milan's Politecnico, 'In the 1980s, when Made In Italy started, it was all about the designers. In the 1990s it was all about the models and now it's all about the people attending the shows.' But nobody is talking about

In the 1990s it was all about the models and now it's all about the people attending the shows. But nobody is talking about how the garments are made and the people behind it. And that's a big mistake. For every one single successful designer, there are at least 100 people working to make his or her ideas become a reality.

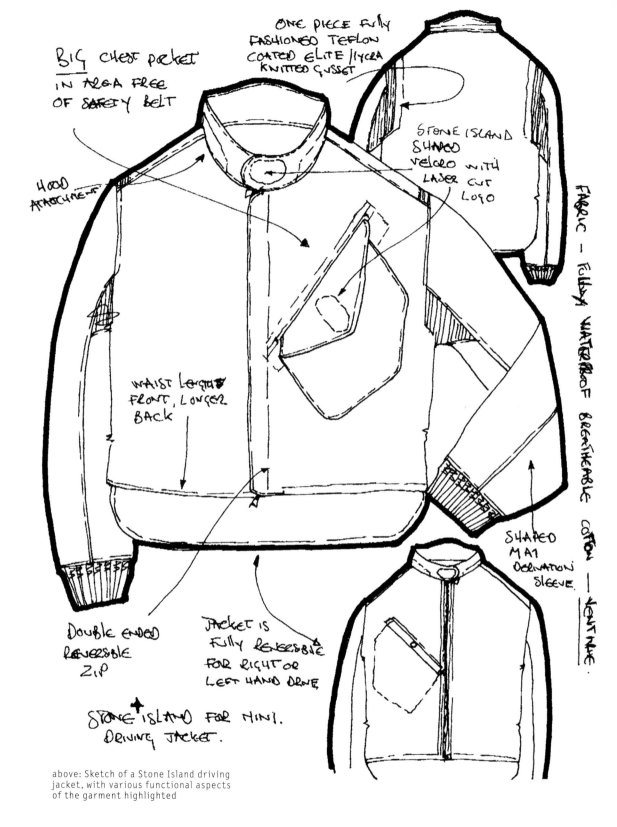

BIG CHEST POCKET
IN AREA FREE
OF SAFETY BELT

ONE PIECE FULLY
FASHIONED TEFLON
COATED ELITE/LYCRA
KNITTED GUSSET

STONE ISLAND
SHAPED
VELCRO WITH
LASER CUT
LOGO

HOOD
ATTACHMENT

WAIST LENGTH
FRONT, LONGER
BACK

FABRIC — FULLY WATERPROOF BREATHEABLE COTTON — VENT NECK.

SHAPED
MA1
DERIVATION
SLEEVE.

DOUBLE ENDED
REVERSIBLE
ZIP

JACKET IS
FULLY REVERSIBLE
FOR RIGHT OR
LEFT HAND DRIVE

STONE ISLAND FOR MINI.
DRIVING JACKET.

above: Sketch of a Stone Island driving
jacket, with various functional aspects
of the garment highlighted

how the garments are made and the people behind it. And that's a big mistake. For every one single successful designer, there are at least 100 people working to make his or her ideas become a reality.

Do you think you need a philosophy to create a successful brand?

Oh, yes. You need philosophy, integrity and consistency. Customers these days are very astute. It's pointless tricking them as you'll end up losing them as a customer. The brand is everything, so it's important to protect the credibility and environment of the brand. Last year, for example, my salespeople asked me to create knitwear with strange designs on it because that was very fashionable at the time, but it didn't have anything to do with our brands. It would have seemed fake, so I didn't do it. Salespeople are terrible. Their only objective is sales and sometimes they don't understand the real product that you've spent so much time and thought on.

What is yours?

Lots of designers say they take ideas from the street, but I think if you do that you're already too late.

> Lots of designers say they take ideas from the street, but I think if you do that you're already too late. I always try to do new things. I want to work with new fabrics, new treatments and that's not always easy as salespeople want to sell what they sold in the past.

I always try to do new things. I want to work with new fabrics, new treatments and that's not always easy as salespeople want to sell what they sold in the past, i.e., garments they already know and are confident about. But this company has a special DNA. It was founded by a designer and Sportswear Company has always supported the research behind it. So our philosophy is about following our own ideas and not becoming corrupted by the market.

You speak about 'design as research' rather than 'design as fashion' for your brands – could you explain what you mean by this and how this sets you apart from other brands?

I feel much more comfortable in the world of design than in the world of fashion. I have a personal dream, which is to have one our products in the Museum of Modern Art in New York, next to the Olivetti typewriter, Lettera 22. Most fashion items are old after six months, but in my opinion this isn't true with our pieces. We have a completely different approach to design than the rest of the fashion world. When I'm researching, I never think about the following season, but merely about doing my research. Also, we never really know in advance when or if we're ever going to get to the bottom of our research. But when that stage does come, when we've cracked something, we'll put it in a new collection.

Where do you get inspiration for new collections?

Our starting point is always the fabric and the treatment of the fabric. When we start working with a fabric, we don't know what we're going to do with it, but we look to the fabric for answers. Ninety per cent of our customers are men, so the component of pure fashion design is less important. We are constantly thinking about the function of the garment. You will never find a pocket that doesn't have a meaning on one of our garments. Every single detail has a function and reason for being there. In Italy we use our hands to talk. And in the last 20 years, the way we use our hands has changed dramatically due to mobile phones, personal computers, etc. Because we are using our hands in a different way, we need different pockets.

How do Stone Island and C.P. Company go about designing a collection?

Collections from one season to the next must evolve; they can't just jump. So you might have a fabric that you used the season before and you might use it in a new way. It's a mixture of innovation and fine tuning elements you had in previous collections. But we get a very concrete briefing at the beginning of the season in terms of quantities and quality, price range and the number of fabrics. As all prototypes are engineered in-house, we are confined to the number our structure is able to develop each season. Seventy per cent of our staff work on the research and development aspect of the brands. I think it helps not to have a totally blank canvas. You really have to hone your creativity when you are bound by a set of restrictions.

Is military wear and work wear still a big inspiration when it comes to how your collections are constructed?

Not in terms of fabric, but in terms of function, yes. Military wear and work wear is certainly still an inspiration for our collections as they are very functional clothes. But active sports such as motorcycling, skiing, sailing, hiking are also very interesting to us as every detail in those clothes is functional. We try to think of it as transforming work wear from a professional use to a civil, everyday use. Pockets, shoulders, zippers, the opening of a garment…these things are all very important to us. We don't research textiles purely from a fashion point of view, but from the point of view of alternative applications. If there's a guy in the world who has a new exciting idea linked to research in fabric he'll come here and we'll explore it together.

Your company's manifesto states: 'there should be no use for the word impossible'. How does that translate into your collections?

Research is so firmly ingrained in our mentality that we are very open to trying new things even if we have no idea whether they will ever come to anything. For example, for the last five or six years we've been working on non-stitching. Through our research we've come into contact with really interesting people from other sectors. While researching gluing I have met some incredibly fascinating people. The skills they have worked on weren't linked to fashion but, say, keeping boats afloat.

If your design approach is so unique, why do you create Autumn/Winter and Spring/Summer collections like every one else?

The companies that can work really quickly no longer adhere to the seasonal approach: they move much more quickly. But working in a seasonal way helps the industry and it helps to sustain your business. I'm not sure what will happen to distribution in the next couple of years: will regular shops still exist or will everything happen online? I think the financial crisis

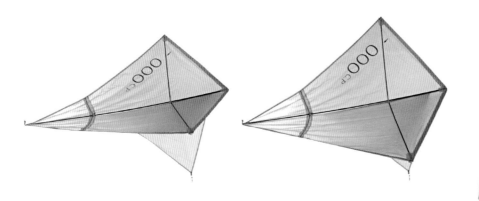

we're in at the moment will change the way consumers spend. I think people will start buying fewer pieces but they will be better quality. The approach will be seen more as an investment. It won't only be about the beauty of the garment, at least I hope it won't. Our consumption has been out of control in the last few years. We don't need all those garments in our wardrobe. I think formal wear will also undergo a change as people are much more into casualwear.

C.P. Company's original designer, Massimo Osti, was attracted to research and creating clothes as tools to live in and with. A completely different approach from someone like Tom Ford who claims he cannot separate the creative side from the commercial, in other words creating clothes that appeal – is this still the case now?
To be honest, we try to follow both. Of course we have to take the commercial aspect into consideration, but we try to do it in a special way. So we don't go by what the market is expecting or asking of us, we try to do our own thing.

Stone Island was created in 1982 and specialized in the surface treatment of fabric and the use of dyes – how has that evolved?
Stone Island came about following a mistake. One day we received a beautiful fabric and when we dyed the jacket we saw that it was quite 'fashion'.

below: In 2000 C.P. Company created 'transformables' – coats that turned, among other things, into tents and kites

One side was polyamide and the other side was cotton and after the dyeing process, one side came out orange and the other side green. It looked really strong. It was incredibly beautiful, but it didn't fit into the C.P. Company brand. The first collection we did consisted of seven shoulder pieces made from one fabric in 19 colours. That's how Stone Island started. To this day 90 per cent of Stone Island and C.P. Company garments are garment dyed, i.e., made in white fabric and then dyed. Six months ago, a gentleman said to me, 'Stone Island is to the fashion business what Oakley is in sunglasses.' Oakley was something totally new. From the very beginning Stone Island

Research is so firmly ingrained in our mentality that we are very open to trying new things even if we have no idea whether they will ever come to anything.

> It's a really strange thing, but if you put colour on a flat surface or on a fabric, the colour comes out completely differently from when you put that same colour on a 3D product...
> It helps and changes your approach to creativity when you are not linked to the supplier, but can build your own colour.

was a departure from the norm, it had a different point of view then and still does to this day.

What is the interest in applying dye to the finished garment rather than the fabric?

It's a really strange thing, but if you put colour on a flat surface or on a fabric, the colour comes out completely differently from when you put that same colour on a 3D product. In our laboratory we can do 11 different colours with one dye bath by playing with fibres and fibres mixing as all fibres take the dye differently allowing different shades of the same colour and/or also contrasting colours. The temperature, the acidity of the water, the type of colouring fabric, the print, etc., also have an effect on the final outcome. It helps and changes your approach to creativity when you are not linked to the supplier, but can build your own colour. It's the closest thing to being a Renaissance artist. We have all the colours of the world: we're like cooks. We work with temperatures ranging from 80 to 130°C and rather

than throwing spaghetti in the pot, we throw our garments in. And because of the way we cook the garments, we need high-quality stitching.

In 2000 and 2001 C.P. Company created 'transformables' coats that turned into tents, jackets that turned into inflatable chairs and you have now created the Shadow Project with Stone Island. Can you tell me about the idea behind these special projects?

We create special projects because sometimes the thing you are researching doesn't link in with the collection and so we create a special capsule collection or idea. It's nice to be able to open the field of research without having to be linked to the main collection. It's a way of staying flexible and that flexibility is my business advantage. My competitors might be able to invest huge amounts of money in advertising, but they can't compete with me when it comes to research. I always think like a surfer: I'm always trying to

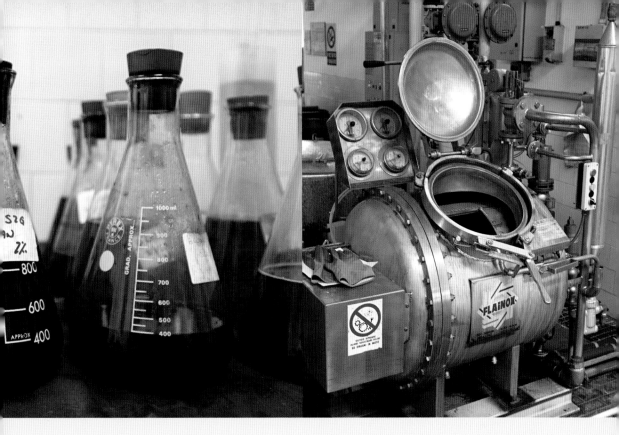

stay on the edge of the wave and jump from one wave to the next.

In your company key staff have been with you for decades, for instance, Giuliano Balboni who has been in charge of the dyeing section for 30 years and Paola Rimondi, who is now head of the fabric research and quality department... What's more all the people involved in the creation and manufacturing process are valued. To what degree is that structure and belief system part of Sportswear Company's success?

Sportswear Company is based in the small town of Ravarino, which is not an industrial district. So we all live together as a community. A lot of the people who started working here when they were young are still here. Currently, the first generation is about to retire, for example, Giuliano. It's a problem because with them goes the experience. It could have been a problem but thankfully Giuliano has some excellent apprentices who are able to carry on and implement

our research. But, and thankfully, he only lives 10 minutes away and is happy to come back if we need advice. I think the people in a company are the single most important element in that company. I always say, 'A one man band is not a band.' People are proud to work here and they really push themselves to the limit of their capabilities. We don't know the word 'impossible' here. If there is a problem my staff would never come to me and say, 'There is a problem.' They would say, 'There is a problem and here's the idea we came up with to solve it.' Because 70 per cent of the company is working on research and development that means 70 per cent of people have a creative approach. People in other companies often say, 'We always do it this way.' That statement doesn't apply here because each time it's a new way.

Ravarino, the village where we work, is 30 km from Maranello, where Ferrari cars are made. Ferraris,

I think, are not cars, they are dreams. In a similar way, we don't create fashion, we create dreams.

In the book *Stardust* you are quoted as saying 'in an industry governed by distrust, arrogance and aloofness': is this your experience of the fashion world?

I always listen to other people because I feel we can learn from them and then we have to interpret what we have learned. But sometimes in the fashion business people feel that by the mere fact of being in the business they know the answer. I think my approach is very different. I attempt things, but am never sure whether they will work out or not.

Do you feel like the industry has changed a lot?

Absolutely. And thank god. I started more than 30 years ago and back in the 1980s when the 'Made in Italy' concept started Italian designers were able to sign everything – even tiles for bathrooms. The problem wasn't so much that they designed and signed everything, but that people were actually buying these things! In the beginning designers had an aesthetic role: they were teaching people how to dress. That's when the 'fashion victim' phenomenon started, i.e., people who would dress in designer gear head to toe because they didn't trust their own judgment. But these days the customer knows what he or she wants. Dressing is a way of communicating something about yourself, it is no longer about designers dressing you. Mind you, there are still kids in Japan who dress in one brand head to toe. They'll wear a British brand with checks and they'll have the hat, the underwear, the blanket, the mobile phone pouch, etc. Why? Because they are unable to choose what they really like.

You claim your greatest successes have been when you have gone against the grain of what retailers have predicted will sell. Can you give some examples...

Retailers always want to sell what they already know. They always ask me to make that jacket that sold so well two seasons ago. But that's a terrible way of thinking. If you follow that type of strategy everyone would be wearing exactly the same thing within five years, like China with President Mao. Same jacket, same colour, same fabric – because it's easy to sell. So if they say one thing to me, I always try to do the opposite. It's the times when I really don't care what people want or expect from my brand that the approach ends up being successful. For example, nobody thought it was going to be possible to make a 100 per cent stainless-steel jacket. I always try to do things my own way. In general people can only desire what they already know. So if you want to make new things, you have to walk alone.

How do you get people to desire what they don't know?

You teach them about a new aesthetic.

Do you still produce your garments in Italy?

Seventy per cent of our production is based in Italy. And the only reason it's not 100 per cent is that we simply don't have the resources here: because the younger generation don't want to work with sewing machines any more, all the sub-contractors are closing down in Italy. My students say to me, 'I don't want to be a tailor.' Manufacturing just isn't a popular job choice here any more. I'm not optimistic that there will still be a manufacturing industry in Italy in 10 years' time. However, the 30 per cent of production that is done abroad in Romania, Tunisia

opposite: Duffle coat in stainless-steel mesh by Stone Island. This garment oxidates over time, becoming less bright, Autumn/Winter 1999–2000

Nobody thought it was going to be possible to make a 100 per cent stainless-steel jacket. I always try to do things my own way. In general people can only desire what they already know. So if you want to make new things, you have to walk alone.

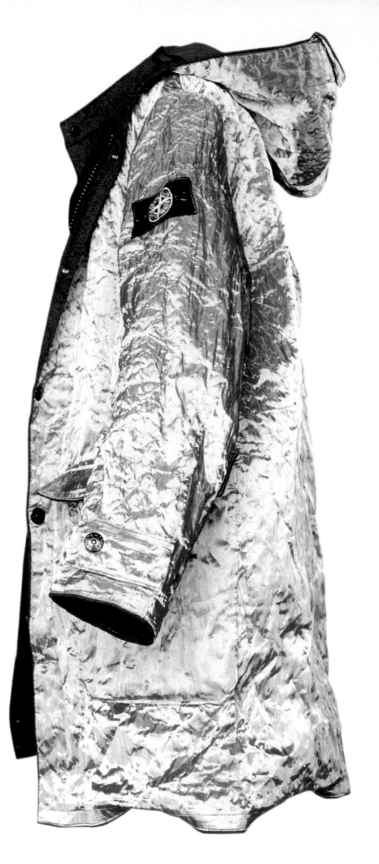

and Indonesia is not there because of low labour costs: on the contrary, the quality of stitching is too important to me. Once I've sourced a factory abroad, I teach them how to improve the quality of the garment construction. It's not about quantity for me: if it was, I'd be producing in China where they are only interested in numbers. To me it's about quality. There is always someone from Sportswear Company present on location before the production can start. I'm sure that some of the manufacturers have lost money working with me because the production numbers are lower, but my man in Indonesia says it's like a business card working with our brands. It opens other doors for them.

How do you go about marketing your brands?

We try to find a specific approach for each country we sell to. Seventy per cent of our turnover is export. We sell in the UK, Japan, Holland, Greece, Korea, China and so on. You have to learn about the different markets. Our main market is still Italy and in the UK we invest in advertising together with our distributors, Fourmarketing, but it's not a huge amount. Generally speaking, I'm not that confident when it comes to advertising because you can never see the return on your investment. I think there are more sophisticated ways of communicating what your brand is about. For example, that can be done on the garment itself by, say, hanging on small booklets or labels that explain the function of particular aspects of the garment and also particular treatments that have been applied. The people who buy my stuff are very sophisticated. We are not inexpensive, so they only understand the quality if they've been wearing it for a long time. The people who buy Stone Island or C.P. Company will always come back.

What makes one brand more successful than the next?

I have to admit something terrible: sometimes the fortune of a brand is determined by sheer luck. Do you know why we became so famous in the UK? Because Eric Cantona was wearing Stone Island one day when he went to the shops and everybody saw pictures of him. There was no strategy there. It was luck. Why does a brand become famous? Investing lots of money in marketing can certainly help. Do the brands that do that become successful? Yes. But can they sustain it for a long time on marketing alone? I don't know. I don't like that type of success. There were brands around in the 1980s and 1990s that became really popular all of a sudden, but they were gone just as quickly. You can fabricate lies for one season, but not forever. If you are not consistent the customer will leave you.

What advice would you give a budding designer?

The first thing I always say to my students is, 'Be humble and don't be too quick.' Young kids these days are very demanding and expect too much too quickly. Companies can't change as quickly as they can. Another thing I tell my students is: learn English. I think my business is the best in the world. Why? I work 24 hours a day. Whether I go and see a movie, or watch a football match, or sit in the pub, I'm doing research. The fashion business is so exciting. Thank god I'm in textiles and not in the steel industry.

What do you hate about the fashion industry?

I hate people who think they know the truth. Not knowing the truth is much better.

opposite, right and below, left: From the Stone Island Shadow Project, Autumn/Winter 2008–2009; opposite, left and below, right: Stone Island ad campaign, 2008

Folk

Cathal McAteer

Founder and creative director, Folk and Shofolk

Cathal McAteer began his fashion career aged 15, working as a Saturday boy in Glasgow's renowned menswear boutique Ichi Ni San. In 1997 he started a fashion agency, Macandi, representing labels such as YMC, Zakee Shariff, Puma Black Station, Blue Blood and Humanoid. The agency provided him with the necessary budget to launch his own menswear label, Folk, in 2001 and the shoe label, Shofolk in 2005. Folk and Shofolk are currently sold in 105 shops worldwide. The first Folk shop opened in Lamb's Conduit Street, London.

When did you first get into fashion?

I was frolicking with a lovely lass from the fairground who was wearing interesting gear. I asked her where she got it and she told me about a shop in Glasgow called Ichi Ni San. When I walked into the shop they asked me to model for them, so I did. After that, they took me on as a Saturday boy. I was 15 at the time, but I had been interested in fashion – or let's say small-town threads, since I was from the purpose-built new town Cumbernauld outside Glasgow – even before then. I had a job as a milkboy from the age of 11 and I used to spend the £12 I made each week on the newest Nike training shoe or burgundy stay-press trousers – whatever was on trend. The money didn't quite stretch to big labels. I didn't exactly know what they were then, and I wouldn't have been able to afford it, so I bought what I could find in the local shopping centre.

How long did you work in Ichi Ni San?

I worked there between the ages of 15 and 21. I started out as a Saturday boy, then went full time and at one point I was made the manager and I also started buying for the shop. Buying trips were very exciting. Back then we bought labels like Helmut Lang, Costume National, Thierry Mugler, John Richmond, Vivienne Westwood, Dries Van Noten, Joe Casely-Hayford, Fujiwara. Leaving my new town and moving to the city, the shop became my base and home. The owners, Michael, Linda and Stephen, had this wonderful family vibe – slightly dysfunctional, but hella fun.

How did working in the shop influence your aesthetic judgement and style?

During my seven years there, I learnt all about ready-to-wear fashion and the wow factor of amazing labels being sold at high prices. It was just a different league from what was

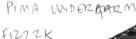

PIMA UNDERARM
FIZZZK

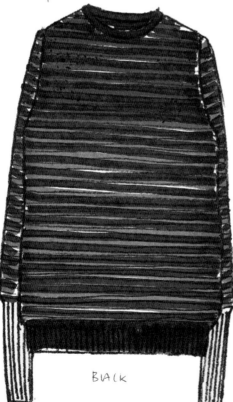

BLACK

LIPSTICK ORANGE

on sale in my home town. It gave me a taste of what fashion could be like: the fabric, the cut, the quality of the garments and all the twists and virtues of the designers. At first, of course, the clothes wore me because I was romanced by the whole thing. I was putting on different styles until I found my own. I learnt how to dress myself and how to build a wardrobe for someone else. I felt very confident building and advising on collections, i.e., what needed to be done to improve and give life to a collection, what would sell and what wouldn't.

I enjoyed advising people what to buy. They walk out happy and they come again. Buying for the shop was great because you could buy things for specific people because it was a small boutique. There were quite a few wealthy guys who came in regularly like chefs, band members, the guy who served up coke for the city. We knew exactly who could pull off what and we'd buy with those customers in mind.

How would you describe your own style?

My nickname in the shop of such finery was trampy... That was 18 years ago. Things have changed slightly, but not that much.

When and why did you start the fashion agency Macandi?

I was looking for an avenue to go on my own. What, I wasn't sure. But in 1997 a friend Jimmy called asking whether I'd represent his brand YMC. That was that. The agency started and then I was fortunate enough to sign a new dawn of sportswear: Puma's collaborative arm called Black Station who worked in conjunction with designers such as Mihara, Neil Barrett, Alexander McQueen and so on to create high-end sportswear.

below: Sketches of Folk knitwear for Autumn/Winter 2008–2009

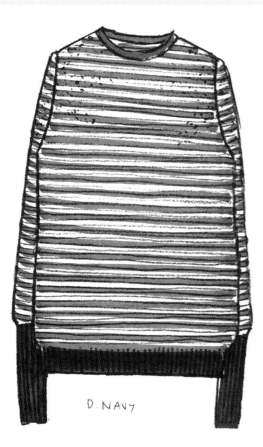

D. NAVY

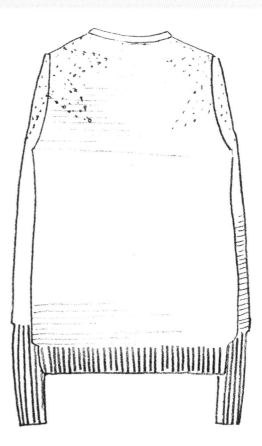

What made you launch your own label, Folk, in 2001?

I'd been travelling in Japan with Zakee Shariff, working on her collection and our partners in Japan said that I should do a menswear collection. So I did. I made four shirts. And if I remember correctly, they were really shit.

Why were they shit?

They were so flawed, it was ridiculous. I find it hard to look at the collection I did last season and enjoy it, let alone something I did so long ago. I always see faults in everything that we've done. I can big the collection up for a two-week period, then I just want to make improvements everywhere.

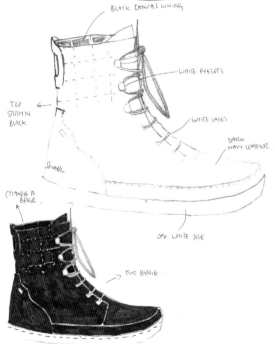

BLACK CANVAS LINING

TOP STITCH IN BLACK

WHITE EYELETS

WHITE LACES

DARK NAVY LEATHER

Shank

CHANGE TO BEIGE

OFF WHITE SOLE

FUR BEIGE

You started your label having had no formal training – how did not going to school help/ hinder your cause?

The owners of the store Ichi Ni San, Michael, Linda and Stephen, served as my teachers. I am sure my sporadic attendance at college assisted in some way but the three aforementioned characters gave me so much. But a hindrance is now apparent due to my lack of formal training, but it's mainly on the business side, not in fashion-related stuff.

Did having an agency first help you learn about the industry and what it takes to launch a label?

I already had a grasp of this from managing and buying for Ichi Ni San. Truth be told, having an agency served a purpose at the time. The money we made with the agency went towards funding Folk. The agency helps labels and stores make money, and they help us make money. Having an agency was valuable in the sense that when we were selling say Mihara and Neil Barrett shoes, we sold them to 130 different shops in the UK. It allowed me to have meetings with those buyers, they got to know me and make money from what I was offering. When they came to the showroom they would also catch a glimpse of this little project that was growing into something. I was not yet offering it to them at the time because I knew it was too early. It wasn't the finished article. It was a side project at the time. Slowly Folk grew into something. Only in the last few years have we been able to offer it the full care and love that it deserves. And now it enjoys the success that we'd intended for it.

What is your vision for the label?

There was always one clear concept for me: making simple, non-restrictive clothes as affordable as we can. The clothes need to have a personality in their total look, and this could be a painfully subtle detail on a shirt or it could be a shocking-pink alpaca cardigan. We also always look to add or take away,

left: Shofolk for men, designed for Autumn/Winter 2008–2009; opposite: Famed for its non-restrictive shirts and knitwear with subtle detail changes, Folk is now sold in over 100 shops worldwide, Autumn/Winter 2008–2009

whether it be sewing vintage buttons on to cardigans, or changing thread colours to give a garment a flash of colour. Following the lines of the body is always attractive, like a stroke with a paint brush, or changing the fabric, or adding a bit of colour. Or we might take a garment, wash it and put old rusted rivets on it: trying to give it age before a guy has actually put it on. We like to give garments a small personality. How we try to make our garments come to life is part of our philosophy.

Where is Folk sold today?

It's sold in a hundred or so shops all over the world, including in America, Canada, Italy, Japan, UK, Scandinavia, Germany.

Do you think you need a philosophy to create interesting clothes?

No. You can and I think I do, but I haven't studied my reasons in great depth as I'm not looking to define myself that way. I like living a lot and want to make clothes for people to live in.

Folk focuses on creating shirts, jackets and cardigans. How do your designs differ from other contemporary labels?

We've got a reputation for making great shirts and knitwear, but when you talk about the pieces people come back for again and again, it's the hand-knitted cardigans made in say Peru, Bolivia or Scotland. We always add a special detail. Our next collection of cardigans will include these beautiful organic leather wallets that you can take out and use elsewhere. The colours and yarn we use add personality. We tend to sell to blokes who are anti high fashion. They don't want to look like a peacock. So we try to encourage them to wear colour, and the best place to drop some in is in knitwear because it's a softer garment and guys are more receptive to that.

You often involve friends in your projects. Is that part of Folk's philosophy?

When you do something like launching your own label a lot of people want to get involved because it's exciting. The concept of using friends in the photo

shoots was born when the photographer Neil Stewart and I first met and had a pint together. We needed to create images that represented the brand and its philosophy. In the beginning, a lot of wearers of the brand happened to be friends. Neil suggested getting a bunch of mates together and going on a road trip. Every season we'd go on a different trip with different friends and always had a lot of fun. We went to Sicily, Mammoth Mountain, Cape Cod, Cornwall, etc. The atmosphere was always fun and adventurous. We try to bring that personality to Folk because that's what the wearers of the label will be doing. But friends have been involved in various projects. For example, Sam Miller has been involved from very early on in the design of the great showrooms we've had and the original last for our first shoe. We tried to come at it from a different perspective. My friend and artist Sidsel Top designed the artwork for the shoe collections as well as the shoeboxes for Shofolk. The sculptor Paul Van Stone gave us three beautiful marble heads on loan for the shop, James Holliday is a constant collaborator because he's a highly talented designer and also because he's part of my family.

Who is your favourite customer?

It's nice when someone comes into the shop who has never bought Folk before and walks out a convert. It's also great seeing strangers wear Folk on the street. But at the moment it has to be my mate Des Hamilton, who is a casting director. Thank you for your support. Every week he buys and buys.

What has having a shop added to the brand?

It allowed us to re-enact the picture we painted in those early photo shoots within the store's personality. We used wood we bought off a trapper in Epping Forest. We've got Paul Van Stone's beautiful sculptures in the shop. We've got bits we picked up at Kempton Market. We used rope I had in a bag somewhere – because we had budget constraints, we had to get down and dirty and be innovative. Friends

below: From the Folk lookbook, Spring/Summer 2009. Illustration by Liza Corsillo

We tend to sell to blokes who are anti high fashion. They don't want to look like a peacock. So we try to encourage them to wear colour, and the best place to drop some in is in knitwear because it's a softer garment and guys are more receptive to that.

helped out creating the store and you can see and feel that when you walk in. There's a really friendly vibe without being cheesy. Having the shop has, of course, also provided us with cash flow.

Where do you get inspiration for a new collection?
Usually the inspiration comes from within myself and Elbe Lealman, a Folk and Shofolk designer. We discuss inspiration, throw ideas around. We tend not to have themes, we get great ideas from looking at fabrics, colours and pictures and whatever is happening around us. It could be anything: for Spring/Summer 2009 we'd like to thank David Hockney, but generally the ideas are endless. So it's almost a case of restraining them by imposing restrictions on, say, the price of fabrics, the time frame, the number of pieces we can design because it's all the business can cope with. We're a self-financed company so we have to be quite strict. In some ways this saying sums up the philosophy: 'When we long for life without woes,

above: Cathal McAteer says, 'I like living a lot and want to make clothes for people to live in.' This image was shot in Cape Cod by Neil Stewart using friends of Folk, Autumn/Winter 2006

remember that oaks grow strong in contrary winds and diamonds are made under pressure.'

What makes a good collection?
It's a living and breathing entity that you edit as you go along. Adding things, removing things, but always improving. There's a mastery to making a good collection by way of balance, 'wow' factor, quantity, more is not better, less is not more. Timing is essential. Certain ideas are not right for the moment even if they are gems because it might be too early or too late. Those get kept in the little black book for another time. Our own store gives me an added tool as I can re-merchandise the current collection, which assists in the building process of any new collection.

Do you think it's important to go to fashion school to be a designer?

Yes. But if you want to do it on your own, do a small business course, learn how money works and cash flows work. It's vital.

How did your shoe label Shofolk come about?

UEFA Cup Final, May 2003. I met a bloke, Scott McHugh, in Seville. What an experience. We shared tears of pain and joy watching Celtic. Not long after that Scott came to London and asked whether I had an idea that needed backing. The artist Sam Miller and I had come up with this idea that we wanted to create shoes that were so so comfortable, where you could replace the sole so they would never wear out. I told Scott about the shoe company idea and he said, 'How much do you need?' and I created a bit of a cowboy business plan and that was it.

Are Folk and Shofolk linked style wise?

They are as one. They're part of the same brand. The same team design it, style it, price it and push it forward. Shofolk is basically 'Shoes by Folk'.

How does an independent label manage to stay alive in this age of advertising and luxury brands?

It's difficult. We've survived through real determination. But I was also lucky enough to meet a couple of people who really believed in the brand such as Fraser Shand, our financial director, and our sales director, Maggie McAteer, who are both partners in the company. Fraser is essentially the brains behind the business now as he manages the company and Maggie is our front of house. I would advise anyone who wants to set up their own label to make sure they have a lot of financial backing. As a creative, you need to be able to look forward and think about the future of the label. I need to be left in my world to make sure that what we put out there is right. Fraser questions that sometimes. Ideas are cheap...and having a strong director assists in seeing which ideas have maximum effect and which ones should be canned because they are shit. It might sound boring but you need that kind of advice. Maybe even more importantly, you need to

be able to take that kind of advice. It's taken me a while to understand that.

You don't pay for any advertising – how does that affect your editorial coverage?

We invite the press to come and see our collections, but generally we have more luck with newspapers because they're genuine in the sense that you can't buy them. Lee Holmes from the *Independent*, for example, was in today. He featured Folk in a recent weekend supplement. We had two pieces in the 'top 50 things to buy this summer'. He featured clothes from Gucci to YMC. It was a true reflection of the market place. It's more difficult with the big glossy magazines because a lot of them have an unspoken rule about using advertisers in their editorial. It's quite sad. But those big fashion houses know exactly what they're doing. They have to ensure the shareholders get their dividends, so they buy ad space in magazines and with that comes great editorial coverage.

Where is fashion heading?

In the UK I think we're heading towards the shopping mall, unfortunately. The boutique that I was brought up in, Ichi Ni San, for example, doesn't exist any more. In the past, people came to small shops because they trusted the owner's choice. Now people are heading to Bluewater, Lakeside and Westfield shopping malls. I think fashion is becoming more and more label-oriented because of celebrity endorsements and advertising. It will narrow people's perception of what they desire, and it will narrow people's choice too. More and more celebrities such as Victoria Beckham and Kanye West are putting out their own labels. And, strangely, people want their clothes. They want to buy into the dream. I wonder how many graduates will be able to start their own label straight out of fashion school now, and make it a success. Very few, I imagine.

What makes one designer stand out more than the next?

Dries Van Noten being a genius. Alexander McQueen being a genius. There are more out there. What seems to make them stand out is that they are single-minded and they don't compromise. They're doing

their shit and they would be doing it if they were poor too. I hope that's true because it keeps the dream alive. But, standing out as a designer can be as simple as some crap star signing a deal to endorse a brand. Money. Advertising. Paying people to wear your gear. Paying for editorial. All the other stuff that goes with any sizeable business. Money talks.

Do you need to be innovative?
Absolutely. It's a pre-requisite, in the sense that people have to be attracted to your work. But that side of the job is a piece of piss, it's about managing the innovations. You need to know how to manage your business, build a collection, be patient, not spend too much money, all the boring stuff that keeps you in business and keeps you alive.

What advice would you give a budding designer?
It seems to me that the route to success these days is to work for a big brand, make a name for yourself and then start your own label. Many people get used to the money and safety of working for a label and never

above: Shot by Neil Stewart in Sicily for the Autumn/ Winter 2006–2007 lookbook. Vibrant colours on knitwear and some detailing are an essential part of Folk's voice

leave. Otherwise you could always marry someone famous or rich, that could help. But essentially it depends what you need in your life. If you want to buy a new car or a new sofa from Skandium, then work for the big guys. If you want to go on a journey that contains many doubts and questions, where you may not be able to pay yourself a salary at times, do your own thing. You have to constantly encourage yourself to keep going. You might get one bit of good news and five bits of bad news in a day, but you learn to thrive on that too. I had to do it on my own. It's my ball and chain, but also my sanity. But I have to say, don't do it *all* on your own because you've got to be ****ing mad unless you've got a stack of cash either to burn or buy friends and influence with. If you truly believe you're a genius, then go for it because people will notice you if you're that good.

Boundless

Zhang Da
Founder, owner and creative director

A favourite of Vogue China, *Zhang Da grew up in the north-west of China. In 1997 he won an award, which allowed him to spend a year as an intern for the Rome-based couture house, Sarli. He later spent some time in Antwerp, where he was influenced by the Belgian conceptual designers. His label, Boundless, is sold in selected boutiques such as Younik in China. Zhang Da believes that for Chinese fashion to progress it cannot look solely at the trends emerging on the American and European catwalks, it must also look at daily life in China.*

opposite: One hundred per cent wool dress made for the Autumn/Winter 2002–2003 collection

You studied traditional Chinese painting, when did you first get interested in fashion?
I studied Chinese painting at high school and had planned to continue at university. In my first year at university, in the library, I discovered foreign fashion books and magazines for the first time, but at that time I was still interested in painting. It wasn't until my second year, when I got my hands on some books about Japanese fashion, that I changed my view on fashion and discovered it as a method to express attitude. From that moment on I became interested in fashion design.

Do you have any formal training?
I studied fashion for four years at the Textile and Garment Institute in Changzhou.

To what degree is the flat construction of your designs influenced by your painting background?
Traditional Chinese painting is a means for Chinese artists to express their viewpoint and the relationship they have with life and the world. It is this different viewpoint that made traditional Chinese painting so different from the works of art of other countries. The way Chinese people view the world is reflected in the way they view the body, which in turn can be seen in the way they dress. My designs are directly influenced by these ideas. 'Flatness' or two-dimensionality is a strong visual characteristic in Chinese painting and clothing.

Do you think the Chinese use clothes/fashion differently from Western countries?
These days the Chinese dress in Western clothes. The cultural divide in terms of aesthetics, climate and society is much smaller. All the people who now live in countries that do not form part of the world's fashion capitals can easily keep up with trends, as it's much easier to collect information. The essential difference is traditional Chinese culture, which still influences contemporary fashion to a degree, but nowhere near as much as before. The attitude and understanding of 'the body' in traditional Chinese culture is extremely different from that in Western culture, which is part of the reason there was a big gap between traditional clothes in the East and West.

How does the Chinese approach to fashion influence your design process?
I guess I have a Chinese thought process, which influences me when I am coming up with the design concept, but it's not so apparent when it comes to turning the concept into real clothes.

What would you like people to think and feel when they wear your clothes?
I hope my designs will make people understand the potential and possibilities clothes provide and the freedom that brings. I want to help people become a part of that freedom.

Which designers have influenced and inspired the way you work?
Martin Margiela, Bless, Wendy & Jim, Rei Kawakubo and the design agency Droog.

How do you go about designing a collection? What is the process involved?
Most of my former designs were abstract. I was either re-designing or re-interpreting items that were already out there or abandoning existing models and trying to create new possibilities for them.

I used to think of the concept first, then decide what material/fabric would work best and finally I would start working on the tailoring. Now I usually start by collecting materials first. Then I find out

opposite: In 2004 Zhang Da designed an entire collection of T-shirts and dresses based around the concept of 'flatness' or two dimensionality found in traditional Chinese painting

I hope my designs will make people understand the potential and possibilities clothes provide and the freedom that brings. I want to help people become a part of that freedom.

what the relationship is between them and I go onto designing and tailoring. I'm thereby hoping to find a new methodology of coming up with a design concept and/or collection.

Where do your clothes retail and at what price? Do you also sell outside China?

Boundless retails in Beijing and Shanghai. I am hoping to sell out of more shops in China. I'd like to break into the overseas market in the near future. The price ranges from 500RMB to 4000RMB ($75–$500). Selling outside China is my goal.

What is your vision for your label?

I'd like to remain independently owned, stay curious. And continue to exist.

To what extent do you need a philosophy to create inspiring clothes?

Great design can help express a person's understanding of life and their environment. Some good ideas or philosophies are helpful for us to understand the world. However, it seems there is no existing philosophy, which could help us to understand today's China.

Fake products are by no means a secret in China. My collection was based around this phenomenon, but it wasn't just about fake brands. It was also about fake certificates and even the fictitious world of the website. This collection will be continued and I'm going to expand the 'fictitious' element.

Where do you get your inspiration?

From abstract ideas but also from the cities I lived in at the time of each design, and the people and things I encountered in daily life.

What was your thinking behind the 0-shirt collection you did in 2004?

This format is not special or fresh. I had three ideas when I designed that collection. First of all, I wanted to create the maximum amount of style with the simplest of elements. I wanted to reach the extreme limit of design's possibility and ended up creating eight styles. Secondly, I wanted to make a T-shirt, which doesn't look like one at all in order to break through the common notion of a T-shirt. And thirdly, I wanted to make flat clothes, like traditional Chinese clothes. My aim was that I wanted to create something that looked totally different when worn compared to what it looked like on display. This is also a kind of Chinese way of thinking that what you see may not be what you get. Like Tai Chi, which looks slow and gentle, but could take life away.

How did you come up with the 'Bogus accessories' collection: the fake Omega wristbands and Gucci wallets in 2006?

Fake products are by no means a secret in China. My collection was based around this phenomenon, but it wasn't just about fake brands. It was also about fake certificates and even the fictitious world of the website. This collection will be continued and I'm going to expand the 'fictitious' element.

How do you go about getting press coverage in China and worldwide?

I haven't made any efforts to do so but the Chinese press have supported me quite a lot.

How do you finance your label?

I break even and work as a consultant designer for other fashion brands to make more money

opposite: In 2006 Zhang Da created a collection of accessories based around the concept of counterfeit designs. The collection included a fake Gucci wallet made from cotton (centre, left), a fake Omega wristband (bottom) and finger covers which had lavish jewels printed on them (top left)

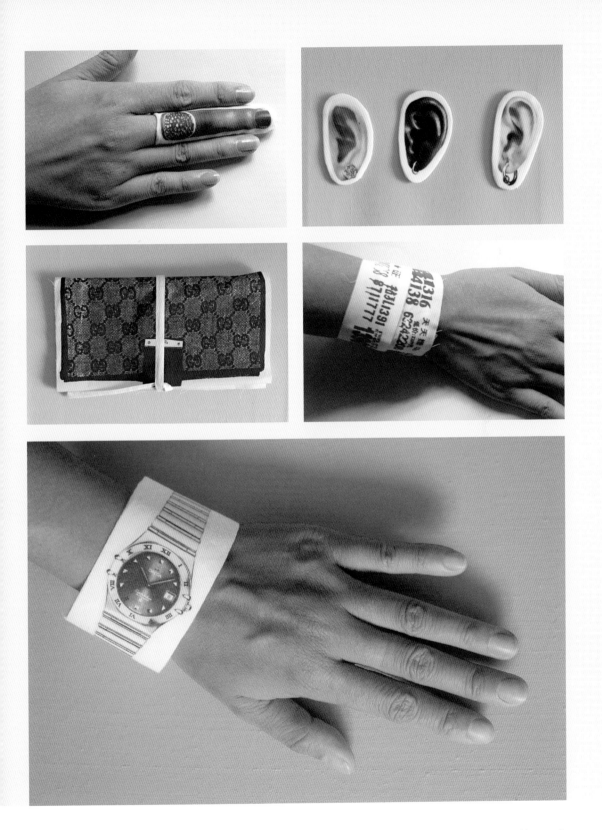

8 Tees

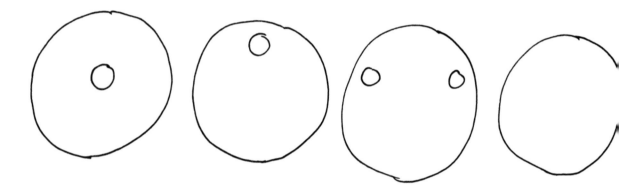

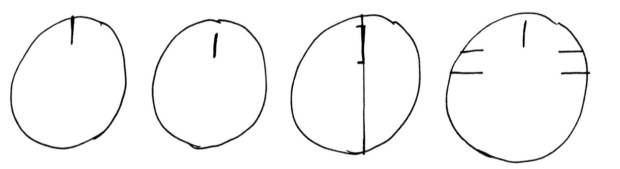

to support my brand. Hopefully the situation will improve.

How many collections do you design per year?
Two seasons a year.

What do you think should be done to improve the visibility of Chinese designers in the West?
First of all, I think people are generally happy to welcome a good product. We just need to try our best to make optimum products. And secondly, we have to focus on putting these products into places where more and more people can actually reach them.

Your clothes are quite conceptual, to what degree is fashion like art to you?
I don't believe fashion can ever be art, or that design is an art form. Only rarely is there a common ground: it is when a designer hopes to use fashion design as a way to express his or her personal idea about the world, and that design thus becomes the medium for its creator's means of expression. That is when art and design seem to share some common ground so that the design becomes a way of seeing truth.

What do you love about fashion?
Fashion is a way for both the designer and the dresser to express themselves.

What do you hate about fashion?
Pretension and excess.

What makes one brand/designer more successful than another?
It, he or she is someone who is able to identify a need or is a great medium.

What advice would you give to a budding designer?
I haven't been managing my own brand for a long time, so I'm not sure I'm qualified to comment on that. What I can say is to make sure you spend your energy and time on what you feel is most worthy. If it happens to be something the customer is also interested in then even better.

preceding pages: In an attempt to reach the extreme limits of the possibilities in design and to break through the common notion of a T-shirt, Zhang Da created eight different styles of garment from one original shape; left: Showing front, back and side views of a dress created for the 'Flat' collection in 2004. The collection was based around the concept of two dimensionality also found in traditional Chinese painting

Rodarte

Kate and Laura Mulleavy

left: Kate and Laura Mulleavy; opposite: From the Autumn/ Winter 2008–2009 catwalk show held in New York

In February 2005 Kate and Laura Mulleavy travelled from Pasadena to New York with nothing more than a box containing half a dozen dresses and a few coats they had created under the label Rodarte. By day, they were visiting the most important fashion buyers and editors in the city, by night they were crashing on their friend's sofa. A week after their arrival, they made the cover of WWD (Women's Wear Daily) *and shortly thereafter American* Vogue's *Anna Wintour came to view their collection in Los Angeles. Since then, Rodarte has appeared in numerous fashion magazines including American* Vogue, i-D *and* W *magazine. The sisters also won the coveted CFDA Swarovski Award for Womenswear in 2008, following two nominations in 2006 and 2007. Their label, known for its intricate couture-like creations, is currently sold in the most up-scale shops in the world, including Barneys New York and Colette in Paris.*

You both did undergraduate degrees that had nothing to do with fashion. Kate, you studied History of Art and Laura, you studied Literature at Berkeley in California. How did you go from there to designing your first collection?

Laura: Kate started sketching really early on when she was young, but we've both always sketched and designed things. We wanted to learn about so many subject matters. My father had done post-doctorate work in botany at Berkeley. It was sort of a family tradition to go there. Laura and I wanted to go to college to study so many different things, everything from 19th-century French photography to physics. Our parents really wanted us to start with a general education. In the end, our education played an important role in the way we design. We had leading scholars teaching us. My favourite course was on James Joyce where I was taught by one of the top James Joyce scholars in the world with seven other students. Art History with Anne Wagner and T. J. Clark was also brilliant. Our time there was amazing. We were exposed to so many things. I think you can benefit from doing a non-fashion degree as you have a much larger frame of reference in terms of visuals, history, culture, etc. It was during our time at school, however, that we realized we wanted to go into designing, but we just figured we'd graduate first and take it from there. We never felt like we had to go to design school.

What propelled you to design your own collection?

In some ways we were exposed to fashion from a very young age through our mother who is an artist and our grandmother who was an opera singer. I also loved the pictures of my parents when they were younger and living in northern California. They had an interesting style. Lots of grey sweatshirts and combat boots. Sort of Yoko Ono. And my grandmother also had amazing costumes. We also used to sit and watch old films with my parents: Cary Grant, Catherine Deneuve and so on. So very early on we built a strong relationship with fashion through film and music. When we graduated we decided to go home and immerse ourselves into researching what we were going to do. We read books on the subject matter, saved up money, watched loads of horror films. Our parents probably thought we were weird. We were sort of making it up as we went along. We didn't really know what we were doing. It was a natural process that went from not knowing anything about the industry to attacking each new question as it came along. We didn't really grasp how you came up with an idea and then made it ready for production. There was no industry guide to understanding how that side of the business works. And the organizational side seemed completely foreign to us.

Did you enjoy putting an outfit together when you were at college?

In college I spent half my time thinking about what clothes I was going to wear. It was all about dressing up. But as soon as I started designing, the creative thought went into something else. I think female designers are given a hard time because people immediately think you are designing for yourself. But that concept is completely foreign to me. What's more, that way of thinking would never be applied to a male designer. For us it's not about creating something for ourselves, but about creating something beautiful and interesting. It's about exploring certain questions. I now like to dress simply. I don't wear dresses and never really have, but it's my favourite thing to create. We can design very freely. It's personal in one sense because it comes through your story and frame of reference, but at the same time it's not about you. It's the best of both worlds.

What was your vision for the label?

We didn't really have a vision as such. We just sat down and tried to create ten pieces of clothing. As we had no formal training, we didn't understand the notion of putting together a 'concept'. Our first collection was inspired by things we really loved like Edward Weston's second wife Charis Wilson,

opposite and left: Inspired by bones, skeletons and an Olafur Eliasson colour palette, Spring/Summer 2009

northern California, washed landscapes... These were the things that lived in our minds, that we wanted to use as a reference point.

Legend has it that you arrived in New York with a suitcase full of dresses and went to see all the up-scale buyers and fashion editors within the space of a week – how did you possibly manage to get through to them?

We didn't have that thing where we'd interned for someone before. Our world was totally removed. We came from a different state, had never been to New York before and arrived with a box of clothes containing ten pieces. We stayed at a friend's house, who was at graduate school for art conservation. She had a cat and a dog and she was working on a Byzantine icon while Kate and I slept on her couch. We managed to get a few appointments with some amazing stores like Barneys where we saw Julie Gilhart, Nieman Marcus etc., but the main thing that happened was that Kate managed to speak to some-one at *WWD* (*Women's Wear Daily*). We went in to see them and we talked about our clothes and they ended up taking a photograph. Bridget Foley was even there. I knew they might do a small story on us, but three days later and a couple of days before Fashion Week started, we ended up on the cover of *WWD*.

I think calling people is a really good tool and also following up what you've done. It's really the only way to communicate because it's so easy not to get emails and post. Kate had made these paper dolls wearing our dresses and she'd made armoires out of paper as well, which we'd sent to the editors. But I don't think anyone actually ever got them. I think when you're posting things to a big magazine, you never know if it ever gets to the right person.

What is your approach to designing collections now?

I think our approach changes every season because we learn so much in-between. I don't believe in following rules for anything. We think about what

left and opposite: Rodarte's version of the future inspired by movies such as *Donnie Darko* and *Star Wars*, Spring/Summer 2009

we're excited by and what we've learnt and we try to combine it. We don't work with trend forecasters. I think if you have a voice, you have to be strong or loud enough to make your own trend.

Your Spring/Summer 2009 collection was inspired by bones, skeletons and an Olafur Eliasson colour palate. How did it come about?

The collection was our version of the future. We love sci-fi and we were inspired by *The Man Who Fell to Earth*, THX, *Donnie Darko* and *Star Wars*. We wanted to relate sci-fi to something much more human specific. We were looking at artists such as Robert Smithson, Dan Flavin and Olafur Eliasson. We wanted to understand the relationship between outer space and earth. What would be left behind if we were to look into the future? Skeletal forms, metal bones holding broken ribs together... We had Eliasson's watercolour sculpture in mind and thought about how those colours are also in the Aurora Borealis star formation, an earth-bound and extra-terrestrial combination. At once foreign and strange, but human and skeletal.

The clothes were very intricate and layered using different materials, knits, leathers, chains and Swarovski crystals – how do they actually get made?

The knits are all hand made and the pieces are made one at a time, so they all have hand-made elements. Each garment is treated individually.

What is the thinking behind using Swarovski crystals in your designs?

If you could see the details on the clothes you could immediately picture how we like to use them. We like to play with colour and texture. A garment might be missing something like sheen, a highlight or some extra depth. For the Autumn/Winter 2008 collection we used mohair to create texture. By embroidering the mohair with Swarovski crystals we made it come to life. We probably use crystals on at least half of our looks.

It seems like you have a more idiosyncratic point of view compared to other designers. Moreover

you are less involved with the lovey-dovey side of the industry and more interested in thinking. How do you see yourself in that fashion world?

I do notice a difference. I don't know if it's because we live in LA. Our world here is either very insular and about our work, or it's about being with our friends who are all in a different industry. They are either writers, or artists, or photographers, but doing something in a creative way. Our experience is very different from lots of other people's and it has given us a different point of view.

Where do you get your inspiration?

It usually happens as an aftermath of something we've seen or have been talking about. We're in a constant dialogue about each choice we make, whether it's colour or silhouette.

Four years after its inception Rodarte is sold in the most prestigious shops in the world including Colette in Paris, 10 Corso Como in Milan, Barneys in New York and Dover Street Market in London. A lot of small labels go bust because they don't have the cash flow to produce the sudden increase in orders. How do you go about financing production now that your orders have sky-rocketed?

For the Autumn/Winter 2008 collection we used mohair to create texture. By embroidering the mohair with Swarovski crystals we made it come to life.

We used our own savings to start our label. We've not had backing from anyone else to date. So far we've managed to produce the garments season to season. Because we create high-end luxury garments we've never been pushed to produce large quantities. We have the capacity to control it internally and not build on it too quickly. It gives us a chance to refine our craft.

Do you feel any pressure to produce more 'wearable' everyday pieces from a commercial point of view?

I don't think there's any pressure because, ultimately, people want to wear creative, interesting clothing. I think any pressure we've ever felt was from ourselves. Every season we try to do more in terms of diversifying the collection, but that is more a result of wanting to broaden our vocabulary as designers. As a designer building your own label, it is crucial to develop a unique voice that can cross over into everything that you do. You have to have a strong opinion and you know what is right for you.

What do your clothes retail at?

It depends on the garment, but it can be anywhere from $1,500 to $25,000 for some of our gowns. There's a wide range.

Did you always know you were going to create luxury clothing?

I think we knew that the only fashion we were ever in love with was high fashion. But at the same time, the process of creating something in the way that we do always develops from an idea and the ideas are always pretty complicated. So then we realized we could only create what we wanted to make in a certain way. So it sort of works hand in hand.

below: Rodarte designs always include handmade elements and are often embroidered using Swarovski crystals, Spring/Summer 2009

You're self taught in both aspects of the industry, i.e., the creative side and the business side – do you have anyone or anything you go to for guidance?

I think that role is really within ourselves because there are two of us. We're always bouncing ideas off each other and it's the kind of relationship where you co-exist. The only person that is in my life that's like that is Kate and I think she'd say the same of me.

Do you ever argue?

Only sisterly bickering every once in a while. But no.

Have you ever considered moving to New York and out of your parents' house?

Laura and I have always been attached to California and close to our family. Living in LA allows us to create in a very personal space. Times are such now that we can go for the shows and be in a different location for the rest of the time. In the end, if we needed to move we would, but for now everything works well for us in LA.

Celebrities such as Cate Blanchett, Tilda Swinton, Natalie Portman, Kirsten Dunst, Keira Knightley, Chloe Sevigny and Kim Gordon, etc., have all worn Rodarte to red carpet events. How do you feel about celebrity dressing?

It's complicated. Because we were from LA people immediately said, 'you should be dressing people', and we thought that we didn't really want to have our clothes on everyone. And we decided early on that there were probably 10 people who we wanted to work with. The fact that we worked with Cate Blanchett was amazing. The others have come either through personal relationships, such as with Nathalie Portman or with Dita Von Teese. I think for whoever is going to wear our clothes there has to be a right match. The personality has to be there. Our dresses are complicated. We'd always hoped we'd be dressing interesting women – that was our goal. You have to be careful with the understanding of your brand. I view our clothes as special and I would want the people wearing them to feel that they are special.

Rodarte, Doo.Ri and Thakoon all worked on a collaboration with Gap after your nominations for the CFDA award. What was it like working with a big corporation?

That came about after winning runner up for the CFDA/Vogue Fashion Fund in 2006. It was really exciting for Kate and me because we'd never approached design in that way. It was an opportunity to understand design from a different perspective and realize that we could do something in that manner. In other words, designing with a team that can make things happen for you. We would basically provide a sketch and then work in their methods of working, so it was breaking down the creative process into different segments. We found that we could assimilate. Having our portraits taken with Inez Van Lamsweerde & Vinoodh Matadin was also really exciting.

How do you go about marketing your label, besides having a PR agency?

Ad campaigns aren't really feasible for us right now. I think marketing really comes from doing your collection and people coming to see your show. It sort of stems from there. We use the press office to maintain the momentum following the shows in order to get coverage in magazines and so on, but also to think about what special projects we might want to be involved in.

So magazines don't expect you to buy ad space in return for editorial?

I think if you're doing something creative enough, hopefully, there will be a space for you. Magazines and media in general are very supportive of younger labels.

What advice would you give a budding designer?

Above all else, follow your creative instincts and never give up believing in your vision no matter what the obstacle.

right: Rodarte garments cost between $1,500 and $25,000 for some gowns. This dress was created for Spring/Summer 2009

PART II
CREATION, STYLING, MODELLING
IMAGE, PRESS, SALES

Alexandre de Betak

Founder of the fashion show production company Bureau Betak

Alexandre de Betak began his career in fashion by doing PR for the Spanish designer Sybilla in the early 1990s. He then went on to create Bureau Betak, a production company specializing in fashion shows, with offices in Paris and New York. Today, De Betak is one of the most celebrated fashion show producers in the world, creating shows for the likes of John Galliano, Viktor & Rolf, Hussein Chalayan, Diane von Furstenberg and Victoria's Secret.

above: Self-portrait by Alexandre de Betak; opposite: Black Calvados lounge in Paris, designed by Alexandre de Betak

How did you first get involved with producing fashion shows?

I started doing PR for Sybilla, a Spanish designer, whom I met shooting pictures for *Primera Línea* magazine when I was 17, just over 20 years ago. It was the times of the Movida Madrileña, the rise of Madrid and Spain. The PR went pretty well and from there I moved on to direct her shows. When I stopped working for her I decided to focus solely on producing and art directing fashion shows. I started in Paris and then moved to New York 15 years ago.

Do you think that doing PR for Sybilla helped you understand the fashion industry and what is needed to sell clothes on the catwalk?

Doing PR wasn't my thing at all and I only did it briefly, but it taught me a lot about what journalists see and don't see, and how to ensure they are touched by a show. A big part of my job today is about creating the material such as media-savvy, memorable images that will help generate PR.

When you take on a project for clients how much is your vision and how much is theirs?

There is no formula. It's a creative collaboration. Each designer has a drastically different approach. My role is to help people understand the designer's inspiration and vision, as well as their creations. I try to enhance the collection we're showing at that time. It works creatively with my subjective point of view, I guess.

What is the working process when you are working with someone like John Galliano?

John Galliano might give me a few words to work with before he even shows me any of his collection. Eventually, he may tell me what his inspiration is at that moment. I'll then come back to him and suggest various ideas, but you can never second guess someone creative like John Galliano. He gives me his inspiration, I give him mine and then the process advances and I try subtly to enhance what I feel should be magnified and shown more. I also always have the desire to portray an emotion. I believe a show should be moving in some way.

What about when you are working with Viktor & Rolf or Hussein Chalayan?

When it comes to Viktor & Rolf their brief to me might be that they are doing a collection they want presented in a 'menacing' way; you might get the Black Show, where everything was black and the girls were painted black. Hussein Chalayan who I've been working with for 12 years, on the other hand, is a very cerebral designer. He might give me an elaborate brief, with a lot of words. His inspirations are often deeply intellectual, and might be historical or socio-political, etc. Using

above: Hussein Chalayan's Autumn 2008 catwalk show,
produced by Bureau Betak

that I develop the format of the show. It will
always be his and have some permanent parameters
such as live music, a choreography inspired by
the outlines of the garments, and the emotional
aspect of the show will be based on the political
message that inspired him at the time. But it all
becomes incredibly abstract. And with a brand
like Victoria's Secret it's a completely different
ball game again. As there is not a designer as such,

Hussein Chalayan's
inspirations are often
deeply intellectual, and
might be historical or
socio-political, etc. Using
that I develop the format
of the show... But it all
becomes incredibly
abstract.

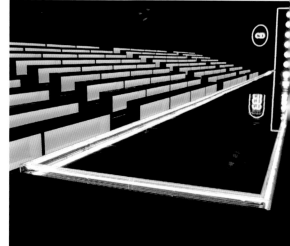

but rather a brand. The idea is to create an entire environment; to create that dream of the angel that doesn't really exist – the Victoria's Secret angel.

What is involved in the production of a show from start to finish?

Everything. The designer brings in the collection and the brief and we bring in the rest. The first thing that needs to be done is to look for a venue. Because there are so few around we often book the venue before we even know what we're actually going to do in it. Then comes the creative phase for me, which is probably the most stressful part. The designers give me a brief and I have very little time to come up with a global concept. The briefs are usually drastically different. John Galliano's may be one word or one colour, e.g., 'dangerous and sexy' or he may just say 'red'. It's very unpredictable. Hussein, on the other hand, may send a 10-page brief of very abstract and political ideas and Viktor & Rolf may just want a single emotion at the heart of the show and often have a precise vision about how to show it.

Once I've got the brief I come up with a global team and set up for the show, which includes the set, the lights, the music, the atmosphere, the seating, the choreography, the special effects and so on. I suggest it to the designers and then we refine it together. I write and I draw a brief and we do 3-D renderings, which include many different points of view, including the kind of TV shots we'll get. And then ultimately, at the very end of the process, comes the fashion side of the booking. This includes the models, the hair and make-up, and what we call collection co-ordination, which means we supply a team

opposite, top left: Donna Karan catwalk, Autumn 2004; opposite, top right: Dior catwalk, 2003; opposite, centre, left: Finale at a Sybilla show, 1991; opposite, centre, right: H&M show with Kylie Minogue in Shanghai, 2006; opposite, bottom, left: Computer-generated visual of Victoria's Secret show, 2003; opposite, bottom, right: Rodarte catwalk show, Autumn 2008

of people to help the designer's team. A week prior to the show they help them with the casting, the fitting, the scheduling, the polaroiding of the look, etc. At this stage there is also a technical team onsite overseeing the build up of the venue. On the days leading up to the show I go and spend a little bit of time on everybody's set up and in everybody's studio.

What is your job on the day of the show?

The day before the show, or sometimes on the day of the show itself, I do the cuing, which is the arranging between the music, the lights, the special effects, the choreography and the timing leading up to the show. I do it technically first and ultimately before the show I take all the models and brief them together once on stage. I might take individuals out if I feel they need a specific briefing. During the actual show I'm the one backstage at the edge of the stage, sending the models out and briefing them one last time before they go on. Timing in a fashion show is very important. In 10 to 20 minutes you have to help deliver the designer's message in a timely and moving manner.

Are there a maximum number of shows you can produce in a week?

Yes and no. We tend to do one every day in Paris and in New York during fashion weeks. You could always hire more people and do more, but ultimately I don't want to be a fashion show factory. The way I work is based on a very personal relationship with all the designers. So far I've always been very involved and attended every show I've produced.

How do you ensure that you maintain a brand's identity from season to season, while coming up with an original concept for a show?

The most important part of my job is to come up with a long-term vision, a visual identity for the shows and then to maintain it every season. It's very important to me that people recognize, for instance, 'I'm at a Galliano show', 'I'm at a Hussein Chalayan show', etc. Certain elements are set, but you need to make them evolve every season otherwise you don't have a reason to go anymore. But there isn't really a formula: I try to maintain parameters that I believe to be important as part of the designer's DNA, or the fashion show's DNA.

In the case of Chalayan, for example, we always try to work within the parameters we impose on ourselves: live music, the choreography, the tension. In a Galliano show, for example, the designer's exits are always very important. There is a lot of energy and strength in the main character of the models: Galliano is a very generous designer, who loves women and loves showing that. Whatever the theme, the story and the set up we still try to express that strength, generosity and power coming out of the girls, as well as the generosity and intrigue coming out of John at the end of the show. We always try to have the energy central in one of his fashion shows. All the designers we work with are determined, talented and successful, but when you're watching Galliano, you know you're watching Galliano. My role is to help maintain that.

Do you ever say to a designer, 'I like your idea but we're moving away from what's essentially a Galliano/Viktor & Rolf fashion show?'
A fashion show is not just one isolated piece of work, it's part of the body of work of a designer or house. Whether I say it to them or myself, sure, it happens that you feel that something is a great idea but it doesn't really work in the framework of the greater whole.

What is the main aim of a fashion show for you, besides showcasing new collections?
There are so many fashion shows these days and they are so visible because you can see them live online, or within seconds of being staged. So it's a bit different from how it used to be. The aim is to a) enhance the distinctive features of that one collection you're showing; b) enhance the collection but within the line of the identity of the designer; c) make it a moving and memorable experience –

it doesn't even matter whether one likes it or not; d) ensure you create the maximum number of images for press and TV. There is only so much the press can cover. To have been successful, you have to have given the designer of the house sufficient material for enough press, TV and web coverage.

How do you ensure you create a memorable show that will generate the most positive and plentiful press coverage and sales?
You can never really ensure anything, but in my part of the creative process there are a few tools I enjoy using more than others such as light. What I call cuing, i.e., creating very calculated moments where the music, the lights, the choreography and the expression of the model come together. You try to get them to a very specific place on stage, in a specific dress, at a very specific point in the music and, for example, a very specific rolling of the eye or expression or smile. I try to synchronize all the tools I have. For Hussein, if it's successful, you know that that moment will create emotion and an image the media will want to use.

What kind of budgets are usually involved?
It ranges from between €200,000 for the smallest show to half a million euros for the medium-sized ones to €1 million for the bigger ones. But then we spend up to €5 or €10 million for shows such as Victoria's Secret, but they only happen once a year so it's a different story. It doesn't mean that you can't do it for less. Smaller designers do it in-house for less.

Do you think a good fashion show needs to be a spectacle?
Not at all. Dior and John Galliano shows have been called spectacular because his creations are so spectacular that they can sustain a spectacular show. Each show I do is very different, but I certainly don't think it should ever be forced. I get called quite a lot by brands who would love to work with me; they say we loved what you did for Hussein and Viktor & Rolf, etc., and I say, 'But you're

different, it wouldn't make any sense. You do sportswear, clothes that are beautiful, but that shouldn't be within a spectacle.' There are a lot of brilliant designers who do the opposite of a spectacle and that's why their shows are so good. For example, I just went to see the Azzedine Alaia fashion show. He had 50 people in his house sitting at a table with a drink, and five to 10 models, and he does it the way he's always done it, in a non-spectacular way. But the clothes are so spectacular, not in the sense of size, but in the sense of artistry and quality. It's a brilliant moment and an amazing show. He doesn't show during fashion week, he shows when he wants. Or take someone like Nicolas Ghesquière, whom I highly respect, or Helmut Lang before that: they have always done shows that were

below: Design for Galliano menswear catwalk show, Spring 2007

The most important part of my job is to come up with a long-term vision; a visual identity for the shows and then to maintain it every season. It's very important to me that people recognize, for instance, 'I'm at a Galliano show.'

Often younger brands, such as Viktor & Rolf or Hussein Chalayan, don't advertise their fashion, so the show is very important. It's the one moment of communication in the entire season.

so not spectacular, but so incredibly beautiful and powerful and personal that you can really see their personalities in their collections.

What shows did you produce last season and what concepts did you come up with?

For example, Hussein Chalayan's fall 2008 collection in February 2008 was based on the origins of humanity, from the monkey age to the Stone Age, etc. He gave me descriptions of the evolution of his inspiration, i.e., his vision of the world. He was

below: Models pose for the Flowerbomb show Spring/ Summer 2005, which also launched Viktor & Rolf's Flowerbomb fragrance

influenced by the morphing of humans and I took it one step further towards the origins of lifeforms and set it in a big bang environment. We used a big splash of UV white and we had three girls and two guys beat-boxing live, creating voices for water, monkeys, etc.

Where do you get the inspiration for shows?

I constantly try to feed myself with what interests me. I spend nights losing myself on Google image when I'm jet lagged. Art movements also inspire me, but it could be anything…a dinner I just ate, it can come from anywhere. Once I decide on a subject I do a lot of research.

Do you think it's important to know much about fashion to create a memorable show?

I don't think you necessarily need to know the history of fashion to create a memorable show. I do believe, however, that you need to know enough about the life your audience leads and of the life they live to know what may or may not impress them. You need to know what they've seen before and what they haven't. I don't think you need academic knowledge to create a good fashion show, but cultural knowledge is extremely important. It will help your eye. You'll be able to discern what's spectacular, new, or original in anything you see. And that, in turn, will help you see and enhance things and show them better.

How much preparation goes into the production of a show?

There is no rule as such, but for the fashion houses that we work with on a regular basis we start as soon as the last show has finished. We discuss the date, venue, inspiration, etc., the minute the designer starts the collection, so it's at least three to six months. The minute I finish a fashion show and put down my clearcom headphones I'm already thinking 'God, what are we going to do next?' It's a challenging thought. I'm incredibly lucky in the sense that the function of directing and producing shows is very short lived. It's a 15-minute moment, and yet the adrenaline you get in that moment is enough to give you energy for the next one. And we never do the same thing twice.

You've often stated that you use light as a tool on the catwalk. How does it enhance the shows?

I've done all sorts of shows, from using neons to having just candles, to moving lights. But really it's more the installing and cuing of lights that creates something moving and memorable. It's about using light as an emotional tool: the way you cue and section it and the way you make it travel. It helps people see what you want to show and helps express what you want to express.

How important is a fashion show these days for future sales, press coverage, etc., compared to advertising?

It depends on the size of the brand. Often younger brands, such as Viktor & Rolf or Hussein Chalayan, don't advertise their fashion, so the show is very important. It's the one moment of communication in the entire season and you have six months of up-coming coverage based on that. For mega brands such as Dior a fashion show is not their main way of communication, however it's the most creative and intense. There is more range and freedom of expression within, say, an haute couture fashion show by John Galliano than a page of advertising. So in both cases it's quite important as it's the moment when they can express their personal vision. That's the reason why they still exist. Everybody complains that there are too many shows, but at the end of the day, when you have to show 30 to 80 looks to 500 to 1,000 people and to another 100 lenses and cameras, in the shortest possible time, it's still the best tool there is.

To what extent does the fact that you also design furniture, lights, the interiors of restaurants, etc., help your creativity on the catwalk?

It helps a lot. One thing feeds the other and it also allows me to experience a whole load of ideas, techniques and materials that in turn will be inspiration for the fashion shows that I do.

Do you think you need a philosophy to create a successful brand?

A brand and a designer are two different things. An incredibly talented designer doesn't need to define a philosophy. If you have an approach to a woman's body and come up with creations to dress her that are impressively new, original, personal or magnificent you don't need to have given it a name. When a new designer shows his creations and people go 'Wow' that wow doesn't have to be based on a word or definition if you are touched by what you've seen. For the creation of brand, however, I do certainly think you need a philosophy or a reason to exist as there are so many out there. There is a lot of everything today already. Anything new today, whether it's furniture, a fragrance, etc., needs a reason for being, but that doesn't necessarily mean having a philosophy, it could just mean having a personality.

What else is needed to create a successful fashion brand?

A very strong personality and a whole lot of talent. Fashion is still one of the rare industries where there is a lot of creative spontaneity and freedom, unlike other major consumer industries, which are ruled by marketing results, statistics and research. There are still huge brands out there that may hire thousands of people, and create millions in revenue, but where the ultimate creative decision is made by one person alone with no calculation or reasoning behind it.

How important is fashion to you personally?

We are heading towards a bigger, more gigantic global market. But I think in reaction to that we will also see a more personal, intimate approach to fashion, with people wanting to do things in a less mainstream and more confidential way. I think there is room for every type of creation. Diversity is what I wish for.

Aesthetics are important to me and fashion is part of that spectrum. I long to be aesthetically and visually pleased at all times.

What do you think makes one designer more successful than another?

A mix of talent, dedication and a ton of work. The industry is so fast paced, so you really need to work a lot. It's as simple as that. It takes a lot of effort to get somewhere, nothing happens by chance.

Who would you like to produce a show for in the future?

I strongly believe that the techniques I've developed for fashion shows could be used in a bigger picture to transmit any sort of message, whether it be for a political, humanitarian, environmental or cultural cause. That's what I'd love to do in addition to doing fashion shows.

What made me start dreaming of doing that was the 1989 bicentennial of the French Revolution staged by Jean-Paul Goude. I was a kid in Paris and it was a giant show in the sense of scale and exposure to the world. It addressed many different topics, from the events of Tiananmen Square to the historical meaning of the French Revolution, but done in a very entertaining, non-heavy way. It blew my mind and made me want to do what I do today. I still believe that nothing has topped that. It's a good example of how far you can go with a show. There are lots of places on earth I'd still love to do a fashion show. And a gravity-less fashion show on the moon would be a very sexy thing to do.

With more and more brands emerging in the market place, where do you think fashion is heading?

Fashion is just one of the things that makes the world we live in more fast paced and globalized. We are heading towards a bigger, more gigantic global market. But I think in reaction to that we will also see a more personal, intimate approach to fashion, with people wanting to do things in a less mainstream and more confidential way. I think there is room for every type of creation. Diversity is what I wish for.

What advice would you give to a budding designer?

I spent many years in the States and I saw a lot there which shocked me. Lots of young kids were dreaming of selling tons and trying to find out how you do that. If anything, the only thing I would advise is to take fashion for what it is great at, i.e., it has no rules. Try to be as spontaneous, creative and personal as possible and don't try to think about how you're going to sell more while you're doing that.

left: Lucite bench designed by Alexandre de Betak, 2003

Katy England

Having studied fashion at Manchester Polytechnic, Katy England worked as a fashion assistant at the Mail on Sunday *and the* Evening Standard *for five years, before becoming Alexander McQueen's right-hand woman and the fashion director of* Dazed & Confused *and* Another *magazine. England is currently the design director of Kate Moss's collection for Topshop and a stylist for numerous high-profile ad campaigns and fashion shows. She remains a contributing editor for* Dazed & Confused *and* Another *magazine.*

opposite: Björk styled by Katy England for the cover of *Dazed & Confused*, May 2000, photograph by David Sims

When did you first get interested in fashion?
I can remember being very aware of what I was wearing from about the age of nine or 10. I had two older sisters and I was dying to grow up so I could dress up like them.

Can you remember any of your outfits?
At age 11 I wanted clothes for my birthday so I was allowed to choose an outfit from C&A. I chose green corduroy drainpipes (bags were still around at the time), a tartan shirt and a razor-blade necklace. It was 1977 so I guess it was influenced by punk. My mum always let me wear exactly what I wanted to. By the age of 14 I had started going to nightclubs and really enjoyed the process of getting ready. I made some pretty outrageous things. I once ripped up some cotton bed sheets into strips and then knitted the strips into a top. It was pretty chunky and stiff, but I was determined to wear it and did so with black leather shorts, a black leather peaked hat, pixie boots and loads of cheap chain jewelry.

What made you want to dress up? Were you trying to make a statement?
Very early on I realized how powerful clothes could be. I was experimenting for myself...creating the character I wanted to be through dressing up and then watching how people reacted. It was purely for my own enjoyment and I was confident enough not to mind what any body else thought.

Did you study Fashion?
Yes, I did four years at Manchester Polytechnic.

How did you get your first job as a stylist?
During the final months of college I wrote to *Elle* magazine for a work placement. I was lucky enough to get one. So at 21 I arrived in London and had my first taste of styling there. I just thought 'this is it, this is what I must do!' I found a job in a PR company to earn some money and from there found out about a fashion assistant vacancy at the *Mail on Sunday*. I assisted two fashion editors, Linda McLean and Sandy Williams. It was manic since I was the only assistant and they

opposite: An image from Katy England's first editorial job for *Dazed & Confused*, issue 10, 1995, shot by Rankin

were both shooting every week. I worked really hard for them for four years and thoroughly enjoyed it.

How was working for *Dazed & Confused* different from working for a newspaper supplement?
Well, firstly I didn't get paid. Shoots had to be done with little or no money so we all worked for the love of it. Photographers, hair and make-up artists, and the models too. I liked using 'real' people to model. Because it was such hard work putting things together on a shoe-string budget it brought about the attitude that I should be able to create what I wanted since I was working for free. *Dazed & Confused* welcomed me and I felt more inspired to produce work that was different.

With no regard as to who was paying for ad space in the magazine?
At that time no. It was such a new magazine I don't think it had many advertisers anyway. It was all very cowboy. The first shoot I did with them was with Rankin and he said I could do whatever I wanted.

Can you describe what you did for that shoot?
It was my favourite 'rock girl' subject. I had found this amazing metallic, patchwork leather jacket, where the appliqué on the collar looked like birds' heads. This was my inspiration and the basis of the shoot. At the time there was a great leather design student at Central Saint Martins called Jane Shepherd. Her work was fantastic so I included a lot of her clothes in the story. Rankin was pretty excited about it and found some extra money to print it on silvery paper.

In this day and age of keeping advertisers happy, it's hard to believe a stylist got free reign...
It's true that magazines have to be really business-minded now. It wasn't like that when I first started, probably because there were far fewer magazines around then. Now magazines have to compete for advertisers, which involves making sure their advertisers are kept happy with an editorial pay off.

Does that mean your vision hasn't had to change to suit the new business-minded approach?
I've been incredibly lucky but one of the reasons I've always chosen to work for *Another* magazine and

Dazed & Confused is because I have been allowed to be creative there. I knew that being part of a fashion team on a more commercially minded magazine was not for me.

When you first started out, where did you source clothes for each shoot?

When I first started there were no mobile phones, BlackBerrys or even the Internet. It was a case of tramping around London on foot. Forming relationships with the fashion PRs was incredibly important – and still is – to obtain the designer clothes. I have always scoured vintage shops and markets and so on because that is where you find something really original. I find it difficult to dress a model head to toe in a designer look straight off the catwalk, so they usually wear a combination of designer, high street, vintage and things I might have had made myself.

Did you have any funds from the magazine to buy the clothes?

Absolutely not! I practically begged people to lend me stuff and if that failed often I would spend my own money to buy it anyway.

You were often referred to as part of the 'new wave of 1990s stylists'. What was that wave?

The new wave was my inspiration...David Sims, Corinne Day, Melanie Ward, Venetia Scott, Glen Luchford and Nigel Shafran... They were the backlash from designer-led fashion, creating their ideas from reality. I wasn't part of that generation, but I came straight after it.

How would you describe your style?

Homemade, cool, quirky and sexy if you were to summarize quickly. I'm not interested in fashion for fashion's sake: in those trickily cut garments that might be a clever achievement but that are pretty unflattering on the body, I don't really do minimalist or simplistic either. When I'm styling the Katy England bit comes in when I put the outfit on and work on it and push myself until I feel it has a unique edge.

What is it about you that makes people book you?

I do four different types of work – consultancy, shows, editorial and advertising and each involves very different skills. With 20 years experience I'd like to think they book me because I'm very good at what I do. I bring to each type of work the same attitude though. I enjoy the work; I am confident and clear in my decision making. I don't worry about what anybody else thinks outside of the people I am working directly with. I know very quickly how to make a picture/outfit or look on a runway work. Ultimately, I'm trying to make a woman look gorgeous/cool/confident/relevant and pretty sexy too, given any materials I know how to do that.

And where does that rebelliousness come from?

I think it's just an attitude you are born with. You're either happy to comply or not.

Fashion lore has it that McQueen asked you to work for him when he saw you dressed in a nurse's coat at the Paris shows. Does dressing up help you get noticed by PRs and editors, etc.?

I think it does help. But it was actually just the way I dressed in my 20s. I was happy to make a huge effort every day. I remember going into *Dazed & Confused* looking great. I wanted to make a statement all the time. Alexander had seen me around at fashion shows and he did literally just come up to me and say, 'Do you want to style my next show?' I was absolutely gob smacked because I'd been to one of his shows at Café de Paris and had been blown away. I said, 'I don't know how to style a fashion show.' And he just replied, 'Don't worry, neither do I. We'll do it together.' And that was it.

Do you remember the first Alexander McQueen show you worked on?

It's such a clear memory. I remember having to pick up the entire collection from his house the morning of the show, stuffing it in my car and taking it to this King's Cross warehouse. It was all very haphazard. I was just hoping there'd be rails there to put the clothes on. And of course we didn't have any shoes. There's never any money for shoes. So we came up with the idea of using the soles of cheap second-hand shoes and ripping off the uppers and sellotaping them to the girls' feet. It looked amazing. One of the dresses burst on this girl while we were trying to get her into it, so Lee (Alexander) taped her in it. It looked great. Eugene Souleiman did the hair and he did this fantastic thing where he kept it very simple and long, but frizzed the ends so it kicked out and flew and bounced as the girls walked. The make-up was done by Val Garland and was nothing but bright orange lipstick. It looked very clean and modern. And I remember all the girls lining up and thinking, 'God this looks incredible'.

What were you feeling before they went out?
It was amazing and exciting. I had roped in all my friends to help me because we couldn't pay anyone. My friend Sam Gainsbury, who is now a big fashion producer, was on board and a girl called Trino Ricarda, who is still at McQueen today. And Alister Mackie was there, he's my best friend, so it felt great to be with them too. I was really impressed as it was the first show I had ever been involved in. There was always a huge adrenaline rush building up to the moment the girls walked out on the runway at a McQueen show.

How did the move to Givenchy come about?
Initially, I just worked on McQueen's shows in London. We'd meet up early in the season to discuss ideas and gradually my involvement increased as we moved nearer towards the show. When Lee was offered the position at Givenchy I felt like it came right out of the blue. The company was so small and he had only done a handful of collections. At that time it was a relatively new idea for design houses to appoint young designers to take charge. Lee's confidence meant he wasn't really phased by it; he treated it like a natural progression probably because he thought he deserved it. I suddenly had to give up a lot of my editorial and freelance work to go to Paris with him. We were thrown in at the deep end and for the next three years I did the whole Givenchy thing with him. I found it really tough just being away from home and I had to learn very quickly.

right: From Katy England's first editorial styling job for *Dazed & Confused*, shot by Rankin in 1995

To have 'style' is quite a rare thing. It's when someone's visual senses are heightened. It's instinctively knowing how to put one's whole self – clothes, shoes, hair, make-up, nails, etc., together in harmony and having the self-confidence to do it. It has absolutely nothing to do with money.

preceding pages: Images styled by Katy England and shot by Nick Knight for a window display at Liberty, London. Originally created for Liberty, they later appeared in *Another* magazine, issue 6, Spring/Summer 2004

What did you learn?

We were two young kids in a couture house in Paris with no experience. Now houses probably know how to guide young designers, but it was one of the first such moves and nobody knew how to deal with us. We were very much left alone and nobody really understood us. Just to experience the craftsmanship in a Parisian atelier was something awe inspiring. Helping to turn sketches into reality was a pleasure when there was so much skill and luxury at your fingertips. At one time I was working on six fashion shows a year – two McQueen, two Givenchy couture and two Givenchy ready-to-wear. Going from one collection to the next was pretty demanding. I learnt everything from model-casting, fitting, how to order outfits in a show, the music, the staging as well as design-directing clothes and accessories. In London, Lee was the forerunner of creating a fashion show as a spectacle. His shows were atmospheric, exciting and unique. Achieving that in London was easy since he had the help of his extended family around him, but in Paris it was really hard. They were not willing to embrace this style of show. There were too many official rules and regulations that we had to comply with and so the ideas were always compromised. This was extremely disappointing for Lee at the time and he was often unhappy there because he couldn't realize his fantasies.

Where do you get the inspiration for the fashion editorials you do?

To me the only point of doing an editorial is if you've got something to say. At times, I'll have seen all the shows of the season and not felt particularly inspired. And in those cases, I don't do anything. But inspiration can come from anywhere. Often an entire shoot can be built around one piece of clothing, or it could be based around a movement. For example, I wanted to shoot these girls in music recently because they were so energetic, feisty and experimental with the looks they were creating. I thought they looked fantastic and it seemed to be a whole new underground movement rising up. It was a fashion shoot but they were the inspiration for the shoot.

Are fashion shows your main source of inspiration?

Not really. I always think there can be many parts to an editorial: the fashion content and then the other parts – the characters, the story, the location, the extra characters and so on. It does depend on the type of story you are doing obviously but fashion content isn't generally enough for me. Just presenting the clothes as they have already been presented in a runway show seems dull. When you do go to the shows though often I am inspired by the atmosphere or something I might have seen on the set or a particular new model who makes an impression when you see her for the first time. Subconsciously after the show season a lot of different types of inspiration have sunk in.

Are you trying to say something with the story element?

I have never felt I have to say something political, or deep, or meaningful in a fashion story. After all it's only clothes and dreams we are trying to sell. I'm led completely by my instincts.

Do you tend to work with the same team?

A huge part of the journey through fashion is finding like-minded people to work with. It takes years to find them and form good relationships. There are certain people that I want to work with now and only those people. For example Guido Palau, the hairdresser. He's like an art director. Working with him is a fantastic experience and I also like him as a person. Because I do so few editorials per season now it's important to be with the people I really like. I've worked a lot with Nick Knight and David Sims; one appeals to my reality side, the other to my fantasy.

How have the luxury brand group takeovers changed the magazine world, aside from creating a plethora of handbag shoots?

It has changed a huge amount in the last ten years. Fashion shoots and magazine editorials are led by business decisions instead of purely creative ones. It's all much more considered.

Why did you decide to leave Alexander McQueen in 2007?

I felt I had reached a point where I had stagnated a bit; I was repeating the same work processes season after season. Leaving was both sad and liberating. It was probably one of the most creative environments I might ever work in. I enjoyed walking through the door every day and seeing all this creation going on, from prints, to fabrics, to trimmings and of course designs. I thought Lee was a truly super talented designer who kept me inspired daily by his vision. But now I am ready for a new challenge.

The newspapers claim you are the creative force behind Kate Moss's collection at Topshop – what is your involvement there?

I help Kate develop four collections a year. I'm the design director, which means I'm involved in every aspect of putting the collection together and making it coherent with the designer and buyer at Topshop. Kate is the inspiration. She often goes vintage shopping and she has the most incredible wardrobe she's collected over the years from around the world. The collection is led by her style and what she wears and we develop it. I'm really enjoying it at the moment. I used to be involved with making clothes where a jacket costs thousands of pounds, now I'm working on clothes that are available to young girls, for £50 to £60. It's really nice to see people in the street wearing something that you've been involved with.

Do you do the actual design sketches?

I don't sketch very well, but I can visualize and communicate what a dress should look like. Many of our designs come from vintage pieces. I instantly know when I see something what should be done to turn it into a great new piece. We might just use parts of the garment – whether it's a collar, some lace, the shape or the trim, etc. The design process at Topshop is worlds apart from a design house and

this is why reworking vintage clothes has proven the best way for Kate Moss's collection.

Do you have any hopes for your own collection?

Having studied fashion, I feel like I've kind of come full circle. Being a creative director and working with other designers on shoes, handbags and clothes is a joy to me. It's something I'd like to do more and more I think.

You are also styling Luella's shows. How has that been different from working for McQueen?

I know Luella well and since her shows are in London I thought it could be an easy and fun thing to do. After my total involvement at McQueen I didn't want to get heavily involved with another designer so quickly again so I just do the final days of putting the show together for her and I have really enjoyed it so far. If someone asked me what my skill was, I'd say, 'Doing a show for somebody'. More than editorial or anything else, I love to go into a company and edit their collection, which means pulling out which pieces are more relevant than others and knowing what is going to appeal to people, ordering the show to making it more coherent and then giving it its own attitude through styling, casting and hair and make-up.

What kind of concept did you come up with for the last show in February 2008?

Luella had designed the collection around this pagan theme originally and I just exaggerated it in a young and cute way. It's about pushing something to the max and at the same time understanding how NOT to over do it.

How do you ensure you remain visionary as opposed to reactionary?

I only let myself do a shoot when I've got something to say. I don't feel like I have to have something out there all the time. I quite like doing less, but working on bigger, special projects. For example, I once dressed Liberty's windows. It was a huge challenge for me. It took so long for me to figure out how to do it. In the end I did a shoot with Nick Knight where we photographed real characters in black and white and I then made red clothes to go

on top of the images in 3-D. Working with Nick is fantastic because he really pushes you. I look back on that as a really special project; it was very challenging and hard at the time. If I could do something like that once a year I'd be happy.

Describe the most challenging shoot you've ever worked on?

It was probably the shoot I did for Alexander McQueen's issue of *Dazed & Confused*. He came up with the idea of using severely disabled people as models in the shoot. One of the girls we used was Alison Lapper, the woman whose statue was later exhibited in Trafalgar Square in London. We asked different designers to make clothes for people with particular disabilities. Hussein Chalayan, for example, projected coloured images onto Lapper instead of making actual clothing. When I started approaching people about the project they would take one look at me and think, 'Oh my God, she's from the fashion world, what does she want?' and the barriers were up the minute you talked about it because they were scared of being exploited. Communicating the idea and finding people willing to participate took months; it was the most challenging thing I've ever done, but in the end it was so rewarding. One of the girls, who had one arm and was shot by Nick Knight wearing Comme des Garçons, said, 'I never thought I could look so beautiful.' And that was it for me. That was the whole point of doing it. Because everyone has the ability to look beautiful. I was incredibly moved by the whole experience.

When you do a shoot with a celebrity – such as the Gwyneth Paltrow shoot you did for *Another* – to what degree are you free to style the celebrity as you wish and to what degree are they in control?

The celebrity is ultimately in control since they can't really wear anything they don't feel comfortable wearing. In the case of a styled piece in *Another* magazine, in my opinion the point is for there to be a strong fashion idea – but to marry the celebrity with

> One of the girls, who had one arm and was shot by Nick Knight wearing Comme des Garçons, said, 'I never thought I could look so beautiful.' And that was it for me. That was the whole point of doing it. Because everyone has the ability to look beautiful. I was incredibly moved by the whole experience.

left: Portrait of Katy England, shot by Nick Knight, 2004; opposite: Athlete, actress and model Aimee Mullins styled by Katy England for the cover of *Dazed & Confused*, issue 46, September 1998, shot by Nick Knight

DAZED & CONFUSED

DAZED

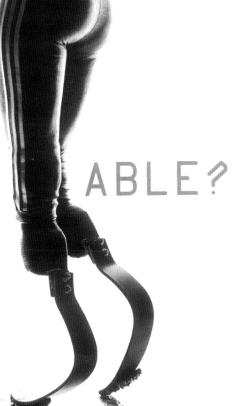

46

ONCE YOU START YOU CAN'T STOP ISSUE

SEPTEMBER 1998 UK£2.50 US$4.50
(45.(R).SAU £2 / RI.1 / DN ABB / 0741

FASHION ABLE?

AIMEE MULLENS BY NICK KNIGHT

9 770961 970063

ALEXANDER
McQUEEN
GUEST
EDITOR
ISSUE

the fashion message can often be really difficult. In many cases you can't even get to talk to that person beforehand even to have a discussion about what they might be up for doing first. In even more cases, Hollywood actresses just want to look 'beautiful'. The better you know the person, the easier it is – working with someone like Björk, for example, is a total joy. At the time I worked with Gwyneth Paltrow she was also happy and willing to put herself in the hands of the 'fashion team'. Being a celebrity stylist, on the other hand, is basically someone paying you to go shopping for them to make them look great, and that's a whole different ball game.

When you style an ad campaign, how much is your vision?

The 'vision' is normally determined by the art director and the client. They pick the team – photographer, stylist, hair, make-up and model according to their vision. It depends on your relationship with the client, and often they need and want your opinion about the choice of clothes to photograph, the model and how the model should eventually look. But in many cases the clothes being shot in an advertising campaign are determined by sales before a stylist is even involved.

Do you have any muses? Whose style do you admire?

I tend to be inspired by 'real' people. Most actresses and women in the public eye these days look so boring and lacking in style it's as if they are all wearing the same uniform. I do get excited when I see young girls who are being experimental with their looks and who don't seem to be afraid to express themselves through their hair, make-up and clothes. It's great to see teenagers not worrying about other people's opinions. We could all do with a shot of style, but real fashion is for young people.

What is style?

To have 'style' is quite a rare thing. It's when someone's visual senses are heightened. It's instinctively knowing how to put one's whole self – clothes, shoes, hair, make-up, nails, etc., together in harmony and having the self-confidence to do it. It has absolutely nothing to do with money.

What makes one designer more successful than another?

That depends on how you measure success... If it's through sales then the bottom line is real women have got to want to wear the clothes in their everyday lives, so the product has to be great and sold at the right price. There must be something about the brand that is so appealing to the customer that they want to be part of it or be associated with it – which comes through marketing and advertising. It's a big question and women have such a great choice now to buy whichever designer they are most comfortable with or who suits their figure type. If success is measured through critical acclaim then that's another matter, but to be able to sustain a company producing clothes and holding twice yearly fashion shows in the international fashion arena I would say is in itself a success. One of the major success stories of the past decade is Nicholas Ghesquière with Balenciaga – he makes cool, beautiful clothes, is loved by the fashion press and keeps the company going through the phenomenal sales of his handbags.

What advice would you give to a budding designer or stylist?

It's easy for kids to say they want to go into fashion – they think they know all about it because it's all around us, to the point where it's practically rammed down our throats. People are so much more aware of how to dress these days. The high street is offering catwalk looks for a fraction of the price and there are thousands of magazines telling us how to dress, so you could say now most teenagers feel they are pretty 'fashionable'. But if you want to make a career out of it, it needs to go a lot deeper than that. There's a lot of hard work to do before things get remotely glamorous and you start making any money. It's about passion, obsession, hard work and dealing with a lot of egos. I think it's either in your blood or not...you can't create it.

opposite: Sue Loosley styled by Katy England and shot by Nick Knight for the *Dazed & Confused* 'One in Ten' shoot, December 2000

Jane Rapley

Jane Rapley OBE was the Dean of Fashion and Textiles at Central Saint Martins College of Art and Design in London from 1989 until 2006. During this period countless students, including Alexander McQueen, Stella McCartney, Hussein Chalayan, Christopher Kane and Alice Temperley, went on to graduate from both the BA and MA courses and make a name for themselves. In 2006 Rapley was appointed head of Central Saint Martins College of Art and Design.

opposite: From the Central Saint Martins' graduate show, Summer 2008; dress designed by Alithia Spuri-Zampetti

What was your fashion background before you went into education?

I did a Diploma in Art and Design and then went on to the Royal College of Art in London to do a research MA on the knitwear industry. After that I worked as a design manager in the knitwear industry for five years and then a group of us started our own business – a design consultancy, which later developed into a menswear brand. It did all the things small businesses in fashion do: it grew, it reduced, it made money, and it lost money... At different times we had our own shops and concessions in say Topman, then we worked as a design consultancy again because we'd built up a track record of knowing where to get things made. Anything to stay alive. During that period I was teaching part time, and eventually in the 1980s, when things got tough, I went into education full time.

What qualities do you look for in prospective students?

Basic talent and for that talent to be suitable for the experience they are applying for. We're also looking for background knowledge, passion and enthusiasm, which sometimes manifests itself as an intensity. You want to know why they want to do it and that has to go beyond 'I just love clothes!' You're also looking for a wider context, i.e., that they understand about the creative world they'll be joining and that it's not just about fashion. We're keen to see a more lateral way of thinking, someone who can think fast and come at things sideways. We want commitment. People who are going to get down and dirty and work hard, which means people with a certain maturity. Putting yourself on a blank page can be quite scary. So the more you have lived, the more you are likely to come up with experiences and ideas that you can expand, explore and research. Most students have done an access or foundation course or have put their portfolio together by attending evening classes and short courses.

Central Saint Martins is a big place with lots of students. They're going to come up against a lot of competition from their peers. They've got to be able to fend for themselves and make the most of what we've got to offer. 'Independent learning' used to be a buzz phrase, but now it's a *force majeure* because the numbers of students is so large and because teaching has become more constrained. It's difficult to take students straight out of school, even if they are very talented, because

The great myth about Central Saint Martins – but myths are always based on some truth – was that students could come up with a great concept, but couldn't sew on a button.

right: Central Saint Martins spends about £130,000 a year on getting pattern-cutters and additional machinists to come in and work with the students

often they can't cope emotionally or London may distract them.

Do students of a certain nationality do better than others?

We have all kinds of nationalities here and they all bring something different. The Japanese students are very interesting because they've often had a sound technical experience but they come to us wanting something else. Their grounding may be good but too linear, so they need to have their imagination and confidence expanded. Recently a group of Chinese students who were here to do some short courses said to me, 'Which course should I do? Which one is the best?' But that's not how we work. The question is what course is best for *you*. Sometimes we turn away talented people because we know we're not the right experience for them. We would damage them. Sometimes we have problems with colleges outside London, who tell their students 'Don't go to CSM, you'll never get in, you'll hate it, etc.' Some students come to us regardless. Sometimes they were right to and other times their college tutor was right.

What do students expect once they've been accepted?

Students often come here with rose-tinted glasses, thinking 'I've got into CSM!' But we don't have wonderful resources, we don't have huge amounts of space, what we do have here is great staff and a huge network of students. And the true value lies in the network, not just of fashion students, but also of fine artists, product, graphic and theatre designers, etc., who will be the movers and shakers of the future. If you're a CSM student sending out your CV, chances are you're sending it to someone who was also at CSM. It may not enable you to walk through the door, but at least it may open the door for you. When I was at college, my network was the Royal College of Art and it affected all my jobs.

Central Saint Martins has been criticized in the past for not focusing enough on dressmaking. Is this still the case?

The great myth about Central Saint Martins – but myths are always based on some truth – was that students could come up with a great concept, but couldn't sew on a button. However, we spend about £130,000 a year on getting pattern-cutters and additional machinists to come in and work with students. In some ways it's a myth and in other ways it's not because you can never learn enough technical skills. We teach skills on a need to know basis, which is driven by projects. If something isn't in fashion while they are at CSM, they won't come across it. If, say, sunray pleated skirts are not in fashion, they won't learn how to make one. What they should learn, however, is how to find out how to do it when it comes back into fashion. In their lives as professionals they will always come across new materials and problems. We're teaching them how to solve these.

But students often think that the technical expertise will solve their design problems. It may give them a greater repertoire but at the end of the day they still have to make a creative and aesthetic judgment. Experience is what helps your design issues fall into place. And we only have three to four years to do that, so in certain respects graduates will always be 'unready' and they have to go on gaining those experiences.

What philosophy do you try to instill in your students?

The basis of our philosophy is finding their own voice and giving them confidence to build on that voice. It's about finding their strengths and weaknesses and their part in the greater context outside. We're not a sausage factory that puts out batches of people with a stock answer to problems.

How do you coax a voice out of someone?

We coax it out by teaching. We set students similar projects but don't expect them all to come up with similar answers. We try to recognize where their interests lie and where they get stuck. Then we say, 'Your work seems to be tending towards X, Y or Z… Have you looked at so and so's work? Have you looked at this for inspiration? Don't you think you should look at, say, active sportswear rather than cocktail dresses? Where are you getting stuck at the minute? Who are your influences?' We're not looking for uniqueness as there is no such thing. We're looking for evolution and distinctiveness.

Do any students end up working in the commercial sector?

We have nearly 200 undergraduates and 40 postgraduates a year and they certainly don't all end up working at design houses. They go all over the world doing all sorts of things at all levels for all kinds of brands, whether that's Adidas, Gap, Donna Karan, Azzedine Alaia or Viktor & Rolf. Not all our students are going to become designers, but the design training will give them the eye, knowledge and confidence to assess other people's work, which is equally valuable.

John Galliano, Alexander McQueen and Stella McCartney have all come out of Central Saint Martins. How much pressure is there for the college to produce the next star designer?

You're on a continuum. Who knows why Galliano decided to come here? Maybe it was because

Katharine Hamnett had graduated 10 years before. Many students who come here do have the ambition to become the next glam front-runner vanguard designer, so we have to spend some time explaining that they're not going to be that, or that it's not that easy.

Galliano was in the 1980s, McQueen was the 1990s and Stella was the mid-1990s. Stella's an interesting and very successful designer but in my view she wouldn't be quite in the Galliano/McQueen category. She's a good designer, who happens to have the whole range of additional skills needed to survive in the outside world. She had the money to back her, the clientele, the name, she had a way straight into the celebrity world, which let's face it drives a lot of our consumption at the moment.

There is certainly pressure, but you don't produce someone of the calibre of Galliano, McQueen or, in my view, Chalayan every year. We may have been lucky. We may have another such designer in Christopher Kane, but it's too early to tell whether he's got the depth of the others. This calibre of person tends to bubble to the top. They tend to be attracted to Central Saint

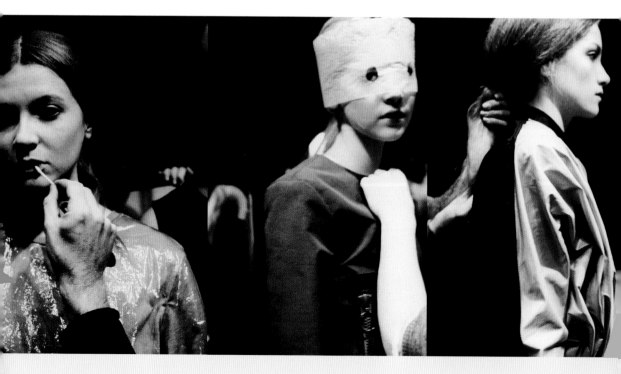

Martins because they think we create star designers, but what they don't realize is that they bring it with them. We just build the paths for them to walk on.

How much business expertise do students learn at Central Saint Martins?

There's been a lot of pressure to get our bright young things to become business-oriented, but my view is that you can't expect students to be everything, just as you can't expect an engineer to be a brilliant businessman, or a writer to be a brilliant publisher. After all, if you look at the most successful businesses in the fashion world, there has always been someone else there, whether it's a life or close business partner who has formed the frame around the really creative designer. We have a business awareness programme. We don't try to teach them how to write cash flows or write business plans, but they have to know that those are things that need to be done.

Do all your students have the opportunity to show their collections at the graduate fashion show?

On the BA course, every student shows his or her work because it's part of the assessment. There are some industry people in the know, who sit through the whole gruelling day of the internal BA show, with a view to employing candidates. From that we select about 40 collections to be shown in the press show. It doesn't mean that there aren't some really good students who didn't get into the show. The show is about showcasing the course, so it has to be balanced across a number of fashion specialities and themes. If you have six really good students working on the same territory, you're not going to put all six in. You can't have only big frocks, or only womenswear in the show, for example. But that doesn't mean that those who aren't in the show won't get jobs. There are a lot of companies that come to us asking us to recommend students, so we line up the suitable students for certain labels.

The time of the shows is tearful, stressful and manic, but then of course that's what the fashion industry is like, so it's an experience they are likely to have in the future. With the MA, it's slightly different. To be chosen, you first of all have to meet

below: Backstage at the Central Saint Martins MA show, February 2008, photographs by Claire Robertson

your deadlines. If you don't meet those you don't get to show. It also depends on the suitability of your clothes for the catwalk. We've had some very brilliant people on the MA who've not shown because their collections were more suitable to display. The MA show is much tighter. Some years we might show as few as 16 or 17 collections. This year we showed 21.

What do you hope your students will exude on the catwalk besides diversity?

Quality, excellence, individuality, confidence and authority. At postgraduate level, their voice has to be strong and authoritative, without being derivative. They need to show a freshness, and hopefully be pushing at the edges of some of the ideas out there.

How important is it to be innovative in fashion?

It's important to be fresh. It's no good going out there and doing a pastiche of what's out there already, but it's not a revolution. It's difficult to be unique. If you're far out no one else will buy into it or identify with it. Designers are designers and not fine artists. There needs to be some resonance. Some of our students in the past have gone quite far out on a limb and it can take time for the public to catch up.

For example, Gareth Pugh is a bit of an eccentric. He did the undergraduate degree here. I don't think he would have responded well to the rigours of the MA: his clothes are somewhat theatrical and costumey. We've yet to see how influential he may become. It may be a pastiche, but he's doing much better than I thought and he's more influential, for example, with his heavy, black, slightly aggressive Goth collection. His attitude reminds me a bit of the Russian futurists. Their work was a bit weird and wonderful and a bit comic, but it had an underlying theme which pushed people's thinking. Whether Gareth actually does push people's thinking and whether he sustains it in the long run, we've yet to see.

Hussein Chalayan, who did the BA, also follows his own agenda. I think the cultural studies we offered here were also important for how he developed his thinking and how he used that philosophical thinking to develop artefacts. He looks at influences in politics, science, technology and society and relates them back to the body. It's quite a difficult and thorny path to follow, but if you're going to follow it, this is the place to try to do it. We can absorb that, just as we can absorb a designer who is going to be incredibly successful working for Gap.

Do design houses snap up your students as soon as they've finished their degrees?

A few do. And of course those are the ones that make the story. Most of the students on the MA course have got significant jobs within the worldwide industry within nine months of graduating. The fashion journalists nearly all get jobs. The textile people almost never get jobs because there are so few employed jobs in the textile industry. The pattern there is to work freelance, or set up your own business like Eley Kishimoto. A lot of the menswear students tend to get jobs too because it's less competitive. For example, Kim Jones, one of our former students, is doing really well working for all sorts of labels from Topman to Hugo Boss.

How different is the UK fashion industry from the French and Italian?

Our buying patterns are completely different from the French and Italian consumers. We're high street dominated and interested in price and design value for money. We're driven by a turnover of ideas in clothes, and we dress less classically compared to the French and Italians, who are still driven by a more conservative, longer-lasting, intrinsic quality and craftsmanship. A greater sector of their buying public is prepared to invest more money in fewer items. Strangely we're quite happy about the fact that you can go from one city to another within the UK and see exactly the same merchandise. Perhaps that's why we turn over stuff faster because the availability of designs is more ubiquitous across the country. And because we industrialized first, we lost our craftsmanship base sooner than in Europe. Virtually all manufacturing is sourced abroad now. Perhaps that's also why we get so many international students. Often they come from textile families in the Far East wanting to learn about European consumer tastes and marketing so that they can be of value in their indigenous industry. A lot of the industry in the Far East was service industry until very recently, and it's now become branded because they see that the profit margin is much greater. China is now obsessed with brands.

Where do you think the fashion industry is heading?

The question is: where is society heading? Because wherever society is heading, that's where fashion will go. Concerns in Western Europe are now about sustainability. We've been talking about sustainable fashion and textiles for 18 years at Central Saint Martins. Big brands have until recently been reluctant to invest in research because they couldn't see the marketing potential or saleability. But we're in a different place now, we're threatened by something so the industry might take it a bit more seriously.

We're probably also going into a recession, so we'll go through an anti-consumerism phase – which is the worst thing in a recession because you need to consume to get out of it. But we're wobbling, we've lost our confidence. America is in a political and economic mess. Who knows what China is going to do? What are the values going to be of the countries with economic power? Because that's where fashion will go. Our aesthetic might become more Asian. If, for example, China becomes the dominant world power our values will shift. All consumerism is a badge about your power.

Do you think it's important to go to college if you want to be a designer?

You can do it without, but you have to be very determined and fight to get through. I think it's

Stella's a good designer, who happens to have the whole range of additional skills needed to survive in the outside world. She had the money to back her, the clientele, the name, she had a way straight into the celebrity world, which let's face it drives a lot of our consumption at the moment.

easier in menswear. There isn't one role called 'fashion designer'. A lot of people who are labelled designers are retailers with great eyes, who know how to create things. Take Luella Bartley. She did the Fashion Communication with Promotion degree and was a journalist who went on a placement at the *Evening Standard* in her second year. She was so successful there that she was offered a job as an assistant and never finished her degree. I think she designs as a journalist. She's got a really good, innate sense of where the gaps are and where the public zeitgeist is. And that's fine too. You can come to design in so many different ways. Paul Smith is a designer, but he also learnt a lot about design from his wife. Essentially, he's an ace retailer with a good eye, who knows how to create things. His success is linked to his savvy sense of what his customers' tastes are.

What do you tell students who are eager to launch straight into their own collections after graduating?

Students often say, 'I don't want to work for anyone else'. They think they're going to be the next Galliano, but when you learn more about the trade, you realize how difficult it is and how special those people are. Your role as a teacher is not just to help them find their voice, but also to aid students with self-realization, which can mean recognizing your limitations as well as your talents and deciding where you want to go with them. Sometimes we hit the spot and we do get people to that stage after three to four years, others have a lot more to learn before they start out on their own. What's encouraging is that some students form partnerships, such as Sinha Stanic, or Felder and Felder. We're not there to dictate to students what they should and shouldn't do. One problem students

have with us is that different members of staff might say different things to them and that confuses some. But the whole point of being here is making a choice as to whom you listen to. You're responsible for your own learning.

Central Saint Martins is moving to a new location in King's Cross in 2011? How will the new space affect teaching?

We hope that the facilities and equipment will be better and we are making huge efforts to maintain our workshops because we're all about making things. We are going to have less space, so we have to be more imaginative about how we use it. We'll be trying to use it 24 hours a day, seven days a week, 48 weeks out of the year. All subjects will be in one building so we're hoping that much more cross-fertilization will take place. Often it's when disciplines start overlapping, such as graphics and fashion or graphics, fine art and performance that interesting, fresh and new things start to happen and at times even engender new areas of study.

Which designers currently inspire you?

The ones I like are already well established. Viktor & Rolf are very interesting and Margiela is always unpredictable. Of the younger ones, the one who is getting a lot of airplay is Christopher Kane. Marios Schwab is another one but on the other end of the scale, with a different sort of aesthetic. There is also Louise Goldin, but I'm not sure any of them will become as hardcore directionist as say Galliano or McQueen. I'm not sure it's the right moment for that. People who come out in a hardcore direction usually come out at the beginning of an 'up'. But we're not on an up. Hopefully we're on a plateau, but we might be on a slope. McQueen came out in 1992 to 1994 when there was a huge rise in confidence, and despite producing wonderful collections in the late 1980s Galliano didn't really take off until he was discovered by Bernard Arnault in the early 1990s. I think it's going to be more a case of going out and learning a lot working for a series of people and then doing your own thing, just like Giles Deacon did, or Tao, who worked for Comme des Garçons first. I think it's going to tighten. If we do go into a recession, retailers will stop taking risks and it will be much harder for equally talented people to go out and actually make a way for themselves. There's a wobble in confidence and fashion is all about confidence.

What advice would you give a budding designer?
Make mistakes on other people's budgets. Remember that you are not the centre of the universe. Maybe if you wait too long to set up on your own, you might never do it because you have to be slightly foolish, brave and wild to do it. But you need the right balance of skills. Talent alone isn't enough. You need the social, inter-personal skills, knowing when to stop, to let go. Perfection is not what's sold in the end. It's all the other balancing factors that make a successful brand. That's why Christopher Kane may well turn out to be incredibly successful because he's got such a lovely personality and people enjoy working with him.

McQueen, on the other hand, had a different approach again. He was really tough, hungry and driven. People wanted to buy into that vision. He came to us asking for work but our course director suggested he do the MA instead because she thought he was very special. Luck is another factor that's needed in the equation for success, whether you're a cabinet minister, a designer or a celebrity. McQueen was lucky in meeting Isabella Blow because she provided an introduction into another network. He chose very interesting people to work with, whether that was his show producers, or the stylist Katy England. Some students will end up being catalysts; others will be the team players helping the catalysts. And there's nothing wrong with that. It's also a terrifically creative skill to

be an ace team player. But that kind of success is a greedy god. It absorbs people's lives and there isn't always space for living a rich private life.

Do you think you can learn to have an aesthetic?
You can learn to hone your eye, but you have to be able to see what you're looking at. You need to have a basic visual literacy and that literacy can be taught just as a written literacy can. The whole point is for students to get inspiration from everywhere, not just magazines and other secondary sources, otherwise fashion goes up its own bottom. The reason we still bleat on about something as antiquated as drawing is not just because it's about making beautiful marks on paper, but because it educates your eye to analyse what you're looking at. You look at things we take for granted: proportions, colour, mood, context, ambience and construction. Students are expected to draw all the time, whether in a sketchbook or in their notes. It's the fastest way of communicating something that words cannot.

opposite and below: Print designs by Frances Lui and Nicola Woolley respectively. Both were Fashion Printed Textile students and winners of the Liberty Project, May 2008

Coco Rocha

Supermodel

above: Coco Rocha at a charity event; opposite: Coco Rocha, photograph by Ben Cope

Discovered at the age of 14 at an Irish dancing competition in Vancouver, Canada, Coco Rocha quickly became one of the world's most photographed models. She has worked with leading fashion photographers, including Steven Meisel, Peter Lindbergh, Annie Liebowitz, Mario Sorrenti and Mert & Marcus and has been in countless ad campaigns, including Dior, Balenciaga, Gap, YSL fragrance and beauté and Dolce & Gabbana. Rocha, who has been a favourite on the catwalk in New York, London, Paris and Milan for several seasons, is represented by Elite Model Management in New York.

When and how did you become a model?

I was spotted at an Irish dance competition in Vancouver when I was 14. I was approached by agent Charles Stuart and asked whether I'd ever thought about being a model. I laughed and told him to go speak to my mom. He asked us a couple of times, and finally we gave in and tried it. It was never my life's ambition to be a model, but here I am.

Did you have lots of dance training growing up?

I started by studying ballet and jazz, then went to singing classes but my first teacher scared the wits out of me. As my mother had already paid for a term, she said, 'we can't waste that money, why don't you take a different class', so I enrolled in an Irish dance class. It was at the time when *Riverdance* had just come out; Nora Pickett was teaching at my school. And 12 years later I think my mom probably wished she'd never told me to pick another class as thousands of dollars went into my obsession with Irish dancing.

What does it take to be a model besides good looks?

I think it's about being yourself. Lots of the girls who make it are true to themselves. I take my work really seriously. I make sure I get to work on time and maintain a good attitude. My dad is quite the comedian, so I also like to joke around and have fun. If a client asks me to do something I'm not comfortable doing, I try to tell them how I feel. My biggest gripe at the moment is linked to the whole notion of 'the anorexic model'. I've been approached or made to worry about what I look like. But I always think to myself, if others appreciate me as I am, I don't need to change in order to fit a dress. Some girls think that if they decline a job they'll never work with that person again, or that it will ruin their career. I've learnt that I may not always be what the client is looking for. If I go to a casting or

below: Coco Rocha away from the catwalk

fitting, and I realize a dress doesn't fit, I just think, 'I'm probably not what they're looking for.' It can be upsetting, but then you may get booked the next day by a designer who does appreciate how you look.

In what way has your dancing background helped your career – in terms of movement and poses, etc.?

I am quite comfortable on the catwalk as I am used to performing in front of crowds due to my Irish dance background, but when I started working with photographers one on one I was a bit nervous. I wasn't sure if I was doing the poses right. Then I realized, you just give it what you've got, and if it's not working for that photographer he or she will just tell you to change the pose. I think dancing gave me courage and presence. However, because Irish dancing is all about the legs, I had to learn to relax my upper body.

Which designers do you like to walk for and why?

I like shows that have a story or theme – where we have to play along. The same goes for editorial:

> Before I began modelling I had nothing to do with fashion. Even my friends think it's weird that I wear heels now. I haven't worn runners for a long time. I went home recently and we were going on a hike and I couldn't bear putting on a pair of jeans and runners. And my family were all like: 'Get over yourself!'

I like it when there's a story or a plot. Otherwise, you feel like you're doing the same thing over and over. Dolce & Gabbana always have a theme, as do Galliano, Dior and Versace. Versace always wants powerful, sexy girls. But it's the whole package together that makes it interesting and powerful: how they have designed the stage, the ambiance, the music.

You did an Irish dance for the opening and the closing of the Jean Paul Gaultier's Autumn 2007 show. How did that come about?

Gaultier had heard that I was a dancer and his collection had been based around Scotland. He thought I was a highland dancer and I told him that it was actually Irish dancing that I did. He said, 'that's good enough.' He asked me if I could go up and down the runway. I think he was surprised by what I did, as he expected me to just do a little shimmy, but it was the real deal.

What is the significance of opening or closing a show for a designer?

It depends. If you're a new girl and you're opening or closing the show, it's a way for the designer to welcome and congratulate a new face. If the girl is established, it's a way of commemorating or celebrating her. Some designers just have their favourites.

You've worked for Dolce & Gabbana, Prada, Louis Vuitton, Chanel – to what degree do you take on a different attitude for each label/campaign?

Dolce always want girls to be powerful and sexy and strong. Chanel is more classic and elegant. But all designers want you to be confident.

What makes a memorable runway image? When can you say that a show went well?

I think it's that dress or design that makes everyone wonder, 'hey, was that actually a good idea, or is it too over the top?' Those are usually the images that are shown around the world. Designers often put their favourite dresses on their favourite girl, or they'll use the model they think will convey that particular look best.

In what way do you think models help sell the clothes?

I don't know. If you're an artistic kind of person and you like looking at images, you'll appreciate much more what models and photographers do. But the average person who is just into clothes and doesn't understand the industry probably wouldn't appreciate an image in the same way. Models always try hard to strike the right pose and create a story. Essentially people want to buy the clothes because the girls make them look good.

Do designers give you clothes to promote out and about?

Some do. I've always appreciated Rag & Bone, Rodarte, Richard Chai: the young and new designers because they're really ambitious about what they're trying to do.

You have Rodarte, Derek Lam and Marc Jacobs in your wardrobe – what do you like about those designers?

Those designers are all different but they're very wearable. I find New York designers more wearable than those from Europe, who often seem to create with red carpet events in mind. The New York designers give off more of a street vibe. It's more everyday wear. I also like the Elizabethan/Tudor look. I like going to vintage stores and buying old jackets and dresses and I like to pair them up with something more modern because I don't want to end up looking like something out of a costume drama. I like high collars and puffy shoulders, long dresses, princess lines, and I'll team it up with a stiletto or modern boot.

What kind of clothes do you like to wear when you are not working?

During the shows we all get decked out to show people what we *can* wear. Everyone from the editors to the buyers and models wear their best pieces. After all why wouldn't you? It's where everyone who loves

left and opposite: Coco Rocha photographed by Liz Collins for the Nicole Farhi ad campaign, Autumn/Winter 2008–2009

A lot of people who aren't in the industry might blame models for what the industry has become, but the girls have no choice. A lot of girls feel that they have to be skinny to get the next pay cheque, but it's not like that... You have to learn to have the confidence to think that if you don't get a job because of your shape this time you'll get it next time because of that same figure.

fashion comes together. Why not wear your best bits around the people who'll appreciate them? At the shows in Paris this season I wore super-high flat riding boots to Chanel that I bought in Canada. I also wore cute American Apparel leggings, a vintage jacket, a top from Topshop and a Longchamp clutch. I don't think you have to wear designers from head to toe. You only need one beautiful designer piece and then the rest will fall into place.

How has your taste for fashion evolved since being in the business?
I think it's still evolving. Before I began modelling I had nothing to do with fashion. Even my friends think it's weird that I wear heels now. I haven't worn runners for a long time. I went home recently and we were going on a hike and I couldn't bear putting on a pair of jeans and runners. And my family were all like: 'Get over yourself!'

Where do you buy your clothes?
It's tricky. I don't really buy a lot as I'm given so much, but I like to go to vintage stores like Cheap Jack on 32nd and 5th in New York. But I never go 'shopping' as such. If I see something I like when I'm out and about, I'll just get it.

What do you think makes someone stylish?
I think you need to take chances to be stylish. Don't copy styles straight out of magazines. Create your own image. Don't abide by the rules.

What do you love about fashion?
I love that I get to travel and see the underground scenes of a city. I get to see how people really live and I get to see things girls my age wouldn't normally get to see. How many 20-year-olds can say they've met Karl Lagerfeld or Steven Meisel or Anna Wintour. Meeting the most important people of a major industry is fascinating to me.

What do you hate about fashion?
I think it's hard to have to grow up much faster than girls your own age. If you're a young girl, who

left: Coco Rocha with her agent, Micki Schneider, at Elite Model Management in New York

doesn't understand the industry, it can be really tricky. You need to make sure you have the right people around you. I was lucky to have my mom around and I have great agents, like Micki Schneider at Elite, who are always honest with me.

You did your first *Vogue* shoot for Steven Meisel – what did he get out of you?
I did that shoot in February 2006. It was with Gemma Ward and Missy Rayder. I had no idea who he was: I'm glad that I didn't know as I would have been a nervous wreck. It's because of Steven that I am where I am today. I worked exclusively with him for a few months. He put my name on the map. After working with him people started saying, 'Who is this Coco and why is he shooting her exclusively?' He introduced me to fashion.

Which fashion photographer do you like working with and why?
I love working with Steven. He knows what he wants and tells you what to do to accomplish it.

What campaigns have you recently worked on?
Last season I did a campaign for PHI, which was shot by Steven Meisel, and a YSL fragrance and beauté campaign shot by Solve Sundsbo and a Nicole Farhi shot by Liz Collins.

What is the most exciting campaign you've worked on and why?
I loved the first Dolce & Gabbana campaign I did, shot by Steven Meisel. It was all period pieces, which I love. It was very luxurious.

What makes a successful fashion campaign?
I think a campaign always needs an idea and concept no matter how great the clothes. The whole image needs to be put together: the hair, the make-up and the clothes have to be cohesive. I loved the Lanvin campaigns, where the model was photographed so it looked like a painting.

What have you learned about the fashion industry since being a model?
It's sort of what I expected. It has its ups and downs. It's not what some people think, i.e., drugs, sex and rock n' roll. It can have its scary moments,

but if you're strong and you know what you want, you can overcome that. You need to make sure you don't get pushed into doing something you don't want to do. Different people have different moral issues. Mine are that I prefer not to be seen in crazy atmospheres, drinking and partying. Even in photos I prefer not to partake in those things.

What are the less beautiful aspects of the fashion industry?
Models and health is something I believe in and have been speaking about recently. A lot of people who aren't in the industry might blame the models for what the industry has become, but the girls have no choice. A lot of girls feel that they have to be skinny to get the next pay cheque, but it's not like that. I feel that could change. You have to learn to have the confidence to think that if you don't get a job because of your shape this time you'll get it next time because of that same figure.

What characteristics do you think you need to survive as a designer or label in the fashion world?
You have to have new ideas. It's hard because you might think everything's been done...but you have to have the confidence to push that envelope forward. In New York lots of designers have the backing of *Vogue* and the CFDA (the Council of Fashion Designers of America). They help newcomers with great talent who work hard. They will often pick the designers who have a great background story. It's good to be backed by these types. You might have the models and the styling all set, but you need that extra helping hand.

What advice would you give a budding fashion designer or budding model?
Stay true to yourself because your time as a model will be over at some point and it'll be much better if you are still the same person as you were when you started. Regarding designers, I think it's important that you stick to what you truly believe in. If you start doing things that don't make you feel comfortable, you're less likely to succeed.

Gino Da'Prato

Founder and co-owner of wholesale fashion distribution company, Fourmarketing

Gino Da'Prato worked as a milkman in Galloway, south-west Scotland, for six years before becoming a sales assistant in the menswear department at Harrods. From there he worked his way up to fashion buyer and later launched his own fashion distribution company with three of his former colleagues: Ben Banks, Charles Perez and Dominique Signoret. In the last ten years, Fourmarketing has become one of the most successful fashion distribution companies in the UK, representing over 26 brands such as C.P. Company and Stone Island, Evisu, Raf by Raf Simons, K by Karl Lagerfeld and McQ. Fourmarketing also manage their own retail divisions with stand-alone stores and an e-commerce team dedicated to pioneering the men's fashion and lifestyle website, oki-ni.com. More recently, Fourmarketing has developed subdivisions that include PR, marketing and media spending. The joint companies currently employ about 100 people.

opposite: Nom de Guerre,
Autumn/Winter 2008–2009

When did you first get interested in fashion?

I fall into a strange position. I come from a big family: I have three younger brothers and three older sisters. My mum was always into dressmaking, upholstering and the whole world of textiles and fabrics. When she was making dresses for the girls I was always there. Apparently, the girls also used to dress me up. Why I'm not gay, I really don't know because I guess I really should be... Later, in the early 1990s, my sister, Rena Da'Prato, became a successful knitwear and fashion designer. It was always our intention to work together at some point because I guess I had the flair you need to sell. I thought it would be best to break into London. I got a job in the menswear fashion department of Harrods. In my first job I was working on the shop floor as a sales assistant. I settled in well and through hard work the doors opened up from there.

How did you go from working on the shop floor to opening your own distribution company?

I was at Harrods for six years and was encouraged to go into the management training scheme. I became an assistant buyer and moved up through the ranks. I was introduced to the higher end of fashion and ready-to-wear. One of my biggest clients was the Italian distributor, GFT, who distributed labels such as C.P. Company, Stone Island, Giorgio Armani

Unless you have a commercial strategy to take the creative ideas forward a brand will never succeed.

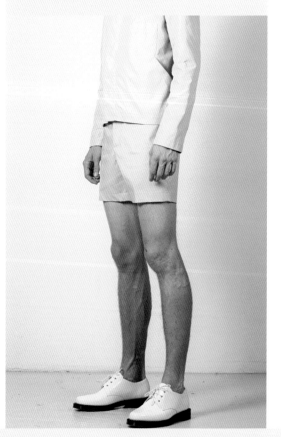

and Katharine Hamnett. I built up a relationship with them through working at Harrods. They offered me a job on the wholesale side in 1991 together with the three other partners who now form Fourmarketing. When their contract expired with GFT in 1997 we were invited by SPW – the owner of C.P. Company and Stone Island – to run their interests in the UK. That was the foundation of Fourmarketing and still is to this day. We set up with quite short notice, so we had to find a showroom and so on. A friend gave us a bedroom-sized basement and that's where we did our first season. We did everything from teas and coffees to sales and we had our best season ever. We were offered a golden egg and we grasped it. To this day we're indebted to Carlo Rivetti, managing director of SPW, for giving us the chance to start up on our own.

Did you spend any time at fashion school?
No, and I don't think it would have been useful to me. My career path related to the wholesale, retail, marketing and internet side of fashion. For me it felt right to get that experience in a working environment, rather than a classroom environment.

How did Fourmarketing grow into the vast business it is today, with 100 odd employees?
After taking on Stone Island and C.P. Company we had a stable base from which to grow. We rented a cool and spacious office in Soho and we needed to bring in complementary brands that would sit well alongside the ones we distributed already. We have since built up Evisu, the Japanese jeans brand, and designer diffusions McQ by Alexander McQueen and K by Karl Lagerfeld. We worked with Fake London for many years on Fake London and on a diffusion licence, Fake London Genius. We now distribute a whole host of different brands.

below: Raf by Raf Simons, Spring/Summer 2009

What does distribution involve?

When we take on brands it's our responsibility to ensure that they are introduced to the appropriate market, that the right balance of stock is sold and that it's delivered well and also marketed well.

How do you go about choosing which brands to represent?

We've never actually gone out and hunted down a brand and are very grateful for that. In the case of Evisu and Fake London, for example, we were offered those brands. It's been an organic process. We have to make sure that any brand we take on fits into the existing structure and complements the brands we already distribute as opposed to competing with them. That's our ethos. We look at opportunities that allow us to build a brand to create a certain level of turnover. But, equally, we may take on a small brand if it looks like it could be beneficial from a marketing and image standpoint. For example, Raf by Raf Simons. It's been a tiny business for the last three years, but it's grown into something quite substantial. In the beginning we just loved what he was doing and at the time it didn't make any financial sense to take it on, but it does now.

One point that lots of people in the lovey-dovey world of fashion tend to forget is that unless you have a commercial strategy to take the creative ideas forward a brand will never succeed. In a way we become ambassadors for a brand as we market the product and make sure they are given an opportunity to succeed. Each brand needs a selling arm that controls and ensures that the right product is sold to the right retailer in the right way. At the end of the day, shops are our holy grail: they have got to sell the product. Such a small amount of emphasis within the fashion industry is put on the distribution side of events, as it's more boring and financial, but it's a crucial part of the workings.

Which territories do you sell to?

We have global distribution rights, except in Japan, for certain brands such as Nom de Guerre – one of my favourites; a tiny new fashion brand a bit like Raf –

who we have global distribution rights for, with the exception of Japan. For some of the other brands we represent, such as Silas, we have European rights. However, our main focus is UK wholesale distribution.

Is it preferable to have a mix of different brands?

We have introduced middle to high-end brands, but our core business is higher-end distribution. With our consumer base some may go more towards jeans, or towards fashion, or technical sportswear, but essentially it's the same market. It's all about disposable income. It doesn't matter whether he's a builder who has £500 in his pocket and wants to spend it on a jacket from C.P. Company or whether he's an architect who will come in and buy a pure piece by another brand. That's where we try and position ourselves without conflicting across the brands. For example, Selfridges probably stocks eight of our brands.

To what degree do you assist the retailers when it comes to selling on the shop floor?

We try to ensure that our retailers are well trained when it comes to the concept of each particular brand they buy from us. I've always had a big thing about this. If you think about the whole chain of events, from the designer who comes up with the concept, through to manufacturing and then marketing, i.e., the people who create the image, through to us who do the wholesale distribution… the chain is not completed until you reach the guy who is working the shop floor. I feel like he is the forgotten hero. If that guy, who earns 18k a year, doesn't get trained up and excited about the brand he is selling, the rest of the chain is pointless.

So what we do is we go to the retailers and get them excited about the brand's concept, history and heritage. We invite shop-floor staff to our showrooms and have training seminars. Our sales team also get in their cars and drive to Hull, Doncaster and Lincoln and so on to train up the shop staff. Essentially, the buyers might come to us and spend a couple of hours on each collection when they write their order, but they don't have the time to go back to their staff and convey what each brand stands for. Usually the boxes of clothes just turn up in August for winter and the shop staff get told 'This dress is going to retail at £440', but they don't know why anyone would go and spend that money if they can get a well-designed dress in Topshop for £60. Our job is to excite them and convey the message behind the brand so they are armed to promote that within the retail environment.

Could you explain whether there are different sales tactics for different brands?

We have 15 product managers who sell different brands. For each we like to ensure that their natural personality shines through. We have a passionate fashion savvy women's brand manager heading up McQ and a team of enthusiastic product-driven guys across C.P. Company and Stone Island. We certainly don't want them to be Fourmarketing clones. We make sure that our sales staff know the collection they are selling very well and encourage the retailer to explain what is new and different in their town; whether there are any new shops opening up and so on so that we can understand the bigger picture as well.

We like to go beyond the fact that a shop may come down and write a 10k order with us. We give them a service throughout the season, for example, if a shop is having a great sell-through, in other words, a great reaction to a collection, we can help support that. Every retailer will hope to achieve a 65 per cent sell-through. It is considered 'good' if they sell 65 per cent of stock before the sales. But we help them further in the season. We find out how they are doing, we see whether we can help them from a promotional or marketing point of view. We might be able to do a point of sale by using imagery to promote the brand, or we may be able to help them with our in-house PR team. Similarly, if they don't get the reaction they had hoped for for a product, we can offer a stock swap on the slow lines, or we can try to help them promote the brand locally. We have marketing budgets that allow us to drive the sales in non-conventional ways. In general, the tendency is that retailers won't come back to

us and buy a brand at the same level if it doesn't do well, but we're actually bucking the trend as we're 20 per cent up on Spring/Summer 09 sales.

How do you choose which shops to sell to or do they choose you?

When we consider which shops to sell to we look at their existing business and what other brands they stock. We consider whether our brand would fit in from a price point and a stylistic point of view as there is no point in selling a basic jeans collection to a high-fashion store and vice versa. You need to know and understand the aesthetic of the shop and what kind of consumer they have in mind. As we travel to do shop visits, we get to know shops better and better.

Is there competition between shops?

It depends on the brand. If a brand is well positioned and well known there's always the feeling that you can make it available to a wider audience straightaway. If, however, you are dealing with a more artisan brand, something like Nom de Guerre, it needs a slower, more cautious approach. It needs to be introduced to the market in a slower way. So we'd start with the retailer who we think would best embrace the brand and introduce it to the right

If you think about the whole chain of events, from the designer who comes up with the concept, through to manufacturing and then marketing...the chain is not completed until you reach the guy who is working the shop floor. I feel like he is the forgotten hero.

EVISU

customer. For Nom de Guerre that was Liberty. Then Harvey Nichols picked it up because they heard of its success at Liberty. In most cases we find that if we give the initial retailer exclusivity to a brand so that they've established the brand with their customer base, they don't mind if another retailer takes on the same brand at a later stage.

How do you maintain a good relationship with the shops that retail your brands and with the designers who create them?

In terms of designers and suppliers, we ensure we give them constant feedback in terms of how the collection is doing. It may be our own personal response to a collection, or information that is conveyed to us by the market. We can build up a catalogue of experiences of what works and what doesn't. Our sales teams also give the brands seasonal reports and outline how the market has

reacted. We also have a post sales meeting with suppliers to outline how buyers reacted to the collection to help them steer their direction forward. The UK is an important market for both designers and suppliers as it's an important barometer for the global market. It's well positioned and very influential, both in terms of how European lines do vis-à-vis America and vice versa. Brands expect a lot from us and we are willing to convey that. If the outcome is, for instance, to steer the brand towards the more commercial, we are the ones who will benefit from helping them figure that out.

Do you ever go back to designers and say 'this and that isn't selling, try doing it differently' or is that not your responsibility?

We get elements of that as the UK market could be different from, say, the Spanish or German market. Suppliers try to keep everyone happy, but that's

above: Evisu campaign

really hard. The real challenge is to develop opportunities within every market to give consumers what they need. But as the UK is influential suppliers tend to listen to us.

What made you launch an in-house press office and do you represent the brands you distribute?

We launched the in-house press office about eight years after we founded Fourmarketing. It was a big development within our wholesale distribution strategy. We're unique in that we maintain a marketing budget for use within the UK. And from that a certain amount of money goes towards the PR activity. We worked with two great PR companies for years, Purple and Modus. But as in most PR companies there is one person looking after a whole heap of brands, so we realized that we had a big opportunity if we controlled the PR ourselves in-house as it would give us complete focus on our brands. We are also in charge of media spending for Stone Island and C.P. Company, which also falls within the remit of our PR department, Four Publicity. So we decide how much is spent on advertising for those brands. If a magazine is willing to write about one of our brands in their editorial, then it proves that they are worthy of consideration for an ad campaign. Within three years of launching Four Publicity we have tripled our media coverage. We currently employ eight people who work on about 12 different brands including Stone Island, C.P. Company, Raf by Raf Simons and Tretorn. We don't represent all the brands we distribute as some have their own global PR and some are covered within the 'maison', i.e., in-house.

How do you ensure the brands you represent get seen and thereby bought?

The PR team help publicize our brands and they work closely with the sales division to make sure key products that retailers have bought into have a good presence within the shops. We also have opportunities to personalize areas within a shop. We have point of sales, we might do a special shop window or in-store installation to promote our brands within a store.

How important is product placement on celebrities?

It's important with certain brands. You can't ignore the power of celebrity these days. If someone is seen to be wearing a brand, then the consumer will be influenced. We tend to approach agents and ask whether their client might be interested in wearing the product. And we try to match the right product to the right celebrity, say, Russell Brand might like Raf by Raf Simons. We don't pay anyone money to wear the brands. Some brands have an arranged contract with celebrities, but we don't have the facility to contact someone to say 'Wear this or that on your album cover or to the opening of your movie.' Noel Gallagher loves C.P. Company, so we'll just give him some clothes and say 'enjoy them' and we normally reap the benefits.

Why do you think Fourmarketing is so successful?

We're actually unique as no other independent wholesale fashion distributor has so many facets

below: From the Tretorn lookbook, Spring/Summer 2006, shot by Neil Stewart, East Coast, USA

to their business. We can pretty much tailor make an opportunity for a brand. If a brand comes to us and says, 'we're a small company and we want to grow slowly', we can do that for them. Similarly, if a brand says, 'we want to open some stand-alone shops', we can do that for them too. We can offer it all. This wasn't our goal when we first set up Fourmarketing: it sort of happened organically. We've bolted on these new aspects to the core business, which is always going to be wholesale fashion distribution.

Also the industry talks kindly of us. A brand might come along and say, 'we've heard about you'. It sounds cheesy, but we care about the brands we distribute. We're ambitious about them and we'd like to do the job right. Take Stone Island or C.P. Company, we've been distributing those brands for years, from the very beginning. We don't just take on brands to see how they do and then drop them if they don't perform well after one season. We like to dedicate a certain amount of space in the showroom to each brand to create a good visual impact. We employ individuals for each brand who understand the identity of the brand and can convey the concept. We've found that if you make an investment, it tends to pay off. I think that's what the industry likes about us. On any given day our sales staff might get into their car to do a shop visit. People appreciate that.

What do you love about fashion?

I'll tell you what I don't like about fashion... I don't like the whole lovey-dovey element. But I can understand why it needs to be there as it creates marketing news. I get criticized by some of my friends in Glasgow who say, 'How can you work in fashion? You used to be a milkman for six years... Don't you get bored of the shallow part of it?' But fashion is an industry, and it employs real people. If you think about the manufacturing side, the sampling side, all the people involved in those less sexy aspects are real people who have families and mortgages just like in any other business. It's not just about the lovey-dovey, airy-fairy world, although that's the world the wider community associates with fashion, but there is actually a real core that benefits from the fashion income stream.

For fashion to work you have to sell a concept before you sell the product. Once you make that product 'wantable', the product will follow. Why should you pay £200 for a McQ shirt if you can buy one for £20? Essentially, you are buying into the lifestyle of that brand. You are hopefully buying into the quality in terms of fabric and manufacturing and you are buying a certain exclusivity. It isn't just a Gap shirt. If less people wear it, it becomes a more desirable, aspirational item.

What makes one budding designer/brand stand out more than the next?

I think every budding designer needs something unique. When you look at most successful designers or brands, they are instantly recognizable. Think of Alexander McQueen...in terms of product, styling and edge he is unique. Then there is the luxury element and the sharper silhouette. Or take Giorgio Armani, you'd never see him designing his menswear collection in lime green. He's all about the blacks, beiges, taupes. It's his signature style. The challenge for every designer is to create a signature and then stick by it. You can evolve but you need to stay true to that core signature.

What advice would you give to a budding designer?

You need to find something unique, whether a detail, the fabrication, a style element...that will become your signature and it will evolve from that. You need to be true to your goals and set up realistic targets. I have people who come to us and say 'we want to open a shop and distribute around the world' and they don't even have a sample collection yet. And remember things don't happen overnight. Obviously the celebrity thing can help, if you are Paris Hilton or Stella McCartney, but at the end of the day even if you're a celebrity you have to deliver a true message and deliver it well. You need to find the right manu-facturer to produce the right product and deliver it at the right price. And, more importantly, you then need to have a selling arm to promote your product.

Armand Hadida

Founder of L'Eclaireur shops in Paris and Tokyo and owner of Tranoï trade fair in Paris

Armand Hadida opened his first shop in a basement retail space on the Champs Elysées in Paris in 1979. He wanted to offer a new buying experience to the customer by offering cutting-edge designers who were yet to become household names. The first French retailer to stock brands such as Prada, Helmut Lang, John Galliano, Ann Demeulemeester and Marithé et François Girbaud, Hadida went on to open four more shops in Paris and one in Tokyo. He is also the owner of the Tranoï trade fair in Paris.

above: Armand Hadida; opposite: An Oscar de la Renta dress at L'Eclaireur, rue Boissy d'Anglais, Paris, 2008

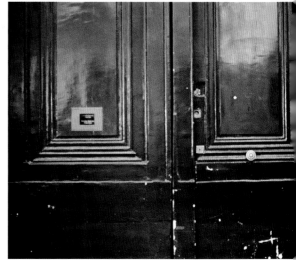

When did you first get interested in fashion?

It was not so much fashion as fabrics that I was interested in. I was born in Morocco and was one of 11 so it was hard for my mother to take care of us all. She sewed all the family's clothes and was always taking me to buy fabric to make the kaftans and dresses with. It was fantastic for me because I learnt how to bargain in a market. In Morocco we had lots of fabrics that came from India and so on with broderie... My mother was always working on the sewing machine, making the clothes; that was my first introduction.

How did your interest develop from there?

When I moved to France I had to start earning money. It hadn't really occurred to me to go into fashion because I was really shy and communicating with others was a real handicap. I came to fashion almost by accident. The first time I worked in a fashion store was when I covered for a friend of mine who was sick. It was Daniel Ho's beautiful shop in St-Germain-des-Prés. It was *the* place for fashion at the time. During that week I helped a few ladies choose their clothes and I later found out they had been Brigitte Bardot and Mireille Mathieu. I was an immigrant, so speaking to people like that was fantastic for me. Every night I'd think about what I'd learnt and the job became a passion for me. Then I became a buyer for a shop called American Bazaar where the boss was buying the wrong things.

When did you open your first shop?

In December 1979 I opened a tiny shop in the basement of a building on the Champs Elysées and called it L'Eclaireur. I had to work really hard for five years to raise the money. I bought a garage and worked 5am–9pm seven days a week in order to open the store. That was the beginning of the retail experience for me. The choice of location and name was very personal to me. L'Eclaireur means 'pathfinder' or 'scout'. It forced me to go my own

way and look at new designers and means of expression. I made it my religion. I was always on the lookout, travelling, never wondering about whether something would be commercial or not. Fashion for me means 'to be different', and not to follow what everyone else is doing.

What was your vision for L'Eclaireur?

My only desire was to share my point of view with my customers. To me it wasn't just about selling products but about selling an attitude, an allure. I've always focused on new designers, something different. I wanted the consumer to follow the story of a brand. Choosing a pair of trousers wasn't good enough, I had to make sure they had the right shoes to go with them. It was a new way of selling. We changed the relationship between the salesperson and the consumer.

What designers were you selling at the time?

When I was a buyer, the first designer I bought was Marithé et François Girbaud. François was incredibly creative, changing the cuts of trousers, etc. Then after a few years, I introduced young, new designers such as Moschino, Vivienne Westwood, John Galliano, Hussein Chalayan, Rifat Ozbek. A few seasons later I brought in the Belgian designers from Antwerp, including Ann Demeulemeester, with their amazing

> L'Eclaireur means 'pathfinder' or 'scout'. It forced me to go my own way and look at new designers and means of expression. I made it my religion... Fashion for me means 'to be different', and not to follow what everyone else is doing.

opposite: Details from Armand Hadida's L'Eclaireur shops in Paris, including the inconspicuous shop front in rue Harold (top right)

new direction. That period was a revelation to me. The market was full of French designers such as Gaultier and the ladies on the street looked very hard, it bordered on the vulgar. This type of fashion is very fragile because it's not easy to combine. If you don't have the right look, it becomes scary. It just didn't correspond with my sensibilities. I was so happy to discover the Flemish designers. I saw another type of silhouette, not a sexy and vulgar one, but a romantic one. It was androgynous, fragile and poetic. It was so deep for me. That was the future. I felt the market needed such designers. But it was tough. The magazines only talked about Azzedine Alaia and Gaultier. They were the kings of Paris at the time. My shop became like an embassy for Belgian designers. I was also carrying Dries Van Noten and Martin Margiela... That was our identity. I then followed the story with the Japanese designers such as Comme des Garçons who introduced a new elegance and femininity.

How did you go about choosing brands for your shop?

I was always travelling to Italy, England, America... looking for something new to show. I wanted to surprise the customer. That was my way of life. In America, back in 1981, I found crazy things such as Timberland shoes and in 1984 I introduced Tod's. Nobody knew those brands at the time.

Was it difficult to sell those new brands?

It was a challenge, but I never felt that I was taking a risk. I bought, say, a thousand pairs of Tod's because I believed in the shoe. I was a salesperson and I believed in my power to sell those quantities. Of course at the beginning nobody wanted them, but I insisted and explained what the story was behind the shoe, how they were made and the press also helped me because they were happy to show the public new items, and provide new stories. After a while we were selling thousands of pairs of shoes. Then Tod's opened their own shop and we went to find something new again. We were also the first to carry Dolce & Gabbana, Prada and Helmut Lang in France.

How has your approach to choosing brands changed over the years?

My vision hasn't changed. I'm always on the lookout for new things, not necessarily new people, but new stories. Two years ago, for example, we wanted to go in another direction and we introduced Oscar de la Renta in Paris. Nobody carried the brand at the time and again everyone said, 'Are you crazy?' Now all those stores, who had doubts, are placing their orders for next season. A lot of buyers don't like to take risks, preferring to follow someone who takes risks before them. Unfortunately, we are polluted by all the ad campaigns in magazines. The big groups have all the power and a lot of people think it's safer to buy brands like that than to go and find a designer with a beautiful story, vision and talent. It's a challenge. We sell some designers that we've been supporting for 15 years, who we love and respect, but only a minority of people understand what they are doing. Years ago it was easier to talk about new names and new people. These days people are not willing to give you their time. They get their inspiration from magazines and then want to buy names like Lanvin and Balenciaga. They don't buy style, creativity or originality, but product names because they don't have the time or inclination to hunt out the different.

Your store in rue Herold spotlights designers of the future? How do you go about choosing those?

I created the shop eight years ago when brands such as Prada spent huge amounts of money opening big stores designed by famous architects, with amazing shop windows, beautiful lighting, etc. I wondered what the future might be for small companies like us and how we could fight against the big companies. My idea was to start something that opposed the marketing codes of the big brands. I wanted to do something completely different so I thought let's go for a retail space with no windows, no name, no passage on the street, no fancy lights, etc. I wanted the success of the space to come merely from the exclusivity of the designers represented there, not the money pushed into its marketing. People thought I was crazy, but it still gives us the best turnover of all our stores. We are the only shop in the world that doesn't offer sales at the end of the season. We preserve all garments at the original price and it's like an investment for our customers and a way of respecting the designer's craft. The fashion world is very sick today. It's hard to think what might happen in the future if we don't find a solution for this type of sales sickness. The environment is not a healthy one for young designers with no power or money. How can they follow their ideas?

What makes one designer stand out more than another?

It's the personal way a designer translates what he thinks. Like with music or painting, it's important to have your own vision, language and vocabulary. If, for example, I go to a collection and I see something that I've seen before I stop looking right away. I need someone with individual work and not ideas from someone else.

Do you think you need a philosophy to create a beautiful garment?

Of course. If you don't have a philosophy you end up following the commercial marketing codes and then you're on to a lost cause.

Have brands that you began stocking exclusively made it big in France because of L'Eclaireur?

No way. Even if it's true I would never say that, it would be too pretentious. It's not because of

below: Buyers at Tranoï trade fair in Paris, March 2008

above: Armand Hadida was one of the first to mix furniture, fashion and design in his shops, creating one of the first concept stores back in 1990

a retailer that a brand becomes successful. It's the people driving the company that make it a success.

How do you fight against the globalization of fashion, i.e., people stocking the same brands in every store?

Globalization is a major problem because it's becoming more and more difficult to surprise the public. Most companies own flagship stores now so you still need to offer very niche garments. Even if you are offering similar brands you need to find your own way of driving the story. If one company has six buyers in different territories you'll have six different stories that have come out of the same collection. It's great when the customer is surprised and says, 'I went to the flagship store but I didn't see these pieces there.'

Where do you think fashion is heading?

It's not about where fashion goes, but how she gets there. I'm afraid that it may not be an elegant or noble path. A lot of brands these days are only thinking, 'how can I make more money?' They don't care how it's done, they only care about the goal. It's all business and marketing. There is no more poetry, no more dreams, less talent. The problem today is that although there are good artists around it's incredibly hard for them to stay alive economically, so they end up working for big companies. There they have to make compromises, but when an artist starts to make compromises he's finished, he's dead. We need to protect and preserve artists and keep them as far away as possible from economic matters. Big brands now pay big money, but they ask for what they want and the designer has to change his or her sensibilities and vision. It's a very sad state for fashion and creativity: the face of true fashion is changing for economic reasons.

Who is your ideal customer?

Either someone who is cultured and really knows what he or she wants, or someone who doesn't have any knowledge of fashion but is very curious and ready to play.

How would you describe the atmosphere in your shops?

I want the customer to feel relaxed and cosy. I'm from an oriental background, so making someone feel welcome is very important to me. We try to give our customer maximum time and service.

You were one of the first to mix fashion with furniture and design in some of your stores, creating a concept store back in 1990. How has this helped fashion sales?

It was very difficult in the beginning because nobody understood what I was trying to do. In Paris at that time people thought fashion was only for selling in boutiques and design objects were for selling in furniture stores, but we wanted to expand the customer's mind and show them something else. I wanted to demonstrate that fashion wasn't just about clothing, but everything that surrounds it. It's a lifestyle. I didn't want to be present only in my customer's wardrobe, but also in their hallway, their lounge, etc. Fashion has become polluted, it's boring. To make people excited and to justify repeated visits to the store, you have to show the customer something new. We've now also opened a restaurant and started a music label.

What is your involvement with the Tranoï trade fair?

We took over the artistic direction of the trade fair five years ago and started a men's fair two years ago as well. It runs four times a year during Paris fashion week and we get buyers coming from all around the world to source for their stores.

How do you choose which brands can show here?

I have a team that selects the brands carefully. We are not looking for jeans labels, we are looking for more contemporary and creative labels. Jeans are too easy, too commercial. Our goal

again is to find new designers. We travel around the world scouting.

Who comes to the trade fair?

Buyers from the most important multi-brand stores from around the world: American, French, Japanese, English, Italian department stores...

What advice would you give to a budding designer?

I think that students coming out of fashion school have generally not matured enough in those three to four years to be able safely to say, 'I'm a designer'. They have just about learnt how to do a drawing and how to cut a pattern, but nothing else. And often it's the fault of the professor. The teacher needs to tell them that they are only learning the basics, that they have to go deeper and deeper. There are only a few schools that speak this language. You need the right combination of teacher and student, you can't make a fire without oxygen. I'd tell a young designer not to limit themselves to fashion school – that's only the first step. If possible they should go to the Beaux Arts: that's the best second step. Fashion is not only about clothing, so immersing themselves in the arts will provide them with the best general knowledge they can have. After that, they might be ready to make a move in the right direction: they might end up a painter or a photographer, but that's OK. There are so many fashion students worldwide who graduate every year and where do they go? They have no direction. Nothing. They don't even get paid an honest salary because they have nothing to say.

It's a very sad state for fashion and creativity: the face of true fashion is changing for economic reasons.

Catriona Macnab

Head of trends, WGSN

After graduating from the Glasgow School of Art with a BA in textiles, Catriona Macnab went on to do an MA in mixed media textiles at the Royal College of Art in London. On leaving college she set up a design studio and moved into consultancy work. She has been working on colour, fashion and textile trends for over 20 years, and became the head of trends at WGSN in 2004.

opposite: Moodboard created for WGSN trend forecasting meetings, Spring/Summer 2009

When did you first get interested in fashion?

At school I was always interested in art and design, but I didn't really know about fashion – I decided to go to art school, and asked my art teacher's advice. He gave me very sound advice, saying I should apply to Glasgow School of Art, which turned out to have a fantastic textile design heritage.

How did you become the head of trends at WGSN?

I've been working on colour, fashion and textile trends for over 20 years now. It was the global aspect that I gained, working with international brands and licensees and the understanding of yarn, fabric and garment production, which was important and helped me to get my role at WGSN.

I used to work for a company called Nigel French and they very much focused on clients in America and Japan so I got to know those markets very well. My experience there was fundamental to finding out how the industry works, and particularly interesting as it was during the era of influential Japanese designers such as Yohji Yamamoto and Comme des Garçons. I worked for mills that developed fabrics for those customers, they were real innovators.

I have also worked with a lot of different companies out there who approached things in a different way. They had large research teams, which was all very new to me. It was an East-meets-West exchange of information. From there I joined the Woolmark Company, working on trends on a global platform. We worked with designers producing collections, initiated design competitions with the Royal College of Art, developed new fibre technology and worked creatively with the marketing and advertising departments. It was an eclectic job, and again a good grounding for my role as head of trends at WGSN.

What does your job involve?

Every day is different. I have a team of thirty trends staff in London, and we also have full-time trends researchers in Los Angeles, Hong Kong, Tokyo and New York, as well as freelancers across Europe, South America and Australia.

It's my team's job to be in touch with everything that relates to product – to keep track of what's happening globally whether it's on the street, in retail, music festivals or key international trade shows. The main areas we cover are menswear, womenswear, kidswear, intimates, swimwear, footwear, accessories and interiors.

Where do you go to pick up on trends? What do you look at for inspiration on what will be *the* thing in the future?

We start with colour. It's an important starting point. Within WGSN we have our core colour team who focus on seasonal colour, researching, analysing and developing key colour palettes for all product areas.

Every season creative content staff will join us from Asia Pacific, Japan, America and Europe where we have our initial inspirational trend presentations showing us what they have found from each region. These ideas may cover political, environmental, social, cultural, design and fashion trends – a multitude of different types of information.

We also invite international speakers to tell us about what's happening in areas we may not be so familiar with such as film, music or a specific country. From there we look at connecting the information which we edit down to three or four big-picture macro trends. From those macro trends each department will develop them further into

below: Street style photographed in 2007 and 2008 in (from left to right) Helsinki, Los Angeles, London, Tokyo, London and Barcelona

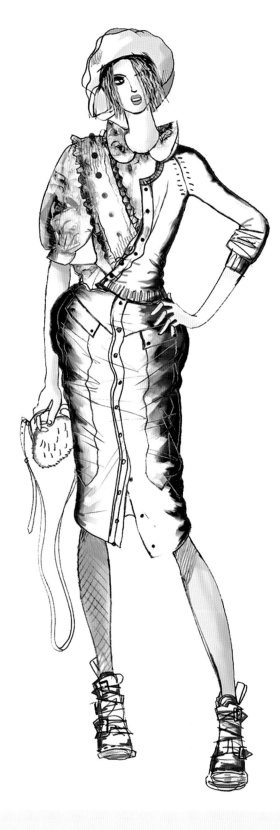

each different product sector. Each season we select different cities where we think there may be new inspirational ideas to find. Recently several of the team travelled to Russia where the emerging domestic arts scene was of particular interest.

We also travel every season to staple cities such as Tokyo – this has become an important and fascinating culture for trends research. What we find in the Tokyo youth and street market can filter through into global fashion trends.

We also look at innovative retail environments, advertising, artists, street looks and, of course, catwalk trends.

How do you decide on, say, what colour will be big next season?

We always start by looking at what happened in the previous seasons. Often it's an evolution from the season before. That's what's exciting about fashion – the evolution and fantasy of the future where we can create something fresh and new whilst always keeping an eye on the season's bestsellers.

We look at what has been selling, what has not and also gut instinct – what we like. It's all in the mix of what's doing well and bringing in fresh new ideas.

How much do fashion, design, jewelry design and so on influence each other?

It's all very much connected. Fashion, media, interiors, cosmetics, cars, toys, food – all respond to the same cultural mood. Shifts in these patterns can act as directional signposts.

Who subscribes to your website?

Our clients range from designer names such as Armani, Burberry and Louis Vuitton to more mainstream brands such as G-Star, Quiksilver, Adidas, Puma or Crocs, and retailers Harrods, Galeries Lafayette, Marks and Spencer and H&M.

left: A sketch used to demonstrate up-coming trends; opposite: Clients of WGSN include designers such as Armani, Burberry and Louis Vuitton

Non-fashion clients range from automotive and electronic to mobile communication and media agencies such as BMW, Ford, Samsung, Electrolux, Sony Ericsson, Leo Burnett and BBH – really any design-conscious company.

Where does the Zeitgeisty phenomenon come from where you may get 20 designers coming out with harem pants the very same season? Do they all sit around in a forest and decide 'this season it's all about the dropped crotch'. To what degree is WGSN responsible for this?

Essentially the industry is often looking at the same references. This could range from the latest blockbuster exhibition at the Victoria and Albert Museum, a new band, a film release, a design exhibition, the hot new cities of the moment, the underground trends that reflect the zeitgeist or a resurgence of a vintage look like Rock-a-billy or Geek Chic. The fashion arena will pick up on what's buying and selling like in any other industry. WGSN is in charge of tracking those influences and cultural moods, looking for what's new and innovative. From

this we create trend directions, which are like mini collections. They will cover mood, fabric, colour and styling inspiration. For a lot of companies those mini collections will help kick start the season's product development – however they will adapt and change the information we give them to make it relevant for their brand or market.

Where did people look to before WGSN?

Small consultancy companies produced printed trend books, which would be published twice

Our clients range from designer names such as Armani, Burberry and Louis Vuitton to more mainstream brands such as G-Star, Quiksilver and Crocs.

a year. That's why when WGSN started ten years ago it broke the mould by going from print to digital – offering daily content.

WGSN is made up of two parts. One side is the creative side, which develops product and inspiration. Then there is the business-to-business information side which reports on trade shows, catwalks and industry related news and analysis – all real-time information.

The creative side is made up of designers who are art school graduates and experts in their field. All have worked previously in the fashion and style industries. The information side is made up of journalists and analysts. It's the combination of the two that makes WGSN such a successful company and a unique one.

Fashion, media, interiors, cosmetics, cars, toys, food – all respond to the same cultural mood. Shifts in these patterns can act as directional signposts.

When does something actually become a trend?
It doesn't really matter whether 20 people are wearing a look, or a particular style was seen on just one person. If you see something that's interesting and you think it's the right product at the right time, it's important to report on it. The basis of a new trend could be an interesting piece of customized hand embroidery on the back pocket of a pair of jeans.

How important are the fabric fairs in determining what next season's trends are going to be?
Each season designers will always begin by looking at colour and then fabrics for their starting point. The main fabric fairs are well attended by all levels of the fashion industry. Designers will develop fabrics with selected mills, but often pick up on new fabrics that have been created for the season.

Over the last few years designers have started sourcing a lot of vintage garments and have asked mills to create similar types of fabrics but using new technology. This has been an important development for both fabric and garment production.

To what degree have celebrities influenced the way fashion works now?
Celebrity endorsements and their influence on collections have always been around, but with the

above: Images compiled by the Trends team which may be used as inspiration for up-coming collections by designers

internet the speed of information is so much faster now. People love seeing what Kate Moss is doing, or what Amy Winehouse is wearing, and everyone loves reading celebrity gossip. Karl Lagerfeld did a homage to Amy Winehouse, so if Karl is influenced by celebrities, who isn't?

To what degree does fashion need to be innovative?

Fashion needs to keep moving and be innovative otherwise consumers get bored. We also need to innovate to become more environmentally friendly and more sustainable. What we're trying to achieve is to innovate and inspire by looking at new innovations in smart textiles or technology – eventually those innovations will trickle down to the consumer market.

What changes have you witnessed in the fashion world in the last ten years?

The one I've particularly witnessed is the growth of China. The shift from West to East has been fundamental. It has had a twofold effect on brands. Not only are companies producing and manufacturing in China, but they are also selling into the Chinese domestic market. There are now many Chinese companies with European creative directors or consultants working for them. Design colleges are producing new designers – so the rise of China has been phenomenal.

What makes one designer or label more successful than another? What does it take to make it in the fast-moving world of fashion?

It's a mix of things. It's not just about design; it's about the whole image. It can also be linked to how much money someone has behind them, financial backing is critical. I think if you want to make it you've got to have lots of ambition and guts and work really hard to keep going as there will be so many obstacles that will come your way. One thing that struck me when I came out of college was that there are so many jobs out there that are not directly linked to what I studied at college. There were a lot of roles that I didn't even know about. You can be a buyer, a merchandiser, a marketer, the industry is complex. It's not just about sketching collections and a lot of students are not so aware of the different opportunities.

What advice would you give a budding fashion designer?

Keep going. Just keep going. Don't give up. If you manage to succeed in this world, it's fascinating.

Purple

Caroline Lynch, Gillian McVey and Nancy Oakley

Purple was founded by Caroline Lynch, Fergus Lawlor and Gillian McVey in 1997. Hallie Logan joined the company as a partner in 1998. Nancy Oakley completed the five-strong team in 1999. Purple's original clients included the master of design minimalism Calvin Klein and Jade Jagger, then an up-coming jewelry designer whose decorative, bohemian style was beautifully contrasting, summing up the conflicting mood of the 1990s. These were soon followed by New York fashion maven Donna Karan and Richard James, with his elegant Savile Row tailoring. Since 2006 the agency has been representing the Dover Street Market, Comme des Garçons' UK flagship store. Moreover, their current client list also includes Belstaff, Roberto Cavalli, Brioni, Kinder Aggugini and Lanvin, as well as 11 luxury beauty brands. Since its inception, the agency has also had an Events division, which organizes high profile events such as the Serpentine Summer Party. Meanwhile, their entertainment division, which represents artists such as Björk, Beyoncé, Mika, Scarlett Johansson and Sharleen Spiteri, was launched in 2005. Purple continues to work creatively on projects that anticipate the future zeitgeist.

opposite: Designed by Kinder Aggugini, Spring/Summer 2009

When and how did you first get into fashion?

Nancy: After leaving art college, my first full-time job in fashion was working for Katharine Hamnett in the early 1980s. I was merely a junior at the time, the incredible Lynne Franks was Katharine's PR, but I got my first glimpse at how powerful PR could be when Katharine decided to wear the anti-nuclear T-shirt '58% don't want pershing' to meet Margaret Thatcher at Downing Street. She was photographed by the press and it made headlines across the world. It was the most used picture of that year, according to Reuters. It was an extraordinary experience to see that happen. There were only six of us working for Katharine at the time and she'd said she wanted that slogan printed on a T-shirt for her meeting with Maggie. Being the pre-digital age, we didn't even have a facility for screen-printing so it was photographically printed onto cloth and stitched onto a T-shirt. Working for Katharine was a steep learning curve and an inspiration. She changed my outlook towards most things in life. I worked with Lynne Franks on the shows and that morphed into me taking over and doing the PR.

Caroline: Following a short stint as a hairdresser, I moved to London to work with Nicole Farhi and French Connection. I then became PR assistant at Emporio Armani and soon became PR manager for Giorgio Armani in the UK. It was a great period in the late 1980s, early 1990s, The company was growing fast and there were store openings, fragrance launches, new media campaigns, film and music events each week, together with a constant flow of film stars, rock stars and royalty passing through the office. I then set up the Club 21 PR & Marketing dept where we launched brands such as Donna Karan (still remembered as one of the best fashion parties ever!) and DKNY into the UK and launched the Metropolitan Hotel.

Gillian: My first job in the business was as a junior press officer for Paul Smith. But it was during a

opposite: Donna Karan, Spring/Summer 2009

time when a job title didn't mean anything, we'd all muck in. If it was busy in the shop, I'd go down and sell the clothes. There were six of us sharing Paul's office at the time. Straight after the show in Paris we'd load up the rails and bag up the collection and put it in a van and speed it back to the showroom to set up for selling – and Paul would be right there with us in the van, this giant skateboard! Back then there was no celebrity culture. Daniel Day-Lewis, John Malkovich and so on would sit in the front row, but it was more a case of art, fashion and film mixing. No one was exploiting the celebrity angle, it was a lovely time. We still work with stylists like Joe McKenna, Mouchette Bell and David Bradshaw who we worked with back then.

Anything was possible. We'd work on ad campaigns, lookbooks, commissioning photographers, booking models. It was a collective consciousness. The PRs were part of the creative process back then. It's changed a lot since: as an agency we no longer get involved with the ad campaigns, etc., it's purely PR now. Nancy and I were the only two UK PRs in Paris at

> PR is hugely important. However, each designer requires a different strategy. If a brand wants to be 'discovered', it's important not to have the same kind of mass-market exposure that some bigger brands would want to have to drive sales. We manage that kind of an approach too.

the time so we'd often end up in the same bars after the shows. We were all great friends – that was the foundation of Purple.

When did you decide to start your own business?

Gillian: We decided to start our own business in 1997. We'd each been in-house PRs for a decade. Nancy and I had both worked for designers that taught us everything we know about fashion. These designers were constantly coming up with bonkers ideas. We were never just working on the collection, but always on special projects too like a book or an exhibition. And always with the kind of thinking: 'What could we do in Ulan Bator?' We learned to think outside of the box and it instilled confidence in us to do the same, so launching our own agency was like a natural progression.

How did you go about acquiring your first clients?

Gillian: It was a small industry back then, pre-email, when everyone knew one another by face and not by text. We moved as a tribe. We were all in London together for the shows, then we'd head to Paris together – in the same way the Polo players follow the sun! Everyone would end up in the same restaurants after the shows so we all became friends. We started our business with Calvin Klein and Jade Jagger who summed up the conflicting moods that are still present in our company today – one was minimalist and one was decorative. We also began working with Ian Schrager early on. We just took the plunge thinking it would take us a couple of months to find our first clients, but it happened straightaway, we were very lucky. Designers such as Calvin Klein were just launching in the UK at the time so it was perfect timing – serendipity even. This was YSL and Gucci pre-Tom Ford and Prada had shown just a couple of seasons. It was a different era and a very exciting time to be starting a business.

What is your company's vision?

Gillian: To work with designers and companies that think differently, laterally. We'd been educated by

amazing designers and we wanted to carry on with people who reflected that same ethos and vision. Designers who challenge the status quo, who don't conform. Dover Street Market, who we have worked with for nearly four years now, reflects everything we aspire to. Even the beauty companies we represent are fantastically innovative: Ren, Jurlique, Laura Mercier.

How do you think Purple sets itself apart from other PR agencies?

Gillian: We don't pay attention to other PR companies or how they work. We don't really think about that, we just do our own thing.

How do you go about choosing which brands to represent?

Caroline: It's instinctive and intuitive. It may be a designer we have loved for years and are delighted at last to have the opportunity to collaborate with or it may be someone starting out whose vision excites us. We know in the first five minutes of meeting a prospective client whether or not we'll end up working with them. We always put our clients first.

What is your agency's role once you've been hired?

Nancy: It's very different from one brand to the next depending on what their needs are, but essentially we communicate their manifesto and vision in as pure a fashion way as possible. We aim to become part of their team. Because of our in-house background, we like to get deeply involved.

How important is PR to the success of a fashion label?

Caroline: PR is hugely important. However, each designer requires a different strategy. If a brand wants to be 'discovered', it's important not to have the same kind of mass-market exposure that some bigger brands would want to have to drive sales. We manage that kind of approach too. We also manage what kind of publication they should be

left: PPQ at London Fashion Week, Spring/Summer 2009

in and we try to control it tightly. There are some designers we advise to do a fashion show and to go out singing and dancing and others where we say, 'The devil is in the detail and we'd like you to do one-on-one appointments with editors. Yours is a collection which would benefit from being discovered and from word of mouth.' We try to give the designers longevity. We have to be able to know when to make a splash. For example, PPQ is a brand that's always about singing and dancing, the show, the drama. They attract the coolest tribes in London. One of our new designers, Kinder Aggugini, on the other hand, has really profited from doing appointments with editors, although he was used to spending lots of money on shows while he was designing for brands like Versace and John Galliano. We like to work with designers who have a sense of conviction, who know where they are going.

How do you ensure optimum exposure for your brands such as Donna Karan, Belstaff, PPQ, Roberto Cavalli?

Nancy: It's not always important to achieve optimum exposure for brands as being elusive can cause equal intrigue. With Roberto Cavalli, for example, we introduced him to London by suggesting he host the Serpentine Summer Party. We combined this with a below-the-line high profile editorial campaign where we were very strict over which editors could feature him and which photographers shot the collection. We worked with only the best in the business. Because this was the first communication in the UK we needed to ensure that it was properly understood in this country as well as reflecting the brand's renaissance. With any collection you can take any route you choose. You can decide to go mass market, or very chic or very trendy... Roberto has a really great balance. He is in a unique position in that he appeals to *Pop*, *Another*, *Vogue*, *Harper's* and *Tatler* readers all at once.

What do you do to keep editors happy?

Nancy: We're honest and efficient. If we've gone to them with a fantastic story, we make sure they've got everything they need. We think ahead.

Is it true that brands buy advertising space in magazines in return for editorial?

Gillian: For us it's church and state – try to ensure that never the twain shall meet. Designers advertise to convey their undiluted image; to ensure there is a global consistency. A good PR doesn't need to leverage editorial with advertising spend. Good design backed up with relevant strategy is the most effective course.

What happens when there is only one sample for a particular designer dress and all the magazines want to feature it?

Nancy: It's the biggest nightmare when there is only one sample. You have to decide should it go to *Vogue India* for a cover or stay in the UK for a *Vogue* editorial? There is a pecking order for each designer. You might be waiting for a dress that is stuck in customs in Mexico to send it on to another magazine. Or you might be waiting for a dress that was shot in a river and you then have to send it on to *Vogue Paris*. And that's not just with couture. Lots of designers only have one sample per collection and it's also used for production, so it can be tricky. Jake and Dinos Chapman once painted a Richard James suit for an *Esquire* shoot...so in that instance we were very happy and so was Richard. We're a fickle lot...

What does a brand need to succeed? Could you explain using your clients as an example?

Nancy: You need a talented designer to begin with. You also need a good product or point of difference. That's what we look for. But you need all the elements to make it work, i.e., you need good salespeople too, and you need the confidence of the press. A lot of shops won't buy unless they have the confidence of the press. Sometimes American *Vogue* might call Julie Gilhart at Barneys in New York and say, 'Go see that collection, you're going to love it,' and then later that collection will be in Barneys.

How do you protect your clients from bad PR?

Caroline: We try to choose the right magazine and the right journalist, who is going to be sympathetic towards our client. We know if they are going to get along and if there's going to be fabulous chemistry. We also do media training with some designers. They are often shy and creative people who don't really want to talk to the press. Some designers don't do interviews, and that's OK too as it adds intrigue to the brand. On the other hand, if something bad had already happened we would do our best to avert further negative publicity. If a client had spoken out of turn we'd set up a complimentary interview as soon as possible afterwards to reinstate confidence in the image. We also sit in on interviews sometimes.

How much money do individual labels invest in PR?
Gillian: It tends to be around 3 per cent of turnover and that covers advertising, PR, fashion shows and all visual marketing tools.

Do you get paid a royalty-type bonus when a brand you assist does well?
Nancy: Our reward is if the brand is selling incredibly well. Take Belstaff, for example, something unbelievable happened there. We re-launched them here in the UK. We had always loved the brand and the product, we knew we just needed to remind everyone how fantastic it was. We began by sending out their classic biker boot to select members of the press. People started calling and asking where they could buy it. It was in every magazine, then on every person walking down the road. And then there were all the copycats, who did imitation biker boots and then there was Ewan McGregor who wore Belstaff during his charity event *The Long Way Round*. Sometimes you just need to remind people how much they love something, that it's right in front of them...that's what we do.

Are there any anecdotes where an idea that has failed has taught you a valuable lesson?
Caroline: The lesson we've all learned is one of Gill's mantras: never assume. And she, in turn, learnt it from Paul Smith. For example, if you send ten invitations out to a press lunch, don't assume the editors have got them... You also have to pre-empt everything that can go wrong, as so many things can go wrong. We NEVER cross our fingers and hope for the best.

To what degree does the agency generate stories for the press? How do you come up with new ideas?
Nancy: We take our ideas from the designers who are creating new collections every three to six months. Often there is a whole story behind a collection that can provide an entire six months of coverage. The designers we work with are really fabulous and very talented and they never cease to surprise us.

To what degree do you get celebrities involved?
Gillian: Whenever it's appropriate and the brand wants it. For example, with Belstaff and Ewan McGregor it was a charity event for UNICEF. But we're not a celebrity agency, we never pay a celebrity to wear the brands we represent. We keep an integrity about it and it's usually more

It's the biggest nightmare when there is only one sample. You have to decide should it go to *Vogue India* for a cover or stay in the UK for a *Vogue* editorial? There is a pecking order for each designer. You might be waiting for a dress that is stuck in customs in Mexico...or was shot in a river and you then have to send it on to *Vogue Paris*.

about a mutual appreciation between a designer and an actor or singer. However, if a dress has been worn by one person for a red carpet event, we would never lend it to anyone else.

Which labels have you launched and how did you go about doing that?

Nancy: We worked closely with Belstaff and with Roberto Cavalli on their UK launches – both were very exciting projects to be involved in. Both brands have very strong and distinct images so we worked with their head offices to implement their global strategies locally. On the other hand, Lanvin was already firmly established as one of the world's most important houses so we just blended into the team, working with the Paris office.

Your company offers services beyond public relations, e.g., events. How important is it to offer a package to the client and keep everything under one roof?

Caroline: There isn't a blueprint – instead we sit down with each designer and discuss where their brand is going or where they would like it to go and together we plan for the future. There is no dictating from the PR to the brand at Purple. We're very old school and respectful of our designers and clients. We tend to slide into the team and work alongside them and decide together what would work best in this country. We think globally, but act locally. It's the best way to translate a vision into the local market. They'll have a different way of doing things in Paris, Milan and New York.

Where do you think the fashion industry is heading?

Gillian: During the recession in 1991 everyone was forced to go back to basics, it was a time of minimalism. It did have an effect on the industry at the time. It was the stealth wealth era, where the people who didn't want to buy Gap would buy an expensive cashmere T-shirt so as not to be seen as splashing out. It was the beginning of the luxury sportswear market. Some great designers came out of that time. The Japanese really rode that wave. They stuck to navys and blacks and block contours. Their silhouette was spectacular.

I think this time round, people will return to great design and flamboyance. People want to dress up again. People going out to dinner on a Saturday night won't be thinking: 'What shall I wear? A T-shirt and black trousers...' I think the opposite will happen. It's going to be good, inventive and creative. People don't want to drown in their misery, they wanted to be lifted out of it. No one wants to buy the same items they already have in their wardrobe anymore. People will look to the smaller designers and want to be individual.

Do you think you need a philosophy to create a successful label?

Gillian: The designers all have that. You can see it. They may not verbalize it, but you can see it. The way we try to explain it to our staff is by saying, 'pretend you speak eight languages when editors come in to view the collections'. Comme des Garçons speak a different language to Lanvin and to Roberto Cavalli. But there is one thread that brings them all together: they are the best in the world at what they do.

What makes one designer stand out more than the next?

Caroline: It's difficult to put into words. It's an extraordinary talent. But sometimes talent is not enough. You also have to be very hard working and know where you are going. You have to have a philosophy and a plan for the future.

What advice would you give a budding designer?

Nancy: Work hard and be yourself. Stick to your original vision. If you work on a collection, it should be about you, not about what you think people want. Be true to yourself otherwise you'll just get frustrated.

opposite: Collette Dinnigan, Spring/Summer 2009

Alexandra Shulman

Editor of British Vogue

Alexandra Shulman was first introduced to the workings of the fashion industry when she was appointed editor of GQ in 1990. She claims she was a 'fashion ignoramus' before she became editor of British Vogue in 1992. But thrown in at the deep end, she found her feet quickly and became instrumental to the magazine's rise in readership to over a million, thanks to her knack of merging couture with the high street, her collector's issues and her continuous collaborations with photographers such as Mario Testino and Tim Walker. In 2005 Shulman was awarded an OBE for her services to the magazine industry.

above: Alexandra Shulman, portrait by Mario Testino © Vogue/The Condé Nast Publications Ltd; right: Editorial featuring Ralph Lauren harem pants, shot by Terry Tsiolis for Vogue, February 2009 © Vogue/The Condé Nast Publications Ltd

Can you tell me a little bit about how you first got into fashion?

I didn't really get into fashion until I came to *Vogue*. I'd been a features journalist at *Tatler* and then I'd gone to the *Sunday Telegraph*. After that I came back to be features editor of *Vogue* and then I was given the job of editing *GQ*. So my first engagement with fashion was actually in men's fashion.

Did you at any point in your journalistic career think, 'Fashion is the way I want to go?'

No. *GQ*, where I was from 1990 to 1992, was all about fashion, cars, sports… Endless things I didn't know about. So fashion per se wasn't particularly obsessing me. I'd never edited so it was all new to me. I only went to the shows once while I was editing *GQ*. Things have changed a lot now in terms of how the industry works.

Was it daunting when you first joined *Vogue*?

I'd worked on *Vogue* for two years as features editor and I'd worked very closely with Liz Tilberis, who had been the editor so I knew the magazine and the offices very well. But I realized when I came to *Vogue* that I had absolutely no idea about how the fashion world worked. I mean no idea at all. I didn't even know that there were two couture collections a year and two ready-to-wear. I was really incredibly ignorant.

How did you pick it all up?

Whatever you are thrown into, you just do it. I was working with lots of people who had been doing it for years. Annoying as it might have been for them to have to take this complete ignoramus around, they were very generous and did it. That's not to say I knew nothing about who the designers were or the trends, I just didn't know about the workings of the industry.

Do you think you can learn about style?

I think style is what you are. You have your own style. Everyone does. I don't think it can be learned, there are just different kinds of styles. Fashion is more of a discipline, whereas style is more amorphous.

Do you think it's important to go to fashion school if you want to become a creative?

I think it's probably hugely helpful because you learn the practical side of things. Secondly, you're exposed to lots of people who have in-depth knowledge of the industry and thirdly, you are introduced to a peer group who are all going to be working in the industry and therefore you can all help each other.

Who gets to go to the fashion shows?

I go. My fashion editors go. Quite a lot of us go. Basically as many people as I think need to go. Besides attending the catwalk shows, we also have lots of appointments to see the collections of people who aren't actually showing on the catwalk in Paris, London, New York and Milan. So in order to cover the ground you actually need quite a lot of people there.

How do you decide which shows to attend?

We only go to Paris, Milan, New York and London with any regularity. We tend to go and see the shows of the big established names. We'll also go to see the shows of people we think might be interesting or of people who are new and coming onto the scene. You just have to make a judgment.

You mentioned going to appointments. How much time and effort goes into seeing the collections of those designers who don't have the money to do shows?

It's more likely to be accessories, but it can be clothing collections. Generally a lot less time as we attend shows all day long.

How do you and your fashion team go about scouting for emerging talent? Where do you look? Who are you looking for?

opposite, left: Backstage at a Burberry Prorsum show, Spring 2009, shot by James Cochrane; opposite, right: Backstage at a Topshop Unique show, Spring 2009, shot by James Cochrane; below, left: Backstage at a Richard Nicoll show, Spring 2009, shot by James Cochrane; below, right: Backstage at a Roksanda Ilincic show, Spring 2009, shot by James Cochrane

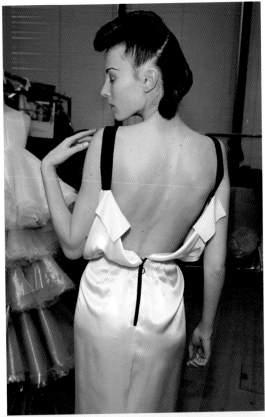

My team are very out there. I'm not, but they are. The fashion assistants and editors spend a lot of time looking out for little people who might be doing something interesting somewhere. They'll cover small shows or people might get in touch and want to show us their collections.

If someone were to call your fashion team and say, 'I'd like to show you my collection', what are the chances of them actually being seen?
You'd have to find a way to make the fashion editors think that it's worth seeing. Either by finding somebody who knows somebody who knows somebody or maybe by writing a really good email or having an interesting calling card. It's about finding a way of getting people's attention in a non-invasive way. Certainly not everybody who calls up and says they want to show a collection of knitwear will be called in.

How do trends like harem pants or gladiator sandals come about? Do all the designers sit in a little forest somewhere and decide, 'this season we're going to go with the Genie in a bottle look'...
I don't really know either. I think on one level, there's just a sort of zeitgeist thing that creates certain movements. There are general preoccupations and people react to those in a certain way.

In terms of clothes, there are the fabric fairs. The first step in making a garment is to buy the fabrics. Designers will go out and see certain types of fabric at the fairs and be influenced by those.

What's more, there are all these millions of people such as trend forecasters and style snappers who go round looking at what people are wearing on the street. I think a lot of the time what tends to happen is that one designer will come forward with a seriously new idea and that's likely to be somebody like Prada, Nicolas Ghesquière or Karl Lagerfeld. And that first season you'll only see it there, but it will be the next season that it'll have really been picked up by a lot of people.

Do you use trend forecasters like WGSN at *Vogue*?
We don't use them at all. What happens is that when we come back from the shows everyone puts their views together to make a list of what we've identified as the important features of those shows.

When you have your big ideas meeting after the shows how do you then decide which themes and styles to feature?
That's where I come in really, in the edit of the ideas. We have a big meeting and go through all the trends and we show those trends in the catwalk supplement we do. So that's the first stage. At the same time, the editors are all feeding me ideas of the kind of fashion stories they want to shoot. These may or may not be the big trends because that's not necessarily what excites them. It's my job to put together a mixture, say, perhaps a slightly left field and inspirational idea, followed by a spread about something that really is a major thing that's going on. Or maybe I'll decide that trends in a particular season are not that valid and so on. Or if there is a strong direction that nobody's suggested then I'll suggest that.

To what degree do the discussions editors have following the catwalk shows create a buzz?
The buzz happens at the shows. It's the gathering of the clans. That's quite an important thing. As you've got all these people there you get instant feedback, not just from your team but from everybody else who attended the shows. There'll be a view like 'wasn't that great' or 'what's happening here?' And that's part of the point of being there and it's very relevant.

To what degree does being featured in your magazine translate into sales?
There are no hard and fast figures other than knowing that it works. We get feedback from advertisers that they've sold either the thing that they've advertised or the thing we've photographed. It's pretty impressive. The front of the book is also very important, people really do buy off the page for that. It's very important for new designers as not only will people go and buy their product, but also shops will be more interested in stocking the thing. The power and influence of the magazine is enormous.

How do you decide which photographer to use for any given story?

The fashion editors tend to think in pictures so they'll usually have an idea of whom they want to use when they come to me with an idea for a story. That's when myself and Robin Derrick, *Vogue*'s creative director, get involved. We look at who would be good for a story, who we want to have in the magazine anyway and what the mix of the issue will be.

Can you give an example of how you matched a theme to a photographer?
For the March 2009 issue, for example, Kate Phelan, the fashion director, wanted to do a story on faded linens. It came out of the Burberry show really, but

above: Editorial shot by Tim Walker for *Vogue*, April 2008

there were lots of linens and dusty colours on the runway. It was very soft and a bit nostalgic. It was an obvious story for Tim Walker to do for us. His very acute sense of traditional Britishness and engagement with nostalgia made him ideal.

The fashion editors tend to think in pictures so they'll usually have an idea of whom they want to use when they come to me with an idea for a story.

What ... *Vogue* does is draw attention to a relatively small selection of what's available. When you have the editorial and the advertising giving you a combined message it does have a big impact.

It seems to me that few readers are actually aware that magazines like *Vogue* get financed by advertising. Can you tell me a little bit about the advertising/editorial divide?

I have no idea what percentage of the magazine is advertising, but I suspect [*laughs*] next year it will be less. We have a core of editorial pages throughout the year. If we sell more advertising pages, we need more facing matter pages at the front and back of the book which means that when the advertising goes up, to some extent the number of editorial pages also go up.

How do you keep the people who pay for the advertising happy in terms of the amount of editorial you give them?

We have a list of advertisers and the way we work is that in the big fashion collections issues we'll do our best to feature all the main advertisers. It seems only reasonable. They won't necessarily be in a big fashion story, but they'll be in there somewhere.

But I also feel it's really important to represent British designers and most of them don't have any budget for advertising so I try to get them in as much as I can as well. It's a complicated thing. We are obliged to feature our advertisers. Luckily most of them are big name designers such as Prada or Dolce & Gabbana – so why would we not feature them? But then there have been times when advertisers have felt that we haven't featured them enough or not in the way they've wanted to be featured and they've pulled their ads. I've always taken the view that we will carry on covering them even if they've stopped advertising with us. I've never known them not to come back because we need each other.

I think compared to a lot of magazines we have a pretty high level of integrity about the advertising/editorial ratio. We never make deals such as if you place 20 pages of ads we'll give you 15 pages of editorial, which some magazines do. Nevertheless,

left: Models backstage at a Prada show, Spring 2009, shot by James Cochrane. This Prada creation was featured in the magazine's editorial and also its ad pages, *Vogue*, February 2009

the advertisers have an implicit understanding that they will be featured in the magazine.

Do you think the general public are aware that what they see featured in the pages often matches up to the ads in the magazine?

Not everybody does. I get a lot of people writing to me to complain about how many advertisements there are in the magazine. They don't understand that the magazine is financed by advertising.

I find it interesting that people, myself included, will read a magazine and flick through the ads and see, say, a Prada bustier jacket and skirt and further on in the magazine that outfit might appear in the editorial spread. And unconsciously we might then head to the shop looking for those exact clothes or something similar and we'll think ourselves 'stylish' and so on.

There are millions of clothes out there and I suppose what a magazine like *Vogue* does is draw attention to a relatively small selection of what's available. When you have the editorial and the advertising giving you a combined message it does have a big impact. I think it's subliminal. From a personal point of view, you might see something in a magazine and think 'that's hideous, nobody is going to wear, say, harem pants' and then by seeing them repeatedly in magazines, in catwalk pictures, in editorials, and maybe even on some celebrities, etc., you get used to them and you may even end up wearing some yourself...

What advice would you give a new designer who would like to be featured in the magazine?

Do a good collection. Think of people like Giambattista Valli. He used to work for Ungaro but now has his own house in Paris and he doesn't have any money to advertise but we still feature him. But aside from the collection, contact with people, personal relationships and networking is the most important thing to get ahead in fashion.

So you have to learn to be a people person?

A bit. But then again there are lots of designers who aren't particularly good people persons. Usually they've found someone who works with

them who is. I don't think someone like Alexander McQueen spends lots of time going out and having chats with magazine editors. But he's so talented and early on people got involved with him who did know other people. You just have to find a way.

Do you think young designers have enough awareness that fashion is not just about being creative but that it's also an industry?

It's certainly an issue. The problem is a lot of designers are artists. That's the way they think about themselves and that's the way their mind operates. But fashion and retail are businesses. Usually, an artist does not have to deal with the whole question of advertising and all the other aspects of the industry a designer has to deal with. As a designer, you have to be able to get into shops and so on. There is a lot of talk at the moment about whether fashion colleges should be emphasizing the practical side of the business more. But you can teach the practical side as much as you want, but it's not the way they're going to think. What happens a lot is that people pair up. Look at someone like Matthew Williamson: he's worked with Joseph Velosa, who has looked after the business side of things. Most of the big designers such as Armani, Lagerfeld and Valentino started off having a business partner. Maybe at some stage that partner moved aside and got bought out, but I think designers don't realize how very important the business side is. But also I'm not sure they can be expected to do everything.

Is there anything you dislike or want to see changed in the industry?

Lots of things. I think that the way the fashion shows currently work is an antiquated and strange anomaly in our society. There are currently 1,000 people travelling around the world two months out of the year, all going and spending a lot of money on hotels, restaurants, cars, flights, etc. All just to sit and watch these shows. I don't want to believe we'll still be doing that in 10 years time. But I don't know what should happen. I think there is something ephemeral, magical and creative about fashion. And when you go and see a show that's really influential, there's something about being there and seeing the whole thing, hearing the music, seeing the hair and make-up, just feeling it happen – it definitely does work like a piece of theatre, or looking at a piece of art. You just don't get that from looking online. But I'm not sure what the answer or solution would be though.

Is that one of the things you find a bit challenging about the job?

I think it's rather self-indulgent in a way. It feels a little bit like a waste of time and it's not environ-mentally friendly. I think sustainability is a key thing and there is an issue there. Nobody loves shopping more than me. I love stuff and I edit a magazine that's all about trying to inspire people to buy more things. So that's my main standpoint, but I also feel that it's not really right to encourage people always to have to have something completely different and new each season. I enjoy showing people what's new, but I don't want people to feel they can't have the same handbag next season. And with the world changing the way it is, I wonder whether there won't be a shift in the next few years. Possibly even in the way people produce their collections because at the moment you've got people producing endless collections not just twice a year but sometimes up to six times a year, feeding the shops with new things all the time. I think we're almost at bursting point in terms of the amount people can buy, the amount of ideas designers have and the amount of stuff that's just being put out there. I think there should be a bit of a reigning back with that.

Where is fashion heading, not just in view of the financial crisis happening now, but also in general?

In the next year there is going to be quite a cull. There are going to be lots of small people who will go under and big businesses will realize they can't carry on putting out as much as they are doing. The question is: what will people learn from that or take away from that? I don't really know the answer.

What advice would you give a budding designer?

Try to find somebody to work with you on the business side. In terms of the clothes, you've got to have an idea about who might want to buy your clothes. I don't think that should be your starting point but some of the young designers just don't seem to have any notion that these clothes have to be bought by people in order for them to survive as a designer.

What makes one designer stand out more than the next?

You might have a personal reaction such as, 'Oh, I love that, it's wonderful.' So part of it operates on that level, but there is another level, which is about having a confident vision. None of the designers I've watched grow up during my time at *Vogue* are similar; they all have their unique vision. Take someone like Alber Elbaz at Lanvin. He used to work at Guy Laroche, then he was at Saint Laurent, where he did perfectly nice collections. But what he's done for Lanvin has been fantastic. It's been really influential, gorgeous and different. What he did for Saint Laurent was good but he was in the wrong place at the wrong time. It had nothing to do with the clothes he produced. That's what's difficult about fashion to some extent. You can be very talented and it can just not work if you don't get all the other bits in place. It's tragic but true.

How did you manage to increase the circulation to 220,000?

There hasn't been such a dramatic rise, but I strengthened the circulation. Although we have many more subscriptions, we judge sales by newsstand sales, i.e., when someone stands there and decides to buy *Vogue* over *Elle* or *Cosmopolitan*. And that has gone up. I think to some extent being journalistic and consciously trying to find things that grab people's attention helped. Everybody knows that *Vogue* is a great fashion magazine and that it will show the season's styles, that it will have opinions and be authoritative, so a certain constituency will always buy it for that. But they don't make up 220,000. They probably make up

right: Models backstage at a Richard Nicoll show, Spring 2009, shot by James Cochrane. Alexandra Shulman is keen to feature homegrown talent. She says, 'most of them don't have any buget for advertising'.

150,000, so there are 70,000 out there who you are trying to encourage to buy the magazine every issue.

One thing I did was introduce a larger price range so that we don't only feature designer clothes. We also began writing more about how real people felt about clothes to make it a bit more personal. And finally, it's about thinking what will sell from month-to-month, such as putting Cheryl Cole on the cover. If we do

something really special with a beautiful cover, such as our Fashion & Fantasy issue in December 2008, the magazine sales increase that month. *Vogue* sales are totally seasonal; you'll never sell as much in May as you will in September. There are lots of people who will buy the magazine twice a year to see the collections.

What do clothes and fashion mean to you?

I love clothes. I don't particularly wear fashion but I see it as something that I work with and I admire. The same way I might admire a film or art or piece of theatre. I'm influenced by it, but don't feel I have to

below: British *Vogue* Fashion & Fantasy issue, December 2008, shot by Nick Knight, © Vogue/The Condé Nast Publications Ltd

wear *the* new thing all the time. Clothes are the way you choose to present yourself to people. Even by deciding you're not interested in clothes you're making a decision that that's what you're going to show the world. I did anthropology at Uni and to some degree I think of fashion in an anthropological way. I find the tribes people belong to really interesting.

What tribe would you put yourself in if you had to give yourself a label?

We did a story years ago called 'Do you dress like the boss?' We realized that in any given office women start dressing the same. People are so tribal. It's about all being together. When I came into *Vogue* my predecessor Liz was always head to toe in designer outfits and the office followed suit. They may have been in the Kookai equivalent, but they dressed in a similar way. Four years after my arrival, everyone walked about in T-shirts and cardigans. There was a terrible decrease in style [*laughs*]. But I guess you hire people because you feel sympathetic towards them and part of the thing that makes you feel sympathetic and/or empathetic is the way people look, I suppose.

"Fashion is my passion"
Kate Moss

BIBLIOGRAPHY

Angeletti, Norberto and Alberto Oliva, *In Vogue: The Illustrated History of the World's Most Famous Fashion Magazine*, New York, 2006

Baudot, François, *Yohji Yamamoto*, London, 1997

Borrelli, Laird, *Fashion Illustration by Fashion Designers*, London and San Francisco, 2008

Bott, Danièle, *Chanel: Collections and Creations*, London, 2007

Brand, Jan, and Jose Teunissen, *Fashion and Accessories*, Warnsveld, 2007

Breward, Christopher, *Fashion*, Oxford and New York, 2003

Casadio, Mariuccia, *Missoni*, London, 1997

Chenoune, Farid, and Laziz Hamani, *Dior: 60 Years of Style: from Christian Dior to John Galliano*, London, 2007

Costantino, Maria, *Marketing and PR: From Product Branding to Catwalk Show*, London, 1998

Danziger, Pamela N., *Let Them Eat Cake: Marketing Luxury to the Masses – As Well as the Classes*, Chicago, 2005

De La Haye, Amy, and Shelley Tobin, *Chanel: the Couturière at Work*, London and Woodstock, New York, 1994

Derrick, Robin and Robin Muir (eds), *Unseen Vogue: The Secret History of Fashion Photography*, London, 2004

————, *Vogue Covers: On Fashion's Front Page*, London, 2007

Dior, Christian, *The Little Dictionary of Fashion: A Guide to Dress Sense for Every Woman*, London, 2008

Drake, Alicia, *The Beautiful Fall: Lagerfeld, Saint Laurent, and Glorious Excess in 1970s Paris*, London and New York, 2007

Ducci, Carlo and Alec Soth, *Fashion Magazine: By Alex Soth*, vol. 3, Paris, 2007

Easey, Mike (ed.), *Fashion Marketing*, Oxford and Ames, Iowa, 2009

Ellis Miller, Lesley, *Cristóbal Balenciaga (1895–1972): the Couturiers' Couturier*, London, 2007

English, Bonnie, *A Cultural History of Fashion in the Twentieth Century: From the Catwalk to the Sidewalk*, New York, 2007

Ewing, Elizabeth, *History of Twentieth Century Fashion*, 3rd edn revised and updated by Alice Mackrell, London, 2005

Finnane, Antonia, *Changing Clothes in China: Fashion, History, Nation*, New York, 2008

Goworek, Helen, *Fashion Buying*, Oxford and Ames, Iowa, 2007

Hartsog, Debbie, *Creative Careers in Fashion: 30 Ways to Make a Living in the World of Couture*, New York, 2007

Huey, Sue and Rebecca Proctor, *New Shoes: Contemporary Footwear Design*, London, 2007

Jackson, Tim, and David Shaw, *Mastering Fashion Buying and Merchandising Management*, Basingstoke, 2000

Jenkyn Jones, Sue, *Fashion Design*, London, 2005

Johnson, Anna L., *Handbags*, New York, 2002

Jones, Terry (ed.), *Fashion Now*, London and Cologne, 2005

————, *Fashion Now 2*, London and Cologne, 2008

Lomas, Clare, *Power Dressing and Sportswear: the 80s & 90s*, Oxford and Milwaukee, Wisconsin, 1999

Lynch, Annette, and Mitchell D. Strauss, *Changing Fashion: A Critical Introduction to Trend Analysis and Cultural Meaning*, Oxford and New York, 2007

McKenzie, Joy, and Sally Gunnell, *The Best in Sportswear Design*, London, 1997

Martin, Richard, Alice Mackrell, Melanie Rickey, Angela Buttolph and Suzy Menkes, *The Fashion Book*, London, 1998

Merceron, Dean L. and Alber Elbaz, *Lanvin*, New York, 2007

O'Keefe, Linda, *Shoes*, New York, 1997

Okonkwo, Uche, *Luxury Fashion Branding: Trends, Tactics, Techniques*, Basingstoke, 2007

Peacock, John, *Shoes: The Complete Sourcebook*, London and New York, 2005

Riello, Giorgio, and Peter McNeil (eds), *Shoes: A History from Sandals to Sneakers*, London and New York, 2006

Scheips, Charles, *American Fashion: Council of Fashion Designers of America*, Paris, 2007

Smith, Paul, *You Can Find Inspiration in Everything* (And If You Can't, Look Again)*, London, 2003

Steele, Valerie, *Fashion, Italian Style*, London and New Haven, 2003

Thomas, Dana, *Deluxe: How Luxury Lost its Lustre*, London and New York, 2007

Tucker, Andrew, *Dries Van Noten: Shape, Print and Fabric*, London and New York, 1999

Tungate, Mark, *Fashion Brands: Branding Style from Armani to Zara*, London and Philadelphia, 2008

Valenti, Stefano (ed.), *Stardust: New Wave*, Stone Island and C.P. Company, Milan, 2001

Vejlgaard, Henrik, *Anatomy of a Trend*, New York, 2008

Vinken, Barbara, *Fashion Zeitgeist: Trends and Cycles in the Fashion System*, Oxford and New York, 2005

Visionaire, No. 20: The Comme des Garçons Issue, 1997

Welters, Linda, and Abby Lillethun (eds), *The Fashion Reader*, Oxford and New York, 2007

Wilcox, Claire (ed.), *The Golden Age of Couture: Paris and London 1947–57*, London, 2007

————, *Radical Fashion*, London, 2003

100: Alexi Lubomirski for H&M; 104: Reeve Banks Photography; 111: J. Grant Brittain; 120–123: Courtesy of Lacoste archive, all rights reserved; 125: Courtesy of Lacoste archive, all rights reserved; 126, 128: Thierry Arensma; 129: Courtesy of Lacoste archive, all rights reserved; 130–31: Courtesy of Lacoste, all rights reserved; 132: Francesco Barasciutti; 133: Sergio Sedano; 135: Marcus Gaab; 138–39: Gabriele Balestra; 140–41: Alessandro Dealberto; 143: Marcus Gaab; 144–45: Simon Thiselton; 146, 147, 150, 151, 152, 153, 155: Neil Stewart; 157: Peng Yang Jun; 158, 161, 162–63, 164: Zhang Da; 166: Autumn de Wilde; 167–71, 173 left, 175: Dan Lecca; 172, 173 right: Claire Robertson; 178: Alexandre de Betak; 179: Luc Boegly; 180–82, 185: Courtesy of Bureau Betak; 186: Peter Stigter; 188: Karl Lagerfeld; 191: David Sims; 192, 195: Rankin; 196–97, 200, 201, 203: Nick Knight; 208–209: Claire Robertson; 214, 216, 220: Courtesy of Coco Rocha (www.coco-rocha.com); 215: Ben Cope; 218–19: Liz Collins for Nicole Farhi Winter 2008; 230: Neil Stewart; 232–34 237, 238: Romina Shama; 241–47: Courtesy of WGSN; 249: Jem Mitchell; 250: Gerardo Somoza; 252–53: Courtesy of Purple; 256: Kym Weston-Arnold; 258: Mario Testino © Vogue/The Condé Nast Publications Ltd; 259: Terry Tsiolis © Vogue/The Condé Nast Publications Ltd; 260–61, 264, 267: Courtesy of James Cochrane; 263: Courtesy of Tim Walker; 268–69: Nick Knight © Vogue/The Condé Nast Publications Ltd

ACKNOWLEDGMENTS

For Niels and Noémie, my vatos, who are there for me. Always.
And, of course, for the spectacularly loco, inimitable, delicious, want-some-more muesli wee man in my life, Bobby Magic, and my beautiful blue-eyed schnitzel, my pixie, my forest-elf, the one and only Miniscules.

Special thanks to Luella Bartley, Zhang Da, Gino Da'Prato, Alexandre de Betak, Katy England, Armand Hadida, Jonny Johansson, Yukihiro Katsuta, Christophe Lemaire, Tory J. Lowitz, Caroline Lynch, Cathal McAteer, Catriona Macnab, Gillian McVey, Angela Missoni, Kate and Laura Mulleavy, Nancy Oakley, Jane Rapley, Coco Rocha, Carlo Rivetti, Alexandra Shulman, Paul Smith, Jean Touitou, Margareta Van Den Bosch, Steve Van Doren and Dries Van Noten for their inspired and honest contributions.

Big thanks also to
Esther Adams, Lilli Anderson, Maddalena Aspes, Jamie Camplin, Marion Cassan, James Cochrane, Liz Collins, Ben Cope, Gemma Corbett, Andrea Covington, James Deeny, Ilona de Nemethy Sanigar, Autumn de Wilde, Claudia Donaldson, Camilla Emilsson-Falk, Helen Farr, Karin Fremer, Alison Gough, J. Grant Brittain, Bernie Harrington, Amanda Harris, James Holliday, Amy Howarth, Hans Jaeger, Bernadette Jaeger-Collet, Helene Keech, Ben Kelway, Nick Knight, Yue Kun, Marie Le Tallec, Sophie Lloyd, Julien Luccioni, Zoe Meads, Chris Moore, Johanna Neurath, Charlotte and Andrea at Nick Knight, Lotta Nilsson, Joanna Ortmans, Chris Overholser, Francesca Picciocchi, Maria Pinto De Sousa, Rankin, Juliana Ribeiro, Sabina Rivetti, Zoë Roberts, Claire Robertson, Gina Sanchez, Micki Schneider, Romina Shama, David Sims, Charlie at Smile Too, Patrice Stable, Alexis Stephenson, Neil Stewart, Clementine Tarnaud, Anne-Emmanuelle Tollu, Kimberley Witcomb and Pauline Wormser for their assistance and support.

INDEX